THE STAKES

Also by Robert Kuttner

Can Democracy Survive Global Capitalism?

Debtors' Prison:
The Politics of Austerity versus Possibility

A Presidency in Peril:
The Inside Story of Obama's Promise, Wall Street's Power,
and the Struggle to Control Our Economic Future

Obama's Challenge:
America's Economic Crisis and the Power of a Transformative Presidency

The Squandering of America:
How the Failure of Our Politics Undermines Our Prosperity

Family Reunion:
Reconnecting Parents and Children in Adulthood (with Sharland Trotter)

Everything for Sale:
The Virtues and Limits of Markets

The End of Laissez-Faire:
National Purpose and the Global Economy after the Cold War

The Life of the Party:
Democratic Prospects in 1988 and Beyond

The Economic Illusion:
False Choices between Prosperity and Social Justice

Revolt of the Haves:
Tax Rebellions and Hard Times

≈ THE ≈
STAKES

2020 and the Survival
of American Democracy

Robert Kuttner

W. W. NORTON & COMPANY
Independent Publishers Since 1923

For information about permission to reproduce selections from this book, write to
Permissions, W. W. Norton & Company, Inc., 500 Fifth Avenue, New York, NY 10110

For information about special discounts for bulk purchases, please contact
W. W. Norton Special Sales at specialsales@wwnorton.com or 800-233-4830

Manufacturing by LSC Communications, Harrisonburg
Book design by Daniel Lagin
Production manager: Anna Oler

ISBN 978-1-324-00365-6

W. W. Norton & Company, Inc., 500 Fifth Avenue, New York, N.Y. 10110
www.wwnorton.com

W. W. Norton & Company Ltd., 15 Carlisle Street, London W1D 3BS

1 2 3 4 5 6 7 8 9 0

To my colleagues at the American Prospect

CONTENTS

≈

INTRODUCTION

W ith the presidency of Donald Trump, we have come very close to losing our democracy. The president has attempted to govern by decree, vilify legitimate opposition, violate long-standing democratic norms, use his office for corrupt personal gain, and exhort supporters to violence. During his first two years the Republicans, with a majority in both houses of Congress, functioned mainly as his enablers. Yet, providentially, our democracy has held.

Despite a potent undertow of state-sponsored voter suppression, Democrats were able take back the House of Representatives in 2018. Special Counsel Robert Mueller was able to complete his investigation in the face of Donald Trump's relentless efforts to destroy it, complemented by investigations initiated by several House committees beginning in February 2019. Trump is at last on the defensive as he tries to resist removal from office, even as Republicans continue to protect him. So we now have a partial firebreak against the worst excesses of Trumpism.

Yet those who were comforted by the containment of Trump have fresh cause for alarm. It took Trump two years to shake off most of his more mainstream minders, but by 2019 Trump managed to install an attorney general in William Barr who sought to censor and distort the findings of the special counsel and advance Trump's extreme view of executive power in other dubious ways. Even the bowdlerized report, once released, made a liar of Barr. But Trump claimed vindication, setting off protracted conflict with the House and something close to a true constitutional confrontation.

Trump also replaced other senior officials who had tried to constrain his more bizarre impulses. These included two more mainstream White House chiefs of staff, Reince Priebus and General John Kelly, as well as White House counsels such as Don McGahn, who refused to break the law. By early 2019, the key White House aides to Trump were acting chief of staff Mick Mulvaney and chief tactician Steve Miller. Their function was to inflame rather than contain their president, to reinforce his worst instincts and encourage Trump to be an even more extreme caricature of himself. Miller, a protégé of Steve Bannon, played the same radicalizing role in the White House that Bannon had played in the 2016 campaign.

At the Department of Homeland Security, Trump replaced anti-immigrant officials who had bent but not broken the law with hand-picked extremists overseen by Steve Miller. As defense secretary, the last of the moderating generals, James Mattis, was ousted in favor of an acting secretary. This was Patrick Shanahan, a former longtime Boeing official with no previous defense experience until he came to the Pentagon in 2017 and a pattern of being deferential to Trump. As national security adviser, the independent-minded

General H. R. McMaster was replaced with the ultrahawk John Bolton.

As a number of scholars have observed, some tyrants succumb to hubris in office while others become more effective over time. It took more than two years, but Trump did get the White House that he wanted and asserted more control over key cabinet departments. In his battle to block investigations by House committees, his assertion of presidential impunity was unlimited. As he attempted to block probes of corrupt financial dealings on other fronts, Trump's behavior became more and more delusional and dictatorial. James Comey, the fired FBI director, observed Trump's method up close. Reflecting on how Trump got serious people to do his bidding, Comey ruefully wrote:

> It starts with your sitting silent while he lies, both in public and private, making you complicit by your silence. . . . From the private circle of assent, it moves to public displays of personal fealty at places like cabinet meetings. . . . Next comes Mr. Trump attacking institutions and values you hold dear—things you have always said must be protected and which you criticized past leaders for not supporting strongly enough. Yet you are silent. Because, after all, what are you supposed to say? He's the president of the United States. . . . You feel this happening. It bothers you, at least to some extent. But his outrageous conduct convinces you that you simply must stay, to preserve and protect the people and institutions and values you hold dear.

By mid-2019, America had a president behaving like a sociopathic tyrant, and the constitutional restraints were under severe stress. It remains to be seen whether the several multiple investigations will culminate in an impeachment or whether the only way to remove Trump from office is via the 2020 election.

The American constitutional system—the "deep state" so reviled by Trump strategist Steve Bannon—has proved just strong enough, so far. However, Trump could get as far as he did only because our democracy was already in serious disrepair. The American republic is in need of massive overhaul. It will take a resounding Democratic victory in 2020 to pull back from the brink of autocracy and begin the process of renewal.

THIS BOOK IS AN ASSESSMENT of the state of American democracy and how it can be revived. The subject is as much economics as politics, because the brutal turning of the economy against ordinary working families over several decades weakened public confidence in affirmative government. The sense of a lost future softened public opinion for the racialization of pocketbook distress, and the appeal of an aspiring tyrant. Democratic administrations that were far too cozy with financial and corporate elites also bear heavy responsibility for the path to Trumpism. People in the forgotten heartland correctly discerned that Democratic presidents and their advisers identified more with Davos than with Dubuque.

American democracy has been fraying for decades. Some of the decay reflects long-term trends independent of either party, such as the crowding out of civic participation by money and by media, and the concentration of wealth that in turn concentrates political power. The growth of an imperial presidency and the expansion of executive power, under presidents of both parties, set the stage for a would-be dictator.

Much of the recent assault, however, is the deliberate and cynical work of the Republican Party. Republican congressional leaders have violated basic norms of democratic process beginning with the speakership of Newt Gingrich in the 1990s and intensifying with the tactics of Senate majority leader Mitch McConnell. As Republicans succeeded all too well in creating a sense of gridlock and blocking the use of the democratic state to temper the extremes and cruelties of the private economy, people increasingly lost faith not just in activist government but in democracy.

If the 2016 election of Donald Trump had aspects of an accident, it was an accident waiting to happen. Neither of the two parties was credibly addressing broad public anxiety; support for the premise that government could solve national problems was at an all-time low. This is the climate that nourishes despots. Autocratic tactics such as suppressing the right to vote, hijacking courts, spreading systematic Big Lies, ridiculing the factual press, and steamrolling legislation with no role for the opposition were on the rise well before Trump. They have now become all too normalized. These tactics and worse would intensify with another four years of Trump or a more competent far-right successor. Trump's first two years are a chilling preview of what he might do with a second term.

The framers of the Constitution were obsessed with containing tyranny, and they devised the separation of powers to that end. "The accumulation of all powers, legislative, executive, and judiciary, in the same hands," James Madison wrote in *Federalist 47*, "may justly be pronounced the very definition of tyranny." But the founders did not prepare for a situation in which a dictatorial leader and a willing party would control all three branches of government. There have been other times when a strong president had a working majority in Congress. Franklin Roosevelt, Lyndon Johnson, and Ronald Reagan were three such chief executives. These leaders each had a clear legislative agenda, but they were not bent on destroying democracy.

Today, by contrast, one of our two major parties has become authoritarian. In 2016, most Republican leaders abhorred Trump. By 2017, each had become the instrument of the other. Republicans in Congress may loathe the man, but they found him to be an expedient enabler of their goals. As late as the spring of 2019, despite mounting evidence of his corruption, most were still defending him. If the Republicans win the presidency in 2020, taking Congress with them, the incumbent regime could destroy much of what remains of the substance of democracy and pursue a permanent lock on power.

≋

RECENT EVENTS THROUGHOUT the West have compelled us to revise our conception of democracy. Despite the popular impression, democracy entails a great deal more than majority rule. It also requires respect for political opposition, the rule of law, and the possibility of the opposition coming to power through free debate and fair elections.

The neofascist parties in Europe have rejected these norms. Viktor Orbán, Hungary's dictator, conveyed the essence of the idea, channeling Mussolini, when he defined and embraced "illiberal democracy"— the leader directly expressing the popular will with no need for a free press or parliamentary niceties. A dictatorial regime may even enjoy wide approval, generated by whipping up nationalism and crippling the opposition, but such a regime is far from a democracy. Vladimir Putin in Russia, Jarosław Kaczyński in Poland, Orbán in Hungary, Recep Tayyip Erdoğan in Turkey—all have broad popular support. But these are not democracies, because the rule of law is revised at the convenience of the regime, and the opposition remains marginalized.

Trump has attempted to do the same. The difference between a Jarosław Kaczyński trying to take over the Polish courts via a mandatory retirement age and Republicans blocking the appointment of liberal judges even under a Democratic president is a difference only of degree. The rigging of parliamentary districts in Hungary by the governing Fidesz party has echoes in the extreme gerrymandering by Republican-led governments in ten US states.* The slide to dictatorship in several nations abroad has been more abrupt. At home it has been slow and relentless, but potentially just as lethal.

If the Republicans win another election in 2020, the supposedly exceptional United States will become more like other nations that display the forms of democracy but little substance. In such nations the incumbent party is effectively the permanent government. The opposition gets to make noise but not to take power. A corrupt alliance between the governing party and its supporters in the corporate plutocracy sustains the incumbent regime.

Looking forward to the 2020 election, the Democrats are blessed and cursed with an enormous field of candidates. They have more

---

* Alabama, Georgia, Indiana, Louisiana, Michigan, North Carolina, Ohio, South Carolina, Tennessee, and Wisconsin. In those states, Democratic candidates for Congress received about 43 percent of the popular vote for Congress in 2016, but only 25 percent of the House seats.

than a year to undermine each other and play into Trump's hands, or to unite behind an effective candidate. The cultural schisms that allowed Trump to edge out Hillary Clinton in 2016 are still there to be inflamed. Trump's popularity fluctuates within a narrow range, from the mid-30s to the mid-40s, the lowest of any modern president. But if events break his way, he could be reelected.

The 2018 midterms were a harbinger of shifting public opinion against Trump. But the presidential election will be harder, since the Democrats are divided among progressives and centrists and among a score of individual candidates. Trump also has the power of incumbency and the power of the courts. And he has the power of having nearly all the Republican presidential money go to him rather than being split twenty ways.

In the 2018 midterm election, there was surprisingly little outright electoral theft—beyond the ongoing systemic theft of Republican voter suppression and gerrymandering. But if the 2020 election is close in key swing states, it could be stolen, as it was in 2000. The federal judiciary today is even more explicitly partisan than it was in 2000, when the Supreme Court called the election for George W. Bush. Democrats not only need to win, but to win by a theft-proof margin.

So, this is necessarily an alarmist book, but a hopeful one. It is also a frankly partisan book. There are times when one can plausibly write about democracy in terms of process reform, good government, comity, and bipartisanship. This is not one of those times. In 2020, a Democrat needs to win, and to win a mandate, in order to rescue America from a Republican Party that has been willing to destroy democracy itself in order to realize its ideological and partisan goals. At stake is nothing less than the survival of American democracy.

THE STAKES

CHAPTER I

Progressive Economics as Democratic Renewal

This book argues that Democrats must win a governing mandate in 2020 to pull the United States back from the brink of something close to incipient fascism—an alliance between an autocratic government and a financial oligarchy, relying on extreme nationalism. But the *way* the Democrats win in 2020 is at least as important as whether they win. They need to win as economic progressives—with a narrative, a manifesto, a rallying of the citizenry, and a set of policies at least as radical as those of Franklin D. Roosevelt.

Why? Because for the last four decades, ordinary Americans have been suffering sickening slides in their economic prospects, and their children face worse. The elements of a decent middle-class life are further and further out of reach—reliable jobs, decent pensions, secure medical care, affordable housing, and college that doesn't require a lifetime of debt. Recent Democratic presidents did not take that reality seriously. This is the soil in which Trumpism grew. The next Democratic president needs to break the cycle. And by winning decisively on popular issues, a progressive Democratic nominee for president is more likely to bring along a working majority in Congress and foil Republican schemes to make the new administration fail. Economic uplift is also the one theme that bridges the Democratic fault lines of race.

Lately, as the economy has recovered on average, there has been a great deal of commentary to the effect of "it's *not* the economy, stupid" (which is the title of several recent articles). The general theme is that the economy is doing well, wages have begun to rise, and most voters do not identify economic issues as their prime concern. "All economic indicators indicate that things are roaring in the country," wrote Chris Cillizza of CNN in a late-2018 op-ed. "Just 12 percent of people say that any aspect of the economy is the most important issue facing the country." Therefore, in this view, echoed by a number of political scientists, economists, and commentators, it would be folly for Democrats to emphasize pocketbook issues.

This assessment strikes me as profoundly wrong as a guide for 2020. The economy may be doing well on average, but for most income groups (except the top) it has barely made up the ground lost since the collapse of 2008. And economic prospects were particularly on the skids in places that voted for Trump. Ben Casselman, the chief economics editor for the website FiveThirtyEight, did some deep digging and produced a superb refutation of the contention that the Trump vote was mostly not about economics. Casselman reported, "The slower a county's economic growth has been since 2007, the more it shifted to Trump." In addition, Trump did better in counties were men had stopped working, and he did better in counties where households had lower credit scores. Casselman adds, "The list goes on: More subprime loans? More Trump support. More residents receiving disability payments? More Trump support. Lower earnings among full-time workers? More Trump support."

As a number of researchers have documented, America had divided into metro areas where a substantial number of workers gained from the new economy and a larger swath of regions and people left behind. The parts of the country where citizens were facing the steepest economic decline were the most likely to gravitate to Trump. This tendency describes whites far more than blacks because Trump mixed his economic message with a racial one. If your life was going to hell, it was because someone of another race (or identity) was usurping your proper place.

People may tell pollsters that the economy is not a pressing concern, but they have a deep sense of unease that the system has been rigged at their expense. Most people are painfully aware that the rules of the game have been turned savagely against working families in the past several decades. Gone are the days when one breadwinner could earn a middle-class standard of living, when a week's pay roughly equaled the monthly mortgage payment on a home in a decent school district, when the standard job came with good health and pension benefits and the assumption of lifetime employment, and when young people who didn't have wealthy parents could attend university without incurring crippling debt. Ask a different set of polling questions and you find that people are painfully aware of this reality.

The Pew Research Center consistently finds that substantial majorities agree with the following statement: "The economic system in the US unfairly favors powerful interests." In late 2018, even 46 percent of self-identified Republicans agreed with that view, as did 84 percent of Democrats and 63 percent of adults as a whole. In the 2016 campaign, even though he personified those powerful economic interests, Trump was able to tap into that unease by doing a variety of head fakes signaling support for Social Security, Medicare, higher taxes on the rich, opposition to globalization, and a pledge to "drain the swamp."

A more authentic version of that politics was available to the Democrats in 2016. Bernie Sanders articulated a version of it. He surprised the experts by nearly wresting the nomination from Hillary Clinton, despite her massive head start, funding, and support from party leaders, as well as Sanders's own liabilities as a seventy-four-year-old professed socialist. Given Trump's proven fraudulence as the paladin of the common American, that potential Democratic politics is still there to be articulated.

Public opinion is not static. It responds to leadership, narrative, and definition. In the same way that Donald Trump could bring to the fore latent racial animosities, a progressive Democrat could give voice and political muscle to tacit economic frustrations.

The past three Democratic presidencies were far too complacent about the corporate domination of American economic life, far too enabling of the excesses of Wall Street, and far too feeble when it came to raising worker wages. Many Democrats in Congress, in contrast to the White House, pressed for stronger efforts on behalf of working families, but this division only confused voters about what Democrats stood for. Contrary to a great deal of commentary, the loss of reliable incomes and jobs was not mainly the result of technol-

ogy, or trade, or education. When most American blue-collar workers earned a middle-class living half a century ago, the majority had
not even graduated high school. Today, the economy is more than
twice as rich on average, but the rules have been changed to favor
the wealthy, and recent Democratic presidents mostly went along.
Different terms of engagement could still lead to different outcomes,
economically and politically.

If the rules of the economy are not radically altered, the wrong
sort of Democratic incumbency would merely continue to slide to
plutocracy. Another corporate Democratic president taking office
in 2021 could well be a weak, one-term interregnum, succeeded by
another Trump—with even more racialization of pocketbook grievances, more defection by working-class voters to the right, more lack
of electoral participation by citizens, more scapegoating of immigrants and minorities. Indeed, the next version of Trump could turn
out to be sane and competent, far more effective and more dangerous.
America would be condemned to a future of mutually reinforcing
civic passivity, kleptocracy, and autocracy.

Race, Class, and Economics

Among journalists, political scientists, and campaign strategists,
there has been an ongoing debate about how much of the appeal of
Trump boiled down to simple racism or tribalism, and how much was
rooted in economic grievance. There have been drastic changes in
American society since the 1950s. These include both the loss of sta-
ble working-class jobs, and the rise of demands from blacks, women,

gays, and lesbians, as well as the increased presence of immigrants. Working-class Americans, especially men, tend to blame the former on the latter. To the extent that the Democratic Party is associated with more solicitude for the demographic rainbow than for the loss of good blue-collar jobs, it is poison to once-loyal white working-class voters. As I suggest in Chapter 6, there are creative ways around this conundrum—if Democratic candidates will use them.

When Donald Trump promised to "Make America Great Again," he was calling for a return to a time when blacks knew their place, immigrants harvested the crops and then went home, traditional values reigned, good blue-collar jobs were plentiful, imports and outsourcing were no threats, and a male breadwinner could bring home a decent paycheck to a traditional wife who served him a hot supper. Trump was brilliant at collapsing issues of lost cultural and economic status into resentments of race and fear of foreigners.

Many commentators have thus insisted that Trumpism, stripped to its essentials, is about cultural and racial identity. The reality is more complex. Political scientist John Sides and colleagues, in an influential postmortem of the 2016 election titled *Identity Crisis*, observe that the election turned on a rejection by Trump voters of identity politics at a time when the Democratic standard-bearer was embracing it. But Sides's deeper story is about the power of latent issues and the ability of politicians to animate and exploit them (Trump) or to stumble on them (Clinton).

In the years before 2016, Sides points out, polls showed there was no increase in racial prejudice. Rather, what occurred in 2016 was that both candidates "activated" latent reservoirs of ethnic and racial identity and made them more intensely felt. Both candidates contributed to this activation, Sides writes. Because the candidates talked so much about identity issues and disagreed so sharply, race and other identity issues, stirred up by both Clinton and Trump, substantially defined differences between the parties—to the advantage of Republicans.

But 2020 does not have to be like 2016. In the midterm elections of 2018, despite Trump's grotesque efforts once again to use identity politics and the demonization of "others" to rally his base and scare swing voters, the American electorate didn't take the bait. His lurid portrayal of the caravan of Central American refugees as a national security threat disgusted more voters than it inspired. In dozens of House districts, voters elected Democrats who kept the focus on pocketbook issues such as health care, Social Security, decent wages, and education. Even deep in Trump country, voters in heavily majority-white districts were willing to vote for African American Democrats who focused on practical economics. The fact that 40 percent of the white working class voted in 2008 for Obama, as an outsider who seemed to offer hope, suggests that lower-income whites are far from merely racist. Their allegiance fluctuates, and depends heavily on what candidates offer them.

I am not contending that progressive economics all by itself can offset the appeals of racism. Unless Democrats abandon support for civil rights, which they must not do, they will never win the votes of hard-core racists. But hard-core racists are far from a majority of Americans. My point, rather, is that *without* a credible economic appeal, race and identity will fragment Democrats and overwhelm what might be common issues that bridge racial divides.

Many Democratic officeholders managed to win in unlikely states and districts by stressing pocketbook and class issues. Senator Sherrod Brown of Ohio won reelection to his third term in 2018 by a margin of 6 points, in a year when every other Democrat running statewide in Ohio lost. Brown is as liberal as any Democrat on issues of civil rights and gender rights. He was the lead Senate sponsor of a resolution to designate June as LGBT month. But socially conservative, working-class Ohioans have long excused Brown for his avant-garde social views because he has been their steadfast economic champion. Brown got the votes of about 45 percent of non-college-educated white voters (the usual definition of the white working class), and made up the ground elsewhere. His ticket-mate, Democratic gubernatorial candidate Richard Cordray, lost the white working-class vote by 22 points, and the election.

Brown is not alone. In Montana, Senator Jon Tester, another economic progressive, was narrowly reelected in a state that had voted for Trump by 23 points in 2016. Dozens of House candidates flipped Republican seats deep in Trump country, by emphasizing health care, drug pricing, expansion of Social Security, and better wages.

It is not necessary (or possible) for the next Democratic candidate to win over the entire Trump electorate via populist economics. Peeling off 10 or 15 percent of Trump voters would make a decisive difference, and would begin to restore the Democrats' historical role as the party of ordinary working Americans of all races. We saw the beginning of this shift in 2018. Conversely, without addressing very legitimate economic grievances as the centerpiece of the campaign, a Democratic candidate would make little headway in winning back those voters.

The great, submerged issue in American politics has been the dominance of both presidential parties by Wall Street. To the extent that a radically different economics has not been on the political menu, cultural issues have filled the vacuum. When pocketbook and class issues are suppressed and racial and cultural issues come to the fore, Republicans win. The alliance between a racist populist like Trump and the corporate backers who are the real beneficiaries of his policies leaves Republicans laughing all the way to the bank. A Rooseveltian Democrat needs to put popular economics back at the center of the national conversation, to rebuild a decent economy, to reclaim democracy—*and to get elected.*

A related core issue is the deep corruption of American political and economic life and the cynicism that it breeds in the electorate. Powerful banks and corporations were permitted to game the system at the expense of workers, consumers, and potential rivals, producing exorbitant profits and incomes for executives and traders. Their allies were appointed to key regulatory positions under corporate Democrats and Republicans alike, though Republicans were more flagrant. The widespread and largely accurate perception that the rules were rigged and that Washington was a swamp set the stage for a radical antisystem figure like Trump. Only a progressive Democrat can revise the national narrative and turn America away from the systemic rot that began long before Trump.

Of course, Trump's radicalism was fake. He epitomized the corruption, and deepened the rot. The next leader needs to drain the swamp for real.

Repairing the economy goes hand in hand with rebuilding the democracy, for reinforcing reasons. The nation's concentration of wealth has produced a concentration of power—generating more policies that favor wealth and even more concentrated power, in a deepening downward spiral. When government does not deliver for ordinary people, they either give up on politics or embrace the far right. But when ordinary people are on the march, the power of citizens can still defeat the power of concentrated wealth—witness the 2018 midterms. Our democracy is bruised and battered, but sufficiently alive that it may yet be redeemed. So, the next Democratic president needs to be an economic radical, as well as a radical democrat.

Could such a person be nominated? Elected? Could a radical Democrat really carry out a transformative economic program in the spirit of Roosevelt, despite structural changes in the modern economy and despite the severe damage to American democracy and the Republican tilt of the courts? Yes, yes, and yes. This book insists that all these can and must be done.

The False Allure of Centrist Moderation

There has been a great deal of commentary to the effect that what ails American democracy is polarization. In this story, Republicans have moved right, Democrats have moved left, there is no common ground, and the cure is the election of a moderate who can bring the country together and restore civility to politics. This argument is made both as an assessment of the road to democratic renewal and as a tactical warning to the Democratic Party: to get elected, better not run too far to the left.

The hero of this story is a mythic creature long celebrated in political science, the "median voter." Supposedly, the political reforms of the 1970s gave too much power to primaries and precinct caucuses in the selection of nominees, resulting in the domination of the Democratic Party by activists to the left of the country as a whole. Leftists could win the nomination but not the presidency.

Yale professor Bruce Ackerman, in an otherwise prophetic volume that warned of the coming of someone like Trump, bought into the median-voter canard. His 2012 book, *The Decline and Fall of the American Republic,* contended that reforms in the nominating process of both parties that gave greater weight to primaries led to greater party polarization. "This removed a crucial moderating element from the system. When party chieftains did the picking, they focused on candidates who might win the support of the median voter in their state." Ackerman's story sums up a lot of the standard wisdom. "The new system," he wrote, "shifted the balance in the direction of extremism—away from the median voter in the general election, toward the median voter in the primary or caucus."

This school of thought, shared by some other political scientists and invoked opportunistically by corporate Democrats, is misleading on several grounds.* For one thing, it misstates what actually occurred. The Democratic Party reforms took effect in 1972, the year that antiwar candidate George McGovern won the Democratic nomination and badly lost the general election. Yet in no election

------

* The median-voter hypothesis conflated a misleading description of what effective politicians supposedly do with dubious advice about what they *should* do. The claim that successful politicians appealed to the median voter ignored "conviction politicians" such as Roosevelt and Reagan, who ran on their principles and succeeded in moving public opinion toward them.

after 1972 was a radical nominated on the Democratic side. In every single case, a mainstream candidate won: Carter, Mondale, Dukakis, Clinton, Gore, and Kerry. The closest thing to an insurgent nominee was Barack Obama in 2008, and he was no leftwinger. So even if the reforms arguably gave greater influence to leftwing activists, they did not succeed in nominating a leftwing presidential candidate. In reality, the radical protests of the 1960s, a popular reaction against structural racism and the Vietnam War, occurred before the reforms, which were intended to give protest a voice inside the system. Even on the Republican side, though the party was moving steadily to the right, most recent nominees until Trump were the candidates of the party establishment (both Bushes, Dole, and Romney).

What actually occurred was an "invisible primary" of big donors and party leaders, which indeed sought moderate nominees and substituted for smoke-filled rooms of an earlier era. These modern party bosses tended to favor establishment nominees. The counter-reform devised by the Democratic Party's Hunt Commission, which took effect in 1992, reinforced these trends by taking power away from state primaries and precinct caucuses in favor of convention "super-delegates," party leaders and elected officials who could be counted on to vote for the establishment candidate. Hillary Clinton was the quintessential example. She won nearly all of the superdelegates and also benefited from the flagrant pro-Clinton intervention by the supposedly neutral party chair, Debbie Wasserman-Schultz. Near-unanimous party establishment support did not save Clinton from being a badly blemished candidate.

In the median-voter story, the premise of anything like symmetrical extremism is preposterous. "Extremism" is a misleading term, because it blurs two meanings. One is ideological distance from the putative median voter; the other is a set of views that are substantively extreme. As several scholars have persuasively demonstrated, the reality is that voting in Congress has indeed become more polarized— Republicans tend to vote with Republicans and Democrats with Democrats, and there are far fewer cases of bipartisan coalitions—but this is not because Democrats have gravitated to the far left and Republicans to the far right in any remotely symmetrical sense.

Dig a little deeper and the reality is that Republicans have moved far right on both economic and cultural issues, while Democrats have moved somewhat left on cultural issues but until the midterm sweep of 2018, they gradually became somewhat more centrist on economics. The typical Democratic legislator of the Lyndon Johnson era favored national health insurance, broader public support for higher education, federal spending on mass transit and housing, full employment, powerful unions, a national commitment to end poverty, and strong gun control. There was no Democratic obsession with budget balance, and scant support for privatization, deregulation, vouchers, and other "market-like" measures that weakened government.

But in the era that spanned Clinton and Obama, the Democrats settled for a market-based, overly complex and inefficient road to broader health coverage, and student debt as a substitute for federal education aid. Fiscal austerity became a badge of virtue. The White House spent little political capital on the labor movement. But this was precisely the period when Republicans moved far right across the board.

The oft-repeated counsel that Democrats should not run too far to the left conflates cultural radicalism with progressive economics. Democrats do need to be careful about how they handle identity issues. But they need to be even more resolutely progressive on economic questions to address the submerged issue of just whom the American economy benefits. It is only by being clear and passionate on the pocketbook issues that Democrats can keep or win back the support of at least some socially conservative, working-class voters.

There is an additional problem with the standard counsel to hew to the center. The premise of a median voter is static, and oblivious to political history. The reality is that effective presidents define new governing coalitions, and they move public sentiment. "Transformational leaders," writes the presidential historian Doris Kearns Goodwin, "inspire followers to identify with something larger than themselves—the organization, the community, the region, the country—and finally to the more abstract identification with the ideals of the country."

Consider the two Roosevelts. In the election of 1900, the reformer Teddy Roosevelt was added to the Republican ticket as the running mate of a very conservative, big-business presidential candidate, the incumbent William McKinley. In that election, McKinley trounced the populist Democrat, William Jennings Bryan. But in September 1901, McKinley was assassinated. Roosevelt, an accidental president, soon made many of the populist demands his own, ushering in what became the Progressive Era, working closely with muckraking journalists, and shifting public opinion in the direction of progressive reform.

By 1904, Roosevelt was phenomenally popular, and he was reelected by a wide margin of 56 to 37 percent of the popular vote against a conservative Democrat. The two parties had, in effect, switched roles, with progressive Republicans becoming the instrument of economic reform. The views of the presumed median voter were influenced by a dynamic president who offered a compelling narrative of what ailed the nation and what needed to be done about it. Public opinion shifted in Roosevelt's direction. Had he not chosen to honor the two-term tradition, TR was on track to handily win a third term in 1908.

Franklin Roosevelt, even more than his cousin, moved public sentiment and defined a new governing coalition based on activist government constraining the excesses of capitalism and creating opportunity and security for ordinary people. What he did not do was meet the Republicans halfway. He excoriated them, often with jaunty good humor, and he mobilized the citizenry to vote Republicans out of office. When the twenty-year reign of progressive Democrats was finally ended by Dwight Eisenhower in 1952, the New Deal was so solidly entrenched in law and in public support that the Republicans, until the 1970s, did not dare mess with it.

Further, the idea of the value of appealing to a median voter places a heroic amount of faith in the clarity of that voter's views and his or her influence, and oddly omits any analysis of the shifting balance of influence. A far more persuasive genre of political science in the past two decades has demonstrated what should be obvious: rich people, banks, and corporations have far more power than ordinary citizens. The more the economy is tilted, the more power they have, to set agendas and capture politicians.

Political scientist Kay Scholzman and colleagues, in research over nearly three decades, have demonstrated that richer people participate in politics far more intensively and effectively than those of modest means. As institutions of working-class recruitment and political mobilization, such as trade unions, have been pummeled and campaign spending has risen starkly, that tilt has only steepened. Some disaffected citizens of modest means, seeing little help from either party, back the Republicans on racial and cultural issues. Others—potential supporters of a progressive populist economic program, if one were on offer—just stay home. Voter turnout among lower-income Americans has been in steady decline, a happy exception being 2018; even then, turnout was higher among upper-income groups. All this, of course, creates a vicious circle in terms of whose voice is heard. Political scientist Martin Gilens, whose book title *Affluence and Influence* conveys the basic point, has demonstrated empirically that the political preferences of the rich, though not the prevailing sentiment, are far more likely to become law. While some well-intentioned ivory-tower social scientists have been worrying about attentiveness to a hypothetical (and malleable) median voter, Wall Street has grabbed democracy by the throat.

The advice to embrace moderation and seek the center makes yet another grave error. It conflates the center in a *statistical* sense—a middle ground between two supposedly equal extremes—with what centrism has looked like in practice. Moderation sounds appealing, but if we look at actual recent history, the reality is less ennobling. The Democratic politicians who have embraced a new center have been allies of the corporate takeover of American politics—at the expense of ordinary working people and the credibility of activist government and its supposed champion, the modern Democratic Party.

Consider some actual prominent Democratic centrists. These are less men of high bipartisan principle than they are close allies of organized finance. In recent political history, self-described Democratic centrists—such as Joe Lieberman of Connecticut, who sabotaged the more robust version of the Affordable Care Act, or enforcers of budget austerity such as former Senate Finance Committee chair Max Baucus of Montana—have epitomized the neutering of the Democratic Party as a compelling opposition to the miseries wrought by corporate capitalism. These people are less principled moderates than they are allies of corporate elites. Their influence in blunting the message of the Democratic Party as champion of regular working Americans is precisely what opened the door to the Tea Party and Trumpism. Lieberman now works as a registered lobbyist for the Chinese telecommunications firm ZTE, a company that has violated US sanctions against Iran and North Korea. The cure for the affliction of Trumpism is not more Democrats like Joe Lieberman or Max Baucus.

In March 2018, when Democrats were presumably united in resisting Trump, sixteen Senate Democrats voted for a Republican bill to weaken the Dodd-Frank Act. These included several of the moderates often praised as seekers of bipartisanship, such as Tim Kaine of Virginia, Tom Carper of Delaware, and Michael Bennet of Colorado. It's not as though constituents of these Senators were clamoring for the government to undercut bank regulation. It was more a case of the senators doing a favor for big business, on an issue that most voters were not paying attention to. As for bipartisanship, Republicans are always happy to have Democratic support—on Republican terms. These Democrats got nothing by way of reciprocal partisan horse trading in return for backing a Republican bill written by the banks to gut Dodd-Frank. What they got were campaign contributions.

In the House, pro-corporate "New Democrats" flock to the tax-writing Ways and Means Committee and to the Financial Services Committee, where they trade favors with potent financial interests and reap campaign money. Of the thirty-three House Democrats who joined Republicans in 2018 to pass the aforementioned bank deregulation bill weakening the Dodd-Frank Act, twenty-seven were members of the centrist New Democrat Caucus. "Progressives come to Congress to change the world," observes Mark Lawson of the group Social Security Works. "New Dems come to Congress to get on the Ways and Means Committee." When Nancy Pelosi quelled a rebellion by the caucus rank and file in December 2018, one of the complaints was that few progressives had been appointed on the most influential committees, such as Ways and Means and Appropriations. Part of the deal that saved Pelosi's speakership was an agreement with progressives that at least 40 percent of the members of the power committees would be from the Congressional Progressive Caucus.

The task of the next Democratic president is not to embrace centrism—we've had far too much centrism by Democratic presidents—much less to build bridges to today's Republican leaders (who are beyond redemption), but to define a plausible public philosophy of progressive populism* that peels away a good part of the current Republican electoral base. The best way to do this is to plant

---

* A note on "populism": Many commentators have tarred all forms of populism with the same brush. This representation is grossly misleading. Far-right and far-left populism tend to be autocratic and demagogic. But the rallying of popular support by Democratic progressives to offset corporate power is essential for reforms to proceed; it is an enhancement of democracy, not an affront. Franklin Roosevelt was the quintessential progressive populist. His presidency left democracy much stronger. Bernie Sanders, Elizabeth Warren, and Sherrod Brown, among others, are principled small-d democrats, not demagogues. For economic elites, branding all politicians who mobilize the people to challenge economic excesses as illegitimate "populists" is extremely convenient. Journalists should know better.

a flag of progressive reform, rally millions of voters to that banner, and create a new progressive center. This is what both Roosevelts did. We will return to this argument in more detail in Chapter 6.

The alternative strategy of cultivating the support of political moderates has a certain intuitive appeal. Many Republican-leaning businesspeople, as well as suburban GOP voters who tend to be moderate on economic issues but more liberal on social issues, are disgusted with Trump. So why not run a moderate Democrat who can pull together traditional Democratic constituencies with defecting Republican ones?

This is the pitch of groups organized by corporate Democrats such as Third Way, a Wall Street–funded lobby that calls for a centrism based on economic moderation and scant regulation of finance. It is also the appeal of a figure such as billionaire Michael Bloomberg, who is conservative on economic issues but liberal on such causes as gun control, climate change, and abortion rights. But the combination of moving to the left on social issues and to the center on economics was tried and found wanting in 2016 by Hillary Clinton. Even if he won, a President Bloomberg would leave the festering economic grievances intact.

The centrist counsel also ignores the key variable of voter turnout, which was severely depressed on the Democratic side in 2016, and which revived in 2018 on a tide of progressive organizing around bread-and-butter issues. It's a mistake to assume that the Democratic base would show up and vote for a centrist as the lesser evil. Many would just stay home, as millions did last time, uninspired by Hillary Clinton's muddled message.

Democrats in socially conservative states do sometimes run as moderates in order to get elected. But it's also the case that Democrats in these states can get elected as progressive economic populists. Montana, North Dakota, and Ohio provide good examples. Montana has elected Wall Street Democrats such as Max Baucus, one of the state's wealthiest men. But it has also elected effective progressive populists such as the current governor, Steve Bullock; the current senator Jon Tester; former governor Brian Schweitzer; and its former, longtime progressive congressman Pat Williams. In 2016, Governor Bullock won by 4 points in the same election in which Trump carried Montana by 23. In neighboring North Dakota, two of the most popular Democratic officials were Senator Byron Dorgan, a progressive populist who came to prominence as the tax commissioner who successfully taxed the antiballistic missile installations; and Kent Conrad, a leading deficit hawk. Ohio has elected centrist Democrats such as former astronaut John Glenn but also pocketbook progressive Democrats like Sherrod Brown and Howard Metzenbaum. There's no good reason for Democrats to elect centrists when they can elect progressives.

The Siren Song of Sweet Conciliation

We know all too well what happens in the current toxic environment when Democrats seek genuine bipartisanship. Barack Obama's entire presidency was a natural experiment in the utter futility of extending olive branches to today's Republicans. The more Obama sought to meet them halfway, the more they took his efforts as a sign of weakness and intensified their obstructionism. Obama was an idealist. He came to national attention with an eloquent speech insisting that there was no red-state America or blue-state America—only the United States of America. But by the time the Republicans got through with Obama, America was more divided than ever. And then Trump came in to expunge any trace of Obama's positive achievements.

What's startling is that a number of serious commentators conclude from this history that Democrats need mainly to try harder to conciliate. For instance, political scientists Steven Levitsky and Daniel Ziblatt, in an otherwise insightful and influential 2017 book, *How Democracies Die*, caution against fighting fire with fire. Levitsky and Ziblatt write, "The weakening of our democratic norms is rooted in extreme partisan polarization." While admitting that this extreme polarization is not symmetrical, they counsel, "In our view, the idea that Democrats should 'fight like Republicans' is misguided." They warn that such a strategy "plays into the hands of authoritarians." And further, "even if Democrats were to succeed in weakening or removing President Trump via hardball tactics, their victory would be Pyrrhic—for they would inherit a democracy stripped of its remaining protective guardrails."

This conclusion strikes me as profoundly and instructively wrong. The framers put impeachment in the Constitution for a reason. Using constitutional means to contain or oust Trump would not be a violation of our democratic guardrails, but an overdue exercise of them. And by exercising constitutional restraints, we would strengthen them. We've now had two moderate Democratic presidents—Bill Clinton and Barack Obama—who went out of their way to conciliate, both ideologically and tactically. But rather than reciprocating, Republican strategists took these moves as vindication of their own scorched-earth tactics. Even short of impeachment, the success of

House Speaker Nancy Pelosi in beginning to contain Trump shows that Republicans respect toughness—and Pelosi did it without violating norms or rules. Indeed, part of her toughness was her insistence that Congress revert to normal procedural order.

The public-minded Republican moderates who often reached across the aisle to work with Democrats are long gone. Great moderate to liberal Republicans provided the key votes for civil rights legislation and Medicare, as well as key consumer and environmental protections. These included Jacob Javits of New York, Clifford Case of New Jersey, Mac Mathias of Maryland, Mark Hatfield and Robert Packwood of Oregon, Chuck Percy of Illinois, Ed Brooke of Massachusetts, John Heinz of Pennsylvania, and several others. The heyday of these liberal Republicans was the 1950s through the 1970s.

The premise that Democrats can conjure up more such Republicans by embracing conciliation is a delusion. Susan Collins of Maine, supposedly one of the last two moderate Republican senators, demonstrated her fraudulence in the endgame of the Kavanaugh confirmation. On issue after issue, Collins's supposed moderation has entailed an elaborate dance in which she withholds judgment on a contentious issue until the last minute, while she gives it elaborate study—and then invariably votes with the Republican side. In 2017, she voted with the Republicans 87 percent of the time, including for the Trump tax bill and the confirmation of Neil Gorsuch. The seventy-one-year-old freshman senator from Utah, Mitt Romney, has appointed himself to play the role of mainstream Republican. It remains to be seen how many converts he will win over.

The moderate liberalism of Republicans of an earlier era was not only the legacy of a once progressive wing of the GOP winding back from New York mayor Fiorello La Guardia and Senator Robert La Follette of Wisconsin to Teddy Roosevelt and Abraham Lincoln. It was also the result of both Roosevelts *defining a progressive center*, in which many Republicans needed to dwell if they were to be elected in states like New York.

Republicans in public life today who call for a new civility, such as former Arizona senator Jeff Flake and former Ohio governor John Kasich, are sadly at the margins of today's Trumpified Republican Party—and even so, they support most of the Republican policy package. In 2016, Kasich tried to run against Trump as a civil, moderate conservative. He attracted almost no support. Flake's final gesture in office—demanding what turned out to be a sham FBI investigation of Brett Kavanaugh, and then voting to confirm him—was pathetic. The far-right Republican stance may change as a result of internal Republican dynamics and the Republican fear of becoming a permanent minority party, but it will not change because Democrats become more conciliatory.

Civility facilitates democracy. But by itself, civility is not a governing philosophy. Nor is civility per se a prime motivator to attract support of voters in down-ticket races. We restore civility by electing a Democratic president who believes in democracy and can make it work for the betterment of ordinary Americans, and who combines respect for democratic norms with shrewd, transformative leadership. When George H. W. Bush died in December 2018, the eulogies praised his civility. Yet it is possible to be both courteous and partisan. Though Bush did seek and find occasional islands of common ground, such as the bipartisan Americans with Disabilities Act, he also cast forty-four vetoes, a modern record for a one-term president.

The ideal of centrism and conciliation is not only a fantasy, but a dangerous one for Democrats—dangerous both as an electoral strategy and as a governing philosophy. The last three Democratic presidents have been liberal on social and cultural issues and centrist on economics, meaning too close to Wall Street and too enamored of budget austerity. Racial and gender justice were a hard enough sell in a period when white working people were prospering. Linked to an economic status quo of downward mobility, they were an impossible sell after the financial collapse. The result was deepening economic insecurity for regular people—followed by the Tea Parties and Donald Trump.

Obama's failure to bridge divisions demonstrated the limits of conciliation. Moderation as an end in itself is harder still when the opposition party is determined to destroy you even at the cost of destroying democratic institutions. Creating and defending a new progressive center becomes feasible when you combine hope and aspiration with strong leadership that delivers tangible benefits to regular people. Jedediah Purdy, the Columbia University law professor and prolific essayist, puts it well: "You define a new center by winning." And, one might add, you win by defining a new progressive center.

If another Wall Street Democrat prevails, progressive economics with real remedies will have no partisan home. A corrupted Democratic Party and a plutocratic, faux-populist Republican Party, with or without Trump, will keep feeding on each other. The only viable alternative is for a radical Democrat to win a mandate and reclaim legitimacy—for democracy, for activist government as an instrument of the common good, and for the Democratic Party as steward. Then the deeper project of rebuilding democracy can continue. It has already begun with the grassroots citizen mobilizations of the Trump era.

≋

CHAPTER 2

Democracy: A Damage Assessment

The weakening of American democracy extends back across several decades, well before it was intensified under Donald Trump. Much of the damage over the past half century was the deliberate work of the Republican Party. Some of it was the consequence of social and technological trends independent of either party. Many of these trends, as we will see, have been exploited more effectively by Republicans. All these shifts softened up American democracy for the shock of 2016. And the assault became more explicit and dangerous with Trump's presidency.

The Long Slide

Executive Power and Secret Government. The abuse of executive power is a concern that goes back to America's constitutional founding. It was vividly demonstrated in the abortive Alien and Sedition Acts of 1798. In a chilling prefiguring of Trumpism, that set of laws made it easier for the president to deport noncitizen residents deemed dangerous to the nation's security. They also criminalized some forms of dissent. Most of this legislation was opposed by the Jeffersonians, and it was not renewed once Jefferson became president in 1801. One provision still on the books allows the president to round up and deport aliens viewed (subjectively) as security threats, with scant due process. This power was invoked during World War II—and by Trump as the legal basis for his restriction of immigration from several Muslim nations.

In the twentieth century, beginning with the World War I "red scare," presidents often invoked national security to justify both substantive policies and secret processes that would not otherwise be tolerated in a democracy. Both parties were implicated. Secrecy and executive power increased dramatically during the Cold War and the Vietnam War. Cold War activities directed overseas often produced blowback that compromised America's own democracy. The FBI extensively spied on leftwing groups, including civil rights groups, on the dubious premise that they were allies of communism. J. Edgar Hoover went well beyond spying and sought to disrupt their constitutionally protected activities. A noted target was Dr. Martin Luther King.

Despite express prohibitions on domestic activity in its authorizing legislation, the CIA underwrote several domestic front groups. These were intended for international Cold War purposes, but they altered domestic politics. The CIA created and underwrote the AFL-CIO's entire international program, which strengthened the role of conservatives in the labor movement's domestic politics. The CIA supported the National Student Association for two decades, ostensibly for Cold War purposes, turning twenty-two-year-old student officers into spies and altering the balance of left and right among the group's officers, staff, and public positions.

For a brief period in the late 1960s and 1970s, Congress reasserted control over executive abuse in response to the exposure of both Cold War and Vietnam excesses, and then Watergate. Congress conducted several investigative hearings, notably those led by Senator Frank Church, and reasserted congressional authority through such measures as the War Powers Act. However, those reforms were short-lived. The pendulum swung sharply back toward secret government and executive excess with George W. Bush's response to the attacks of September 11, 2001.

The centerpiece was the USA PATRIOT Act, a laundry list of shortcuts that legalized secret courts and other forms of extrajudicial surveillance long promoted by police and spy agencies but rejected by Congress until 2001. Bush drastically increased the use of "signing statements" to alter the plain meaning of legislation passed by Congress. Even under Democratic presidents, including Barack Obama, the uses of secret executive power continued to increase. All of this weakened the democratic guardrails against a tyrannical president. Trump has taken executive power to a new extreme, but the stage was set for his actions by earlier excesses. In a second Trump administration, these would be intensified.

A variety of existing laws allow a president to define an emergency, and to exercise virtually dictatorial powers. Even without statutory authority, courts have held that this residual power is implicit in the Constitution, and only presidential self-restraint has contained its abuse. Franklin Roosevelt's internment of American citizens during World War II, Abraham Lincoln's suspension of habeas corpus during the Civil War, and warrantless wiretaps after the attacks of 9/11 were all left unchallenged by the courts. According to an exhaustive review by Liza Goitein of the Brennan Center for Justice, the president has the power to invoke a state of emergency under 123 separate statutory provisions. Literally hundreds of such declarations are currently in effect, and nobody manages to keep track of when they are ended. For instance, the national emergency that President Truman declared in 1950, during the Korean War, stayed in effect and was used by Presidents Kennedy and Johnson to prosecute the Vietnam War without a declaration of war by Congress.

The 1976 National Emergencies Act, passed by Congress in the wake of Watergate, was an attempt to limit abuses. The law stipulated that states of emergency would end after six months unless renewed; they required reports to Congress and gave Congress the right to reject them.* Emergency declarations have been routinely rolled over, and Congress has not played its designated role. At least thirty states of emergency were in effect at the start of 2019. These emergency powers are another accident waiting to happen.

In February 2019, President Trump declared a national emergency in order to divert funds denied him by Congress to build a wall along the US-Mexico border. The House and Senate voted to

---

* The president could veto a congressional rejection, so effectively it took a two-thirds majority in both houses to override a veto and thus to overturn a presidential declaration of emergency.

overrule him, but not by a veto-proof majority. Most Republicans compliantly went along. When few Republicans objected to this most fundamental assault on separation of powers and Congress's constitutional power of the purse, Democratic representative Adam Schiff wrote, tacitly invoking the famous poem of Pastor Martin Niemöller,* who was arrested by the Gestapo in 1937:

> To my Republican colleagues: When the president attacked the independence of the Justice Department by intervening in a case in which he is implicated, you did not speak out. When he attacked the press as the enemy of the people, you again were silent. When he targeted the judiciary, labeling judges and decisions he didn't like as illegitimate, we heard not a word. And now he comes for Congress, the first branch of government, seeking to strip it of its greatest power, that of the purse.

The Growth of the Imperial Presidency. Wartime emergencies were not the only source of expanded and antidemocratic executive power. In the Reagan era, a then obscure rightwing law professor, Antonin Scalia, promoted a dubious and fringe theory known as the

---

* First they came for the socialists, and I did not speak out—because I was not a socialist. / Then they came for the trade unionists, and I did not speak out—because I was not a trade unionist. / Then they came for the Jews, and I did not speak out—because I was not a Jew. / Then they came for me—and there was no one left to speak for me.

"unitary executive." Later, as a Supreme Court justice, Scalia worked the doctrine into his opinions.

The idea is that the president, who is the executive under Article 2 of the Constitution, has absolute authority at the expense of other agencies of the executive branch. The core problem with that premise is that the Constitution also empowers Congress to be a check on the executive. Congress has enacted innumerable laws creating independent regulatory agencies. Though these are technically part of the executive branch, by statute they are not subject to presidential whim. Many such appointees serve fixed terms and cannot be removed for any reason except legitimate cause. The Constitution makes the president the commander in chief of the military, but only Congress can declare or finance war.

The imperial presidency, however, has come up with several subterfuges to assert absolute presidential power. Reagan and his legal advisers invented an extraconstitutional device called signing statements. These have been used and abused by his successors. Under the Constitution, a president may sign or veto a piece of legislation. There is no line-item veto; the president takes or leaves the law in its entirety. But with a signing statement, a president asserts the authority to disagree with part of the law and decline to enforce part of it. Reagan issued 250 signing statements, of which 86 explicitly took exception to one or more provisions of the law he was signing. George W. Bush used signing statements to object to at least 1,200 sections of bills that he signed into law.

Proponents of signing statements even persuaded publishers of law books to include signing statements as part of the "legislative history" of laws. In truth, a legislative history is a well-established legal concept that includes hearing records and committee reports, which can be used by regulatory agencies and courts to clarify legislative intent if the words of the law are ambiguous. But a signing statement is something tacked on by a president after the fact. It has nothing to do with the legislative history and should carry no legal weight.

Another gimmick by which usurped presidential power has undercut the ability of regulatory agencies to enforce the law was the creation of the Office of Information and Regulatory Affairs (OIRA) in 1980 as part of the Office of the President. OIRA, technically part of the Office of Management and Budget, asserts the power to review, revise, or reject proposed regulations issued by executive agencies pursuant to laws created by Congress. This power was invoked under Reagan and both Bushes, all of whom had an antiregulation agenda, but the antidemocratic potential of OIRA was fully realized under Barack Obama. To head OIRA, Obama appointed his friend Cass Sunstein, an ideologically ambiguous law professor who tries to reconcile liberal goals with free-market Chicago economics. Critics have faulted Sunstein for wielding a form of cost-benefit analysis that tends to understate benefits and overstate costs. Under Sunstein's direction, OIRA gutted innumerable regulations of the EPA and other agencies—rules that were legally required to carry explicit standards that were mandated in laws passed by Congress and duly signed by the president.

Yet another dimension of the growth of the imperial presidency was the use of legal opinions written by the Office of Legal Counsel at the Justice Department in concert with the White House legal staff. There reached a peak of abuse under the presidency of George W. Bush, orchestrated mainly by Vice President Dick Cheney. Two key players were Cheney's close allies John Yoo (deputy director and then director of the Office of Legal Council) and David Addington (Cheney's own legal adviser). Among Yoo's more outrageous inventions were his legal memoranda contending that "enhanced interrogations" were something other than the torture prohibited by the Geneva Conventions, and that, in any case, prisoners allegedly associated with Al Qaeda were "enemy combatants" (another invented term) not associated with a state and thus had no protection against torture. Yoo also provided memos contending that despite US exercise of full authority at the Guantánamo prison camp, Guantánamo was not on US soil and thus was not subject to the due process required by US law.

Bush's lawyers also invented a concept called "rendition," in which US-held prisoners of war were spirited to countries known to practice torture, so that the US could disclaim legal responsibility. Most legal scholars found these contentions preposterous, and they were resisted by senior officials at the Departments of State and Defense, as well as the CIA. But they were very convenient to the Cheney-Bush strategy for Al Qaeda and the Iraq War. Since the increasingly rightwing federal courts cut executive power a wide berth, these memoranda were not challenged in court. They were rescinded by Obama, but a new round of inventive extralegal memos justifying executive overreach has spiraled higher under Trump.

Big Money as Constitutionally Protected Speech. The structural shift against democracy marched in tandem with the massive financial investment in politics by corporations, by Wall Street, and by the ideological right wing. Those investments operated not only independently from but increasingly in concert with the Republican Party. The political investments by organized business were a backlash against both the constraints that had begun with the New Deal and the new wave of consumer and environmental regulation that had begun in the 1960s. The case for concerted business engagement to roll back progressive regulation was crystallized in the famous Lewis Powell memo of August 1971, which called for a massive business counterattack. Powell, later a Supreme Court justice, was a corporate lawyer who wrote the memo at the request of the president of the US Chamber of Commerce. It was titled, "Attack on the American Free Enterprise System." Powell lamented "the apathy and default of business," adding:

> What has been the response of business to this massive assault upon its fundamental economics, upon its philosophy, upon its right to continue to manage its own affairs, and indeed upon its integrity?
>
> The painfully sad truth is that business, including the boards of directors and the top executives of corporations great and small and business organizations at all levels, often have responded—if at all—by appeasement, ineptitude and ignoring the problem.

The influence of the Powell memo can be exaggerated, but it crystallized a moment and a shift in strategic thinking. Business groups soon were pouring huge sums into rightwing think tanks and programs to inculcate rightwing ideas into the academy and the courts, as well as into intensified campaign spending and aggressive lobbying of the Nixon administration. In his first two years, Richard Nixon, fancying himself a socially progressive conservative, had been friendly to consumer and environmental legislation. That abruptly changed.

This shift strengthened the Republican Party in several respects. A system that is both democratic and capitalist necessarily reflects the tension between two contradictory first principles: one person/ one vote versus one dollar/one vote. To the extent that the capacity of money to buy votes is constructively suppressed, democracy can thrive. When money crowds out civic participation, not only does the whole system tilt to the right but public confidence in democracy rightly suffers, reinforcing the downward spiral.

Conversely, the increasing role of money as the currency of politics whipsaws Democrats, both as a party and as an ideology. Most very rich people have a fairly conservative view of economics and gravitate to the Republicans, despite the occasional Democratic billionaire. To the extent that Democrats try to compete for big money on essentially Republican terrain, they become more like Republicans. And if they try to court liberal big money by going left on every issue but economics, they distance themselves from their party's workaday base, as 2016 revealed. Small money demonstrated great potential in the 2018 midterms, but the allure of corporate and Wall Street money still exerts a huge undertow on Democrats as well as Republicans.

The corporate investment in politics repeats an unsavory pattern that had been curtailed for much of the twentieth century. Beginning with the Tillman Act of 1907, corporations were flatly prohibited from making political contributions. This reform was enacted in response to the last big wave of corporate money trying to take over politics under President William McKinley. The steady redefinition of money as speech began with the Supreme Court's *Buckley v. Valeo* decision in 1976, allowing unlimited campaign spending as speech, but preserving some limits on permissible donations. The decision gutted much of the reform that Congress had enacted with the Federal Election Campaign Act amendments in 1974, after the Watergate revelations of secret campaign donations that were effectively bribes.

Courts subsequently contrived other rulings that together virtually outlaw the regulation of campaign spending and weaken disclosure as well. In the 2010 *Citizens United* case, the Supreme Court overturned all limits on corporate campaign donations, despite the fact that prohibitions on such corporate spending had been found constitutional ever since the Tillman Act. The ruling inverted the usual meaning of the First Amendment, to give corporations the unlimited right to donate money to candidates, in the name of corporate personhood and free expression. This string of rulings was intensified in the 2014 *McCutcheon* decision, in which the court, by a 5–4 vote, effectively struck down all aggregate limits on campaign donations.

This intensified investment by special interests needs to be seen not as a "money and politics" problem but as an avenue of deeper corruption, in which money has become the principal currency of politics. Dark (secret) money has reached a level where it can be spent on ads and social media campaigns against candidates, spreading lies that targeted candidates simply don't have time or resources to rebut. As money crowds out voting, centrist Democrats raise huge sums from financial elites. Tame Democratic policy makers reciprocate the courtesy with friendly policies.

Media and Civil Society. As observers since Tocqueville have pointed out, it takes strong institutions of civil society to activate a deliberative citizenry and make institutions of formal democracy meaningful. The expansion of democracy in the twentieth century went hand in hand with the growth of voluntary, participatory associations. As Theda Skocpol's research has shown, a century ago there were some fifty-eight democratically accountable grassroots organizations with at least a million members each, ranging from largely apolitical service and fraternal groups like the Elks to more political groups, such as the League of Women Voters. In addition, political scientist Robert Putnam has called attention to the slow decline of what he termed the "long civic generation," the cohort whose views of democracy were shaped by the Great Depression and World War II. Putnam's work correlates social association and "social capital" with civic activity. The two are not identical, but they reflect and reinforce a similar associational state of mind. The same sensibility that led millions of Americans to socialize over bridge games and bowling leagues went hand in hand with participation in the League of Women Voters or the PTA.

For Putnam, one of the major factors that weakened the habits of association was the rise of television, typically a solitary or at best family activity, and also a passive one. Putnam demonstrates that the rise of TV viewing paralleled the decline in civic participation. This analysis can be overstated; other factors were at work.

For instance, the decline in working-class wages and the rise of the two-income family deprived the civic sphere of volunteer resources that were heavily female. The dominance in today's civic life by the elderly is not only because this age cohort is the last remnant of Putnam's long civic generation. Retired people are the only group today with spare time to participate in civic life. Still, there is a lot to the TV part of the story.

Television not only stole civic time that might have been spent at PTA meetings or even bridge games or bowling leagues. It also represented a source of diversion (in both senses of the word) that was far more entertaining than democratic participation. In another era, before radio and television, epic political events such as the Lincoln-Douglas debates provided both. Even in radio's early years, FDR's fireside chats were heard by most of the nation. They were entertaining in the best sense of the word—charming and witty, and also educational, uplifting, and solidarity-building. By the late twentieth century, congressional hearings might be available on C-SPAN, but they were a lot less fun to watch than any of a hundred other televised offerings. When a demagogue finally managed to be elected to the presidency, small wonder that he was first and foremost an entertainer.

The rise of cable and then of social media fragmented the public into many separate, self-isolated publics. Conventionally, Fox News represents the right, and CNN and MSNBC the left, but that framing is far too charitable to Fox. The mainstream press and cable networks dwell in an essentially factual universe, and Fox News largely does not. In its news coverage, Fox News is far more explicitly a propaganda arm of the Republican Party than CNN or even MSNBC is of the Democratic Party. Though commentators on CNN and MSNBC tend to tilt to the left, in their news coverage CNN and MSNBC essentially play it straight, and Fox News coverage does not. Fox also receives and echoes back pure conspiracy theories. In another sense, Fox merely takes to an extreme a fragmentation caused by the plethora of media options. But neither the fragmentation nor the extremism disguised as mainstream TV is good for democracy. In principle, the ability of people to select their own preferred cable channels is a gain for free choice, but democracy is irrevocably a collective endeavor that requires some sense of common conversation and common purpose.

More ominously, by 2018 Fox News had become not just a right-wing echo chamber, but literally a propaganda arm of the Trump White House. Jane Mayer detailed in an investigative piece for *The New Yorker* the multiple ways that Fox executives and on-air figures like Sean Hannity advised the president, boosted the president, and coordinated talking points with the president. Trump, in turn, took much of his material from Fox. It was something previously unknown in the American experience and all too familiar to dictatorships—state TV.

The Internet, Social Media, and Democracy. The displacement of civic life by television was positively benign for political democracy, compared to the next media revolution—namely, the rise of social media. In the early years of TV, the relatively small number of channels and the dominance by three networks meant that Americans could have one civic conversation. When internet affinity groups, followed by social media platforms such as Facebook, became the preferred form of communication and definition for the young, some observers saw a big gain for participatory democracy. People who were disinclined to show up at actual meetings could join virtual ones. A great deal of political organizing could take place via the internet and social media. Some politicians could and did make this work. As the effectiveness of groups such as Indivisible in the 2018 campaign attested, social media used as a communication tool could translate into genuine organizing. A lot of small money could be raised online via groups such as ActBlue, and web communities such as MoveOn could mobilize millions of activists as well as dollars.

But this blessing turned out to be double edged. Participating online via an affinity group or sending money in response to an e-pitch, as any organizer can tell you, does not represent the same level of commitment or engagement as coming to a meeting. Many people who get emails from MoveOn and send money conceive of themselves as activists, but most are passive activists.

Far worse is the fact that social media was ready-made to energize the extremes, such as the alt right. Groups that had lurked at the far fringes now had a new tool to activate hatred and build large networks of haters, based on alarmist and flatly false claims about the global Jewish conspiracy, Obama's birth in Kenya, and a thousand other slanders. By the fall of 2018, when a rabid anti-Semite opened fire with an A-15 assault weapon and massacred worshippers at a Pittsburgh synagogue service, it was all too clear that social media had become a haven for neofascist conspiracy theorists and advocates of violence. In a country whose civic traditions value free speech even for extremists and whose corporations value profits above all else, the big platform companies could not keep up with haters (and did not try all that hard), and civil libertarians were at a loss to know how and where to draw a line defining hate speech that deserved suppression. The venerable wisdom about free speech not allowing one to falsely cry "Fire!" in a crowded theater had no good digital analogy.

An old saying holds that a lie is halfway around the world before the truth gets its boots on. Social media supercharged that dynamic.

Web platforms enabled people to become not just consumers of news but *generators* of news, much of it fake or badly distorted. According to the Pew Research Center, 45 percent of Americans get their news primarily from Facebook. During the same period that social media were proliferating, the internet crowded out the core source of income that sustained traditional newspapers: display and classified advertising. Three essentially national papers have navigated the transition and found digital sources of revenue—the *New York Times*, *Washington Post*, and *Wall Street Journal*—but the shift as been devastating to regional newspapers, whose newsrooms are now a fraction of their former size and whose circulation has dwindled dramatically. This weakening of the factual press has been compounded by the takeover of many regional papers by private-equity owners with no commitment to journalism, and the further shrinkage of their newsrooms. The decline has impoverished the accurate coverage of state and local government and the civic conversation.

And, of course, new media made American democracy a sitting duck for Russian trolls, bots, and fake websites. The internet, and its uses by social media, was also ready-made for both corporate and government spying. Americans, who supposedly value their privacy, have been trained to put every imaginable kind of personal information online. If one-party government and one-party courts continue, it would be child's play for the government to get its hands on this information and use it to disrupt opposition activity and punish opponents. Despite early hopes that social media platforms would energize democracy, on balance they softened up America for a tyrant.

Democratic society finds itself caught between two versions of Big Brother: corporate and state. The giant platform companies, like

Facebook, Google, and Amazon, have massive access to our private information—and government security agencies have even more ability to snoop on citizens. We do not trust social media companies to police themselves, and we rightly are suspicious of proposals to give government more power to police them. Long before the internet, the framers of the Fourth Amendment rightly recognized that invasions of privacy are an assault on liberty. More than a century ago, first as a practicing attorney and later as a Supreme Court justice, Louis Brandeis famously defined "the right to be let alone" as a fundamental democratic freedom. All of this is in electronic jeopardy.

The Rise of the Market Paradigm as a Loss for Democracy. During the past half century, the market has become hegemonic. Institutions of social solidarity, such as trade unions, have been weakened. Reciprocal loyalty on the part of employers to their workers is seen as archaic and inefficient. The dominant ethic of the age is that you are on your own, and you will be paid on the basis of whatever skills you bring to the marketplace, where you are simply in competition with everyone else. Gig employers such as TaskRabbit make that premise explicit. Workers are literally in competition with each other to work for the cheapest pay. Young people are counseled to think of themselves as a brand. Products that used to have one price have a multiplicity of prices, from airline tickets to prescription drugs to hotel rooms, as commerce becomes a bidding market—laissez-faire gone berserk. All this comports with extreme conservative ideology.

Half a century ago, Sears Roebuck and other large, paternalistic employers had generous profit-sharing plans for their workers. A career Sears salesman could retire with a million dollars in profit-sharing savings. Sears provided this benefit out of a sense of civic commitment and loyalty to its workers, and also out of a strategic sense that being known as a good place to work would be good for its brand. The profits funneled to Sears employees came directly out of corporate earnings that might otherwise have gone to shareholders or executives. Sears leaders calculated that the increased effort and gratitude by its sales force might make up the difference, and more. But even if it didn't, the employees were valued as stakeholders.

This sensibility was blown away by the market revolution. In the 1970s, a new Chicago-economics doctrine contended that the only duty of a corporation was to "maximize shareholder value." That, in turn, became a rationale both for bogus manipulation of share prices and sheer greed on the part of executives. In this new world there was no room for Sears-style profit-sharing plans. Amazon, Google, Facebook, and the new wave of staggeringly profitable digital platform companies have no such plans. Amazon founder and leading shareholder Jeff Bezos is the world's richest man, with a net worth upwards of $150 billion. Until 2018, when Bezos was shamed by bad publicity into giving his workers a raise, he was paying some Amazon workers minimum wage. He could finance a profit-sharing plan out of his own petty cash.

But profit maximization just for the boss is the dominant ethic of the market era. The rest of us are on our own. If we did not have the wit to become entrepreneurs, too bad for us.

The conversion of more and more of economic and civic life into a market insidiously undermines democracy, a realm where citizens are supposedly equal. It weakens civic empathy. In a world where we all are on our own, why should I pay for your Medicaid? If my kids are in private school or if I am retired, why should I pay for your kids' public school? Why should I pay into Social Security, when I could be putting the same money into an IRA and getting a higher return? If you recognize these arguments, it's because they are standard Republican talking points in an era when the market model has become dominant, both explicitly and tacitly.

All of this feeds on itself. As public institutions are weakened and underfunded, they deliver less and less, and it becomes rational for people to conclude that we really are all on our own anyway. Ideology, values, and pocketbook realities are mutually reinforcing. This trend also weakens the Democrats as the party of civic and social solidarity and collective purpose. It strengthens the Republicans as the party of the market and self-reliance.

The rise of the market and the increase in public cynicism have gone hand in hand with declining confidence in government; in all large institutions, including the media; and in democracy itself. Just 13 percent of citizens report confidence in Congress. The percentage of people who tell pollsters that they care deeply whether they live in a democracy has fallen from 72 percent for the cohort born before World War II to just 30 percent for millennials. In 2015, some 32 percent of Americans told Pew that it would be better to have "a strong leader" who does not "have to bother" with elections.

The dominance of the market, and the weakening of countervailing institutions, has also widened income extremes. Sages since Aristotle have pointed out that gross inequity in income and wealth is incompatible with democracy.

Half a century ago, the political sociologist Barrington Moore wrote a classic titled *The Social Origins of Dictatorship and Democ-*

racy. Looking back over hundreds of years, Moore makes the point that different societies were more or less predisposed to democracy because of their social structures. In Britain, the constraints on the absolute power of the monarch by feudal lords prefigured modern democracy. In the American colonies, the postfeudal pattern of land-holding and the rise of yeoman farmers predisposed the colonies to democracy. Everywhere, the rise of a strong middle class was essential. In the nations where feudalism and absolute monarchy persisted and the middle class was weak, democracy was more difficult to sustain, and revolutions often ended in dictatorship. By almost any such measure, American society is less hospitable to democracy today than it was in the twentieth century.

The Antidemocratic Party

For the most part, the antidemocratic trends described in the previous section operated independently of the Republican Party, though they helped the Republicans in both a partisan and an ideological sense, as the party that trashes government and wants government to do less and the market to do more. Here we turn to other strategic moves by Republicans that *deliberately* weakened democracy.

The Conversion of Government from Ally to Adversary of the Franchise. Voting is the most fundamental expression of democracy. For most of the American experience, our democracy has steadily expanded the right to vote. In the early nineteenth century, the remaining property requirements for the franchise in some states were repealed. The Fifteenth Amendment extended the franchise to former slaves; the Nineteenth Amendment gave the vote to women. The Twenty-Sixth Amendment extended the vote to eighteen-year-olds. It was only with the Voting Rights Act of 1965 that the putative black right to vote in the Deep South became real, but all of these represented a steady expansion of democracy. This long succession of democratic expansions sponsored and enforced by government would soon be reversed.

The political scientist Richard Valelly refers to the great civil rights era that began in the 1960s as the Second Reconstruction. This progress was built on three great civil rights acts, of 1964, 1965, and 1968. These laws were finally enacted only after a bottom-up social movement—one that was brutally resisted by state-sponsored terror—pricked the conscience of a nation and a president. Unlike the aborted first Reconstruction of Abraham Lincoln, the second one stuck. Or so it seemed. Even Republican presidents supported extensions of the 1965 Voting Rights Act. Black voting in the South dramatically increased. Biracial governing coalitions in much of the Deep South elected political moderates who were liberal on race, such as Jimmy Carter and Bill Clinton. But the racism that has afflicted American democracy since the constitutional founding was only sleeping, and it came roaring back in the twenty-first century, as Republicans became the party of white southerners and of barriers to black voting.

Beginning with George W. Bush, and more intensely at the state level, government under Republicans began suppressing the right to vote. With the Supreme Court decision *Shelby County v. Holder* in June 2013, state voter suppression tactics were largely exempted from the Justice Department's review ("preclearance") of proposed changes in voting systems. Several southern states immediately took advantage of the ruling. They changed voting procedures to reduce voting by minorities and others likely to support Democrats, thus exposing as disingenuous Chief Justice John Roberts's claim in *Shelby* that Justice Department preclearance to prevent voter suppression was no longer necessary. In several northern states, including Wisconsin, Ohio, and Pennsylvania, Republican governors and legislators borrowed tactics long used by the South. All of this intensified under Trump. The story of the extensive suppression of the right to vote—a right that is so fundamental to democracy—deserves its own chapter; it is addressed in detail in Chapter 4.

Excesses by the Congressional Majority. Under successive Republican House Speakers and Senate majority leader Mitch McConnell, the normal rights of the minority party have been trampled. Legislation has been drafted in secret without the usual hearing process, and rushed through on pure party-line votes without opposition legislators even getting a look at the full text. Long-standing congressional norms of how House-Senate conference committees operate (with minority and majority members from both houses) have been violated. The use of special-interest provisions to benefit corporate and political allies has reached a new low.

It has become conventional among many political scientists to speak of the "dysfunction" of Congress as a generic problem. This is misleading and far too polite to Republicans, for whom gridlock has become a prime, deliberate strategy. Abuses of power took one form (to block and undermine presidential initiatives) when Republicans controlled Congress under Obama, and another form (to rush through legislation) under Trump. Under Obama, the Affordable Care Act consumed 25 days of debate, and members of both parties offered 130 amendments. This was after 60 hours of legislative markup in the Senate Finance Committee, all with the full participation of both parties.

By contrast, when the Republicans sought to repeal the ACA, the legislation was prepared in secret, and there were no hearings, McConnell appointed an all-Republican task force of thirteen senators to draft the repeal, and Democrats did not get to participate at all. That measure failed. The Republican-led Congress resorted to similar tactics in successfully jamming through their tax cut. McConnell also violated long-standing practice by refusing to consider any nomination by President Obama to the Supreme Court after the death of Antonin Scalia in February 2016, when Obama's term still had almost eleven months to run.

If bipartisanship is dead, the responsibility is lopsided. The Republican-led House was equally culpable. A key factor was the Republican strategy begun under the Bush presidency that was known as the Hastert Rule, after then-Speaker Dennis Hastert. Under the rule, which eliminated bipartisan coalitions, legislation could be brought to the floor only if it had the support of "a majority of the majority"—more than half of the Republican Caucus. Then other Republicans were expected to loyally support the bill. This rule precluded Democrats getting together with Republicans to cosponsor and possibly enact genuinely bipartisan bills.

Opportunistic Uses of Federalism. In principle, Republicans supposedly value both states' rights and local control. In practice,

Republicans at the national level use federal power to preempt state regulation when that proves expedient, and Republicans at the state level pass laws to preempt and prohibit liberal ordinances by cities. Many states controlled by Republicans have cities governed by progressive Democrats. These include Austin, Charlotte, Atlanta, Memphis, and numerous others. In these states, Republican legislatures and governors have trampled home rule, in order to veto city ordinances on wages, taxes, gay rights, the environment, and other contentious issues. By the same token, the Republican federal administration has selectively tried to preempt state regulation when that is ideologically useful, as in the case of Trump's effort to reverse California's long-established regulatory regime for auto emissions, and the provision of the 2017 Republican tax act capping the deductibility of state and local taxes as a way of punishing high-tax, high-service states typically led by Democrats.

Traditionally, the usual form of federal preemption has been known as "floor preemption." The federal government sets basic standards, and states are free to go further. This has been the case in policy realms as diverse as minimum-wage laws, the estate tax, and environmental regulation. Today's Republicans, however, are situational federalists. They are for federalism when it serves ideological and partisan goals, and against federalism when that is convenient. Both stances are antidemocratic as well as anti-Democratic.

Flagrantly Ideological Uses of the Courts to Weaken Democracy. As the far right has gotten more and more of a lock on the federal appellate courts, culminating with the confirmations of Neil Gorsuch and Brett Kavanaugh to the Supreme Court, purely invented doctrines have been used to serve goals of rightwing ideology and politics, and to entrench the Republican Party. Not only have these decisions undermined voting rights while elevating the role of money in politics, but they have been profoundly antidemocratic in their opportunistic reversals of laws enacted by Congress that earlier Supreme Court decisions found fully constitutional.

These rulings have amounted to a war on government's ability to regulate capitalism, to protect the rights of minorities, to constrain arbitrary presidential power, to respect the ability of states to pass laws that go beyond federal minimums, to safeguard labor rights enacted by Congress, and a good deal more. Both the rulings themselves and the tactics that Republicans used to install far-right partisan judges were profoundly antidemocratic.

Trump's Intensified Assaults

These several trends weakened democracy. Most antedated the election of Donald Trump. Taken together, they undermined the norms of comity and the legitimacy of political opposition, on which robust democracy depends. They weakened public faith in public institutions, in government's basic honesty and its capacity to address public problems. Though nearly all of the obstructionism was the work of Republicans, the media fed a narrative of "partisan bickering" and "gridlock" that suggested symmetrical blame. In the 2016 campaign and in his presidency, Trump intensified the assault. With an aspiring dictator in the White House, the Republican-led Congress doubled down on its own antidemocratic tactics.

Denying the Legitimacy of Political Opponents. During the 2016 campaign Trump encouraged chants of "Lock her up!" Had Hillary Clinton been elected, the Republican Congress was prepared to embark, even before she took office, on impeachment and other harassing investigations. Weirdly, had Clinton won, her presidency would have been treated as less legitimate than Trump's, even though she defeated him by more than 3 million popular votes and Russian influence in flipping several key states has now been well documented. Trump, however, claimed—with no evidence whatever—that 3–5 million votes had been cast illegally for Clinton. All this was an intensification of the relentless denial of Obama's legitimacy by the Republican Congress and the far right well before Trump's election. And Trump, obsessively concerned with extirpating any vestige of Obama's achievements, was part of this pre-2016 mob, in his embrace of the bogus denial of Obama's birth in the United States.

This denial of the legitimacy of one's opponent was something new and ominous in American politics. If any recent president deserved to have his legitimacy questioned, it was George W. Bush. But once the Supreme Court had acted by a party-line 5–4 vote to suspend the 1980 Florida recount (also with dubious legitimacy), Democrats gamely accepted the result for the sake of the republic, led by Al Gore's too-gracious concession speech. Not a single senator rose to challenge the report of the electoral college certifying Bush's election.

Using the Presidency to Incite Violence and Stir Up Hatred. Both as a candidate and then as president, Trump has glorified violence and encouraged mobs to rough up his opponents. Repeatedly in the campaign, he condoned acts of violence, going so far as to suggest that perhaps "the Second Amendment people," meaning gun extremists, could "take care of Hillary Clinton" once and for all. After the August 2017 Charlottesville rally of neo-Nazis and other far-right activists ended in a riot and the death of a peaceful protestor, Trump refused to condemn the violence and insisted that there were good people on both sides. Campaigning in 2018 for the reelection of Montana congressman Greg Gianforte, who had punched out a reporter during the 2016 campaign and pled guilty to misdemeanor assault, Trump declared, "Any guy that can do a body slam, he's my kind of guy." In both the campaign and as president, Trump gave legitimacy to the so-called alt right, a polite term for the racist and anti-Semitic far right. They became his shock troops. These are the classic tactics of a fascist leader. And when impeachment became a political possibility, Trump warned that his supporters would riot in the streets to prevent it. All of these are the maneuvers of a dictator.

Trump has tried to have it both ways, dog whistle style. His remarks legitimize and incite violence. When actual violence ensues, his posture is, "Who, me?" After pipe bombs were mailed to several critics of Trump two weeks before the midterm elections and the perpetrator turned out to be a fanatic Trump supporter, the president initially stuck to the expected script and declared, "We have to come together and send one very clear, strong, unmistakable message that acts or threats of political violence of any kind have no place in the United States of America." Within a day, Trump was back to blasting CNN, one of the targets of the pipe bombs, as purveyor of fake news and hatred. And more than a dozen Trump allies in the far-right media were spreading the story that the bombs were actually sent by Democrats, "false flags, carefully planned for the midterms," as Jacob Wohl, a Trump backer at the website Gateway Pundit, wrote on Twitter. The theme was picked up by Rush Limbaugh on his mass-market radio show. "It's happening in October," Limbaugh said darkly. "There's a reason for this." Just days before a pipe bomb was mailed to billionaire George Soros and a gunman massacred worshippers at a Pittsburgh synagogue, Republican House majority leader Kevin McCarthy tweeted, "Don't let Soros, Bloomberg and Steyer BUY the election." All three Democratic donors are of Jewish origin.

Scapegoating "Others." Trump's characterization of Mexicans as rapists and murderers and his demonization of Muslims are also vintage techniques of tyrants. The damage to democracy is both overt and subtle. The use of scapegoats affirms and stirs up fringe groups. It divides the nation and diverts attention from policy strategies that might unite it. (Why think about how corporations are fleecing working people generally when you can just hate Muslims?) On a more insidious level, Trump's brand of demonization undermines the ability of democracy to address difficult policy challenges, in this case immigration, which then reduces public confidence in democracy itself.

Despite the deep Republican antipathy to Barack Obama, a rare island of constructive bipartisanship between 2013 and 2016 was the compromise immigration reform cosponsored by four Democrats and four Republicans. The package combined tougher border controls with an earned path to citizenship for illegal immigrants who had clean records, plus permission to stay for undocumented migrants who had been brought to the United States as children. But once Trump came on the scene, Republicans other than John McCain jettisoned their support for the bill. This stalemate further served Trump's demagoguery by leaving a policy challenge to fester, while giving him a fatter target.

Dancing with Dictators. As both a candidate and the president, Trump has made clear his admiration for autocrats. His first trip as president, weirdly, was to Saudi Arabia. His first European trip was to Poland, where the Law and Justice party government was under fire from the EU and from local democratic activists for suppressing liberty and democracy. In his speech and his comments to the press there, he mentioned none of this. Trump notoriously had only kind words for Vladimir Putin, and even effusively embraced North Korea's Kim Jong-un and Rodrigo Duterte of the Philippines. Trump's motivation has been a jumble of serving his family's business interests via corrupt conflicts of interest, Russia and Saudi Arabia being prime examples, and genuine regard for strongman leaders in league with local kleptocrats whom he viewed almost as role models. The damage to democracy as a global cause was all too obvious. The damage to American democracy was more tacit. The president of the United States was signaling that it didn't matter whether a nation was a democracy and that autocracies were often better models. His chief political strategist, Steve Bannon, went on to try to construct a new International, made up of autocratic regimes.

Encouraging Russian Interference. Special Counsel Robert Mueller did not even need to document secret meetings between Trump senior aides and Russian operatives. Trump urged the Russians to produce more Democratic emails, *on television*, before tens of millions of witnesses. Not only did Russian intelligence hack and leak embarrassing private emails of Clinton's campaign staff; the Russians timed the leaks to deliberately upstage the most potentially damaging revelation about Trump: the tape of his comment that he could grab women "by the pussy." That story quickly vanished from the front pages in favor of the juicy details of John Podesta's emails, which were leaked immediately following the pussy uproar.

So extensive were Russian operations that fake organizations created by Russian trolls sometimes had more impact than real ones. A bogus social media campaign called Blacktivist was created expressly to discourage black support for Hillary Clinton. At points during the campaign, Blacktivist.com was getting more page views than the real organization, Black Lives Matter. In her exhaustive study of the impact of Russian hacking and trolling in 2016, the political scientist Kathleen Hall Jamieson demonstrated that these Russian tactics changed enough votes to literally flip the election to Trump. Former FBI director James Comey's decision to criticize Hillary Clinton on the eve of the 2016 election, Jamieson documents, was in response to a "news" item that Comey knew to be fake but that some people in the US Attorney's Office thought was real, so Comey felt he needed to take Clinton to task for the sake of his own credibility. Russian intelligence, in effect, got the director of the FBI to make an attack on Clinton that was very likely decisive in Trump's victory. Trump's otherwise bizarre foreign policy moves had one thing in common: returning the favor to Putin.

Vilifying the Free Press. Trump's obsessive lying to the media and denunciations of the truth-telling press as "fake news," and his repeated characterization of the press as "enemies of the people," are also vintage dictator behavior. These assertions play to long-standing public skepticism about the media and undermine one of the core democratic safeguards. I overheard a conversation in which one Trump supporter referred to the extensive documentation by the *New York Times* of the Saudi government's culpability in the execution of *Washington Post* columnist Jamal Khashoggi. The other Trump supporter responded, "They make it up," as if that settled the question.

Attacks on the press by politicians are nothing new, but Trump has made them systematic. He has oscillated between making threats or banishing critical reporters and news organizations such as CNN from the White House pressroom, and trying to charm even the *New York Times* and the *Washington Post* with occasional exclusive interviews. He pressured the Justice Department to block the merger of AT&T and Time Warner, which owns his nemesis, CNN (the Justice Department suit was subsequently thrown out by a federal judge). He blatantly tried to intimidate the *Washington Post* by threatening to have one or more government agencies go after Amazon, whose founder and CEO is also the *Post*'s publisher.

Destroying Government with Malign Neglect. Democrats have been too close to Wall Street, but they have also been competent stewards of the basic functions of government. Indeed, as the political scientist Suzanne Mettler has pointed out in an important book called *The Submerged State*, government has gotten far too little credit for all of the constructive things it quietly does for citizens. Ordinarily, the process of finding well-qualified people to run major agencies begins immediately after Election Day, and presidents who think they have a chance of winning already have a transition team well in place. Obama appointed his in June of 2008.

By contrast, Trump got into a feud with his transition director, former New Jersey governor Chris Christie, on election eve, and blew up the entire transition process. In agency after agency, Obama officials, having prepared to hand over authority to incoming Trump officials, found nobody in place to take charge. The actual appointment of officials was a burlesque process of ad hoc outreach to industry trade associations, the alt right, old cronies, junior campaign staff, and rightwing think tanks. The result was a stealth demolition of government, by chaos, conflicts of interest, and sheer incompetence. Unsung but important positions like the director of the Federal Emergency Management Agency (FEMA) went to people who literally had no idea what they were doing, and the result was all too clear in the aftermath of several hurricanes. With Hurricane Maria, Trump added insult to injury when he blamed Puerto Rican citizens and officials for the failures of his own appointee. At other, lesser-known agencies, there was deep damage below the waterline.

Thankfully, civil service appointees remained. They even worked without pay during the government shutdown of December–January 2018–19. The deep state so reviled by Trump's henchmen has a certain amount of staying power. But the next Democratic government will have a massive repair job.

Dumbing Down Discourse. A decade ago it would have been inconceivable to imagine that a president of the United States would both make major policy announcements and hurl schoolyard insults via tweets. This habit has produced eye rolling about Trump, but worse, it has caused politicians (and opinion leaders) across the political spectrum to use tweets to gain publicity. In a cluttered news environment, where hardly anyone reads press releases, tweets play to the reporter's need for a pithy quote and the politician's need to get quoted. Tweets have become all too normal, pulling other politicians down to Trump's gutter level in a contest that only Trump can win. Tweets reward the inflammatory or snarky remark, and punish anything resembling complexity or nuance. They are the antithesis of the kind of informed public discourse envisioned by the framers of the American republic at Philadelphia. (Imagine the deliberations of the Constitutional Convention being conducted via tweets.) So, Trump even influences his adversaries in the manner in which the public's business is conducted. This is very good for the shareholders of Twitter and good for Trump—not so good for democracy.

Denying Objective Truth. There has never before been a president with a penchant for claiming that black is white and up is down. The *Washington Post* has a full-time team assigned to track Trump's lies. During his first two years, the tally was 8,158 false or misleading statements. Trump has repeatedly insisted that he did not say something, even when video exists of him saying it. He offered Elizabeth Warren a million dollars to be donated to the charity of her choice if she would take a DNA test that demonstrated Native American ancestry. When Warren duly took the test, Trump not only stiffed her for the donation—a long-standing Trump habit—but denied that he had ever made the offer, despite a widely circulated video that shows him making it.

Paradoxically, because of their sheer volume and the short attention span of the media and the public, exposés of Trump's lies did not do the political damage that they would do to an ordinary politician. While the media was reporting one Trump lie, he was on to several others, or he was changing the subject with another headline-grabbing tweet. His intuitive tactic of flooding the zone flummoxed the ability of both the press and his political opposition to hold him accountable.

Before Trump, outright lies in politics were rare occurrences and big stories. When a political figure was caught in a flagrant lie or even a relatively innocent misrepresentation, it would be a major scandal, often a career ender. In 2008, Barack Obama felt he had to pull the nomination of former senator Tom Daschle to be his secretary of health and human services because it came to light that a donor had paid for Daschle's car and driver, and Daschle had neglected to report it as in-kind income. This was penny-ante stuff compared to a multiplicity of Trump lies and conflicts of interest. But because Trump's lies are so extensive and frequent, they are taken for granted; they have lost their power to shock, and the latest lie is not much of a story. Obviously, when lying by a chief executive is merely normal, there is massive damage to democratic accountability.

By the same token, the claim by Trump, his allies, and supporters that objective truth does not exist in many realms makes democratic deliberation all but impossible. Republicans have gone beyond claims that global climate change does not exist or is not a consequence of human actions to shutting down government research projects that might demonstrate the contrary. In North Carolina, the state prohibited public agencies from basing projections or recommendations on the assumption of sea-level rise. The Fox News habit of dwelling in a world made up of its own truths, and Trump's relative success in disparaging more objective, factual media as "fake news," is toxic for democracy itself, since it blurs the distinction between fact and value, and makes debate based on commonly agreed facts impossible.

Would that all of this had begun with Trump. It did not. The Bush administration softened the ground for Trump by basing its case for the Iraq War on made-up facts. Likewise the Reagan administration in the Iran-Contra affair, in which the White House sought to secretly move funds to rightwing Nicaraguan guerrillas, despite explicit prohibition by Congress, through the use of a bizarre money-laundering scheme via Iran. This official lying was not limited to Republicans. One of the biggest government lies of the mid-twentieth century was the fabricated Gulf of Tonkin attack, used by President Lyndon Johnson to stampede Congress into approving escalation of the Vietnam War.

These other presidents, at least, paid a dear political price for their lies. And a few very big lies were easier to bring to public focus and to expose than a blizzard of thousands of lies—large, medium, and small. With some 40 percent of Americans prepared to support Trump no matter what he says or does, it remains to be seen whether he will be called to account, despite serial assaults on democracy that would have undone an ordinary politician.

George Orwell anticipated all of this, both in his celebrated 1946 essay "Politics and the English Language," which gave us the adjective "Orwellian," and in his two dystopian novels, *Animal Farm* and *1984*. He was writing at a time when communists and fascists alike used language in service of Big Lies. If rulers can create their own reality and dominate discourse, then actual reality stands no chance. The leftwing enforcers of politically correct language, an irritation to the broad public that Trump brilliantly hung around the necks of the mainstream Democratic Party, inadvertently helped enable Trump.

The wheel, of course, is still in spin. The good news is that not all of Trump's attempts to destroy democracy have succeeded. The bad news is that all of them—and more—would intensify with a second term for Trump or another Trump-style Republican. We now turn to the firebreaks that have held so far, and the menace of what Trump might do next.

CHAPTER 3

≋

Averting Tyranny

D onald Trump's first two years were a road map to tyranny. A Trump second term or a term under a successor who picked up where Trump left off could be far worse. A good place to start is a refresher on Watergate—what Watergate was actually about, the differences and similarities between Nixon and Trump, why democracy could triumph in 1974, and why it is less resilient today.

From Nixon to Trump

History's verdict on the Watergate affair is that democracy held. The last chapter on Trump remains to be written. Richard Nixon was done in by the collision between his own overreach and the strength of core institutions of American democracy. It also took some elements of luck, most notably the fact that a security guard happened to discover a scrap of tape over a lock at the Democratic National Committee's headquarters in the Watergate complex, placed by Nixon's surprisingly amateurish Plumbers squad as it attempted to steal documents from the Democrats. In the Trump era, no physical break-in was needed to get politically embarrassing materials on the Democrats. It was far more efficient for the Russians, egged on by Trump and his confederates, to hack and make public confidential DNC and Clinton campaign emails.

The reason Nixon needed to set up the Plumbers and kindred extralegal operations in the first place was that the CIA, the FBI, and the IRS refused to become Nixon's personal spy agencies. By the same token, the deep state of the Nixon era included uncorrupted courts and a Republican attorney general, Elliot Richardson, who named a fiercely independent special prosecutor, Archibald Cox, and refused to fire him, setting up the Saturday Night Massacre of October 20, 1973, the event that began Nixon's final downfall. Under Trump, other branches of government are less of a barrier.

Watergate, at bottom, had four strands. One was the use of secret campaign contributions. These came to light as part of the broader investigations, and stimulated congressional reform legislation in 1974. The second element was attempted use of the machinery of the federal government "to screw political enemies," in the choice words of an August 1971 White House memo. The third and best-known strand was the use of extralegal break-ins, most famously the Plumbers' foiled attempt to take documents from Democratic Party headquarters at Watergate. The final aspect was the failed cover-up, which ultimately led to Nixon's impeachment and resignation.

When the agencies of government failed to do Nixon's political bidding, he set out to create a parallel intelligence apparatus to crush both the opposition to the Vietnam War and the Democratic Party, as well as his personal enemies. In addition to the Plumbers, the Nixon White House created a unit known as COINTELPRO (short for "Counterintelligence Program"), to gather intelligence and sow discord among antiwar groups. The success of Daniel Ellsberg in making public the official and often sordid history of the planning for the Vietnam War in the Pentagon Papers made Nixon apoplectic, and the Plumbers' first caper was a break-in at the office of Ellsberg's psychiatrist, Lewis Fielding, in September 1971.

Nixon tried to explicitly politicize the IRS to gather intelligence on his enemies. This was one of the counts in his impeachment. He failed. I wrote about it at the time, in an investigative piece for the *New York Times Magazine*. I found that three traditional Republican commissioners of the IRS, who had a sense of the integrity of the institution, flatly refused to do Nixon's bidding. Nixon also tried and failed to get the FBI to turn off any investigation of the Watergate break-in, and he considered FBI director L. Patrick Gray hopelessly disloyal. In May 1973, Attorney General Richardson appointed Cox as special prosecutor. By late spring of 1973, several White House officials were cooperating with the special prosecutor.

For Watergate to unravel and lead to Nixon's downfall, several elements of our democratic system had to function. One was separation of powers, and it was crucial that Democrats controlled both houses of Congress and launched the needed investigations. It is doubtful that congressional Republicans would have acted. In addition, at least some Republicans in the administration, notably

Richardson and Deputy Attorney General William Ruckelshaus, put loyalty to the republic well ahead of loyalty to the Republican Party or to Nixon personally, and resigned rather than carrying out Nixon's order to fire the special prosecutor. The third-ranking Justice Department official, Robert Bork, did fire Cox, but the firing was ruled illegal by a federal judge, and Nixon soon felt compelled to agree to a successor prosecutor, Leon Jaworski, who proved just as tough and independent as Cox.

Another key element was that the courts did their jobs. Much of the truth about Watergate unfolded in the courtroom of US District Court judge John Sirica. When the existence of Nixon's secret White House taping system came to light, the Supreme Court unanimously ruled that Nixon had to turn over the tapes, which he did.

Last, the press did not succumb to any of the White House threats, including Attorney General John Mitchell's notorious on-the-record warning to Carl Bernstein that *Washington Post* publisher Katharine Graham was going to "get her tit caught in a big fat wringer." In the end, Nixon was duly impeached, dozens of high officials went to jail, and the Republican Party was punished in the 1974 midterms by a Democratic Party gain of 49 House seats.

To compare the Watergate denouement with Trump's assaults on democracy is to realize how far the republic has fallen and how much the democratic guardrails have been weakened since Nixon's day. For one thing, of course, Democrats do not control both houses of Congress and few Republicans are inclined to cross Trump. For another, the special-counsel statute under which Robert Mueller operates is far weaker than the statute that governed Archibald Cox. The Nixon-era law expressly authorized the special prosecutor to tender his report to Congress. The current law requires the special counsel to report to the Justice Department, which is under no obligation to do anything with the information received and may keep it secret or bowdlerized, as Attorney General William Barr sought to do with Robert Mueller's report. Far fewer Republicans in the current administration have the independence and integrity of an Elliot Richardson. The courts are also far more partisan and ideologically rightwing than they were in the 1970s. Finally, the drama of the Watergate break-in, though it was not the only element of Watergate, gave the story a concrete focus. Trump's offenses, if anything, are more impeachable but more diffuse.

The press, at least, still does its job, despite Trump's attempt to vilify and intimidate the media. But unlike in the Watergate era, today's press is fragmented into different bubbles and different realities When mainstream press and the three networks reported on the Watergate affair, there was only White House propaganda to counter those reports, and no segment of the media to insist that the stories were fake news. Today, Fox News is effectively an arm of the White House message machine, seconded by rightwing talk radio and an echo chamber of social media sites, and we lack a single national conversation of the kind that steadily turned public opinion, followed closely by Republican senators, against Nixon.

The grounds for Trump's impeachment have long been hidden in plain view, from his patent violations of the Constitution's emoluments clause, to his public invitation for the Russians to meddle in the election, to serial forms of other corruption. But because our democracy is less robust today, and his party far more slavishly loyal to him, the consequences remain to be seen.

Two Cheers for the Deep State

We have lost major elements of our democracy. But enough of it remains that it may yet be redeemed. Some powerful norms and rules have persisted that Trump could not totally destroy, at least not yet. Elections were not canceled. Courts were partly captured but still functioned. Trump found that there were limits to his ability to govern by decree. Many of his moves backfired politically, and eventually even Republicans began to defect.

Unlike a pure dictator, Trump was unable to fill the entire executive branch with personal loyalists. His own chaotic incompetence undermined his tyrannical zeal.

Effective autocrats take pains to install a personalist regime throughout the government. Yet nearly two years into Trump's presidency, 204 out of 665 major presidential appointments that required Senate confirmation remained unfilled, which meant that civil service or holdover appointees continued to run much of the government.

As several books and articles have revealed, even Trump's own appointees were often appalled by his actions and determined to protect the country from his worst excesses. Despite severe damage to the career foreign service, officials of the national security establishment, at the Pentagon and at the State Department, did what they could to keep foreign policy from coming off the rails. There were times when Trump and his senior appointees were openly contradicting each other on major policy matters, yet he could not fire them all.

The inspectors general at several agencies continued to do their jobs. The inspector general for the General Services Administration, which handles government-owned and government-rented real estate, published a report detailing Trump's personal involvement in decisions concerning the location of government offices that affected his private business interests. The 500-page report of the Justice Department's inspector general confirmed that the FBI was much harsher on Hillary Clinton than on Donald Trump in the closing days of the 2016 election.

The survival of independent science agencies, despite Trump's war on climate change, is more evidence of the resilience of the deep state. Trump did succeed in doing serious damage to the Environmental Protection Agency. On the other hand, the White House kept trying to cut the budgets of the National Institutes of Health and the National Science Foundation, but even under the Republican-led Congress, large majorities in both houses not only kept these agencies whole but increased their funding. Why? Part of the reason is that American private business, from biotech to Silicon Valley, depends on the basic research of these science agencies. The alliance between business and the deep state is toxic when it comes to the failure to regulate the big banks, but it proved useful in protecting basic science from Trump.

Other key agencies continued to be defended by strong public constituencies. With exotic diseases and other effects of climate change increasing (despite the denials of far-right Republicans), it would be insane to cut back the budgets of the Centers for Disease Control or the National Hurricane Center and the other branches of NOAA (the National Oceanographic and Atmospheric Administration). The navy, whose bases are at sea level, became a prime counterweight to the denial of sea-level rise. So, while Trump and his henchmen did their utmost to destroy environmental regulation, the basic mission of the science agencies endured. In late November 2018, thirteen major agencies of the federal government issued a comprehensive 1,656-page report mandated by Congress on the worsening dangers and likely consequences of climate change—which Trump could not block.

Despite all that Trump was able do to the national government, the US is still a federal system. At the level of state and local government, opposition to Trump persisted, not just in states controlled or partially controlled by Democrats but via state prosecutors and courts. Thanks to the midterms, Democrats at the start of 2019 controlled twenty-three of the fifty governorships. Most important, Democratic control of the House opened the door to myriad investigations of Trump's abuse of power, and also blocked several legislative forays, as well as restoring something like normal functioning of a bicameral legislature.

Yet all of these firebreaks could be breached if Trump survives to be reelected, or if he is followed by a Trumpian successor.

As in Watergate, some of the survival of our democracy has reflected luck. We were lucky that Jeff Sessions, a proudly independent (if racist) former senator, was attorney general, and not some factotum who would have bent to Trump's will. Trump's insults of his own attorney general were unprecedented, but Sessions is a proud man with friends and allies in the Senate, who warned Trump not to fire him.

We were similarly fortunate that Rod Rosenstein, a man of integrity and concern for the system, was named deputy attorney general. Sessions and Rosenstein protected the special counsel and enabled

Robert Mueller's investigations and prosecutions to gain traction. This luck was in no way guaranteed. These two positions might have been held by opportunistic hacks like much of the rest of Trump's cabinet, and Mueller could have been gone before his investigation really began.

When Trump finally did fire Sessions, the day after the 2018 midterms, replacing him with an unqualified loyalist, Matthew Whitaker, as acting attorney general, the constitutional antibodies kicked in. Trump had expected that with Sessions gone, Whitaker could exercise his right to approve or disapprove all of Mueller's proposed actions, and to have full access to the special counsel's files, which in turn could be shown to Trump to help with his defense. But the gambit backfired. Whitaker found himself hemmed in by challenges to his authority to function as attorney general, not having been duly confirmed by the Senate, and Mueller proceeded to wrap up his investigation and indictments, as if Whitaker did not exist.

With William Barr, Trump finally got the attorney general he wanted. Prior to his appointment, Barr auditioned for the job with an unsolicited memorandum outlining an extravagant and extraconstitutional view of executive power. At his confirmation hearings, Barr postured as a public-minded sixty-eight-year-old who really didn't need this job, and who would put his loyalty to the republic above his loyalty to the president. That turned out to be a disingenuous feint. When Mueller at last tendered his report, Barr took four weeks to laboriously "redact" (censor) the 448-page document. In the meantime, Barr sounded a lot more like the president's personal lawyer or publicist than the attorney general, spinning the report as a vindication of Trump. But when the heavily censored report was at last made public, there was no way to disguise its damaging findings. Mueller had stopped just short of an indictment, but the report was a virtual invitation to an impeachment and a road map for how Congress should proceed. The report demonstrated in great detail that the "Russian government interfered in the 2016 presidential election in a sweeping and systematic fashion." There were no explicit quid pro quos in Russia's successful effort to throw the election to Trump, but plenty of signaling and plenty of otherwise inexplicable reciprocal favors by Trump to Putin afterward. Mueller included a 128-page summary of the evidence that Trump personally obstructed justice.

The obstruction only intensified when Congress tried to follow up on Mueller's leads. Trump had tried to obstruct justice; he had failed only because some of his underlings had refused to follow his orders. The release of Mueller's report marked the beginning of a new and ominous phase of the Trump presidency. Trump initially tried to depict it as vindication. Then, once even the censored version was made public, it was clear that the report was nothing of the sort. Mueller had declined to indict mainly because the Justice Department guidelines prohibited an indictment of a sitting president. Trump then changed his story. The report, he tweeted, was "bullshit," just the latest phase in a continuing witch hunt. Trump then mounted a wall-to-wall effort to block all of the pending investigations following up on Mueller's leads. He directed officials and former aides not to testify. He filed suits to block other probes, such as the investigation of Deutsche Bank's possible corrupt financing of Trump's empire. As these cases reach the Supreme Court, the rule of law could hinge on Chief Justice Roberts—and whether Trump tries to defy the court.

The Unfinished Trump Agenda

Consider the several things that Trump wanted to do but didn't—and what he or a more systematic successor might accomplish in a second term.

Shackling the Free Press. Trump has demonized the media, but has not succeeded in destroying a free and critical press. However, there is a playbook for doing just that. Dictators manipulate broadcast licenses and the financial viability of the print press, so that friendly media dominate and only token opposition survives. In semi-democracies, friends of the regime invest in supportive media. In Russia, there is a nominal opposition press, but opponents of the regime risk being murdered. The killing of Saudi journalist Jamal Khashoggi became an international scandal in part because he was a US resident and *Washington Post* columnist, and in part because the killing by a high-level Saudi hit squad took place in the Saudi consulate on Turkish soil. But hundreds of dissident journalists inside Saudi Arabia are in prison or dead.

In Hungary, the regime has created a Media Council. All the major newspapers and broadcast outlets give favorable coverage to the government. In Turkey, after an alleged coup attempt in July 2016, the government seized the assets of more than 150 media organizations. These were closed, causing some 2,700 journalists to lose their jobs. In Israel, the pro-Netanyahu paper *Israel Hayom* is lavishly subsidized by American billionaire and Trump supporter Sheldon Adelson and given away free, while the chronically strapped independent *Ha'aretz* has to watch its back.

Even in well-established democracies such as Britain's, the press suffers the effect of constraints that have never hobbled the American media. Britain has much tougher libel laws, as well as an official secrets act that puts journalists at personal risk for disclosing confidential information, even if they have never signed a national security oath promising to keep knowledge secret. By tradition and long-standing constitutional doctrine, the media in the US have not been subject to prior restraints of items that the executive branch contends might harm "national security" (a term so vague as to invite all manner of abuse), except in the most extreme circumstances. Even these last-resort restraints have been successfully resisted by the press. That situation could also change, by statute.

One area of ambiguity is the right of the press to protect confidential sources who have leaked classified material, or to protect itself from litigants who seek to compel testimony in civil suits from reporters or their sources. The United States does not have a press shield law on the right of journalists to protect whistle-blowers. In a few cases, judges have held reporters in contempt. But given long-standing norms of press freedom, judges have not pushed this too far. Only a tiny handful of reporters have ever had to go to prison to protect sources. And their sources have largely escaped retribution as well. Even Daniel Ellsberg was spared prison. In the Pentagon Papers case, the Supreme Court ruled that the government had not met the very high burden of proving national harm necessary to justify prior restraint. But that was in the heyday of the Warren court. It is all too easy to imagine the Roberts court, despite all of its contrived solicitude for corporate speech, going the other way in deferring to executive branch claims of national security, when it comes to real free speech.

The Espionage Act of 1917, the governing statute in such cases, is alarmingly general and ambiguous. The Act makes it a crime to communicate information that could harm the national defense or help a foreign power. Knowingly receiving and passing along classified information is potentially a crime under the Act. The case of Julian Assange, the mastermind of WikiLeaks, demonstrates what a slippery slope this could be. WikiLeaks was the conduit for distributing a huge archive of classified information stolen by intelligence analyst Chelsea Manning. This preceded the 2013 information leak by Edward Snowden, a former NSA contractor. In 2016, Assange distributed hacked emails provided by the Russians. Until now, the government has successfully prosecuted a small number of leakers, including Manning, but it has never successfully prosecuted a journalist for disseminating leaked material.

Assange is a facilitator of leaked information, some of it highly classified and some of it provided by the Russians. But is he a bona fide journalist? The Obama Justice Department concluded that Assange could not be prosecuted. After much delay, the Trump administration in late 2018 decided to prosecute Assange. In April 2019, Assange was hauled out of the Ecuadoran Embassy in London and jailed pending extradition to the United States. The indictment against him charges him with criminal conspiracy with his source, Chelsea Manning, a former US Army intelligence analyst who was convicted of leaking classified information. The indictment, unsealed after Assange's arrest, alleges that the conspiracy served "to facilitate Manning's acquisition and transmission of classified information." As further evidence of conspiracy, the indictment cites Assange's efforts to protect his source. There is no worse poster child for the First

Amendment than Assange, the reckless founder of WikiLeaks. But disseminating leaked information and protecting sources are activities that bona fide journalists do all the time. If the government were to win a conviction of Assange under the Espionage Act as an illegal purveyor of damaging classified information, it's not hard to see how rightwing courts could extend the precedent to bona fide journalists.

The current Supreme Court has shown great, crocodile-tear deference to the First Amendment claims of corporations, to justify unlimited campaign spending and to constrain abortion rights allegedly to protect the First Amendment rights of doctors and health plans that oppose abortion. But the court is likely to be far less protective of speech when the executive branch wraps itself in national security. The stakes could extend well beyond situations like the Snowden case, in which a leaker deliberately made public massive amounts of highly sensitive classified information. The government—under Obama—prosecuted Snowden, who fled the country. It did not prosecute his media ally, Glenn Greenwald. Such protections for the press could also change.

A more insidious strategy used by rightwing allies of Trump has been deep-pockets litigation intended to bankrupt target media. A defamation suit by the wrestler Hulk Hogan (the stage name of Terry Gene Bollea) bankrolled by billionaire Trump supporter Peter Thiel drove the website Gawker out of business.

When the Nixon administration tried to get the courts to restrain publication of the Pentagon Papers that had been leaked by Daniel Ellsberg, the courts initially sided with the administration. But after the White House won a restraining order enjoining continued publication by the *New York Times*, one newspaper after another began publishing the papers in solidarity with the *Times* and in defense of a free press. It was a magnificent display of civil disobedience eventually accepted by the courts. Just to be sure, Senator Mike Gravel of Alaska read most of the Pentagon Papers into the *Congressional Record*. The Constitution held. With enactment of an official secrets act and the risk of prison time for editors and publishers, it might not hold next time if Trump is reelected.

Unlike Orbán, Erdoğan, and Putin, Trump has not tried to use bogus national security violations to silence, arrest, or even murder his critics. But all the pieces of a hyper national security state are in place to increase the level of intimidation or incarceration. We don't have an official secrets act in the United States—yet. But it would not be hard to build on the apparatus that exists, especially with sympathetic courts. So far, the courts have had little sympathy for prior restraint of the press except in the most extreme cases. Changes in the law could bar publication of information deemed sensitive to the national security, so that journalists who published investigations of government excesses would be risking prison time and the bankruptcy of their media institutions. Their publishers could well have second thoughts. In her decision to publish the Pentagon Papers, Katharine Graham famously defied the wishes of the *Washington Post*'s board of directors, who were alarmed about how a prosecution might affect the *Post*'s stock price.

A more strategically competent Republican government unrestrained by Congress could change the libel laws to resemble Britain's, making press exposés of government wrongdoing much more difficult. It could effectively repeal *New York Times v. Sullivan*, the landmark case that set a very high bar for public figures to win libel suits. In that 1964 case, the *Times* had published an ad soliciting donations to defend Martin Luther King from a perjury charge. The ad contained minor errors. One of King's racist abusers, Public Safety Commissioner L. B. Sullivan of Montgomery, Alabama, contended that the ad defamed him and sued for damages. A lower court awarded Sullivan $500,000. But the Supreme Court unanimously held, in a decision written by Justice William Brennan, that in the case of public figures where the press is doing its job in good faith, only "reckless disregard" for the truth or "actual malice" can justify libel suits. Thanks to *Times v. Sullivan*, the press has gone on doing its job.[*]

Other nations, including Russia, Brazil, Hungary, and Poland, have criminal libel laws designed to repress the press. In Anglo-American law, prior to the famous free speech case of the printer John Peter Zenger in 1735, even truth was not a defense against libel if publication was deemed to harm or embarrass the plaintiff. A jury found Zenger innocent, but the issue of whether truth was an absolute defense against libel remained in contention at the state level throughout the nineteenth century.

The First Amendment, in short, means what the Supreme Court says it means. In a second Trump administration, if a willing Congress revised the libel laws to overturn *Times v. Sullivan*, it is hard to imagine the Roberts court objecting. Indeed, one could imagine an increasingly hard-right court doing so on its own initiative.

---

* I wrote these words before Justice Clarence Thomas, in a concurring opinion written in February 2019, contended that the court had erred in *Times v. Sullivan* and should overturn it. "Thomas, J., Concurring, Kathrine Mae McKee *v.* William H. Cosby, Jr.," Supreme Court of the United States, decided February 19, 2019, https://www.supremecourt.gov/opinions/18pdf/17-1542_ihdk.pdf.

Trump has also fulminated against publishers who have other business interests, again taking his lead from other dictators. Thus far, he has gained little traction against publishers such as Jeff Bezos, or CNN, which is owned by Time Warner. That, however, could also change for the worse in a second Trump administration. Silicon Valley is not known for political courage on behalf of liberty. On the contrary, the big platform companies have been on the wrong side of one issue after another—from net neutrality to privacy to turning a blind eye to fake news sites. They have constrained the freedoms of their own engineers by demanding draconian noncompete clauses. Who knows how they might buckle if Trump got more strategic about threatening their core profit machines. For now, Time Warner management has protected CNN chief Jeff Zucker. What would top management do if Trump got serious about squeezing Time Warner's business interests? When it comes to safeguarding democracy, big business is a slender reed, as has been shown in country after country where the corporate elite made its peace with tyrants.

Given another four years, a more systematic and competent neo-fascist government could mount a multipronged attack on a free opposition press. This could include one part stronger libel and official secrecy laws to intimidate and silence both journalists and publishers, one part rightwing subsidy and presidential coziness for more propaganda outlets, one part threats to tax-exempt independent media such as NPR, and one part assaults on media organizations as businesses.

Except for the outsized role of Fox News, why didn't more of this happen during Trump's first two years? Not because he values a free press. Trump did make some forays, but his short attention span has been one of the best allies of American democracy. In a second term, the march to dictatorship could be orchestrated far more systematically by more competent strategists.

Using Government Agencies for Partisan and Personal Ends. The failure of the FBI to do Nixon's bidding offers an alarming contrast with Trump's presidency, in which Trump fired FBI director James Comey for failing to protect him from the investigation of Russian influence in his campaign. Before Comey was ousted, he was pressured in a phone call by then–White House chief of staff Reince Priebus to refute a report (which turned out to be accurate) on contacts between Trump senior campaign aides and Russians. Trump has repeatedly sought to get the Justice Department to initiate purely political prosecutions. Trump personally interviewed several candidates for US attorney—something utterly unprecedented.

Trump went on to use the FBI for political purposes in the sham investigation of sexual abuse allegations against Brett Kavanaugh. The FBI's narrow remit was orchestrated by White House Counsel Don McGahn, whose prime client was the president. In May 2019, Trump directed Attorney General William Barr to selectively declassify secret FBI and CIA materials over the strenuous objection of the chiefs of those agencies. This was a flagrantly political manipulation of intelligence agencies to back up Trump's false story that they had spied on his 2016 campaign.

Trump repeatedly tried to get the Justice Department to launch prosecutions of two political enemies: Hillary Clinton and former FBI chief James Comey. He relented temporarily when McGahn warned in 2018 that this pursuit could lead to Trump's impeachment and had White House lawyers draft a memo to that effect. McGahn is now gone. Trump's ouster of Jeff Sessions was evidently motivated not only by Sessions's protection of Mueller but also by his refusal to politicize prosecutions on Trump's orders. In a second Trump administration, we could expect more selective prosecutions, and more fishing expeditions. Norms of professionalism and respect for the Constitution traditionally have prevented this sort of banana-republic behavior. Given the wide latitude that a prosecutor has, selective prosecutions used for political purposes would technically be legal.

In a despotic presidency with one-party control of all three branches, the fragility of these norms is all too apparent. One core element of democracy is the concept of a loyal opposition. Dictators throw their opponents in jail. Here again, as in so many areas, Trump's contempt for constitutional democracy was hidden in plain view. In one of the presidential debates in the 2016 campaign, this dialogue played out before a hundred million witnesses:

> Trump: "If I win, I am going to instruct my attorney general to get a special prosecutor to look into your situation."

> Clinton: "It's just awfully good that someone with the temperament of Donald Trump is not in charge of the law in our country,"

> Trump: "Because you would be in jail."

Trump's subsequent behavior as president made it all too clear that he meant what he said.

The politicizing of nonpartisan government agencies goes well beyond the area of criminal justice. An egregious case is Trump's effort to rig the 2020 census by depressing the count of foreign-born residents. This measure would reduce the reported population and congressional representation in predominantly Democratic areas and, by extension, their votes in the electoral college. A depressed census count would also reduce federal spending and public services.

This plot was hatched by the always inventive Steve Bannon and his deputy, Steve Miller, who succeeded to Bannon's political strategist role at the White House after Bannon was fired in August 2017. According to court documents in pending litigation, Bannon and Miller, working with then–Kansas secretary of state Kris Kobach, a notorious architect of voter suppression techniques (see Chapter 4), came up with the idea of adding a question to the census asking whether the respondent is a US citizen. The White House aides directed commerce secretary Ross to order the Census Bureau, which is part of the Commerce Department, to add the citizenship question.

After extensively studying the idea, senior technical experts at the Census Bureau had concluded that the question would depress the response rate by about 6.5 percent, since immigrants, both documented and unauthorized, had good reason to fear divulging this data to a federal agency. Ross gave sworn testimony to a congressional committee in March 2018 that the sole purpose of the question was to collect data requested by the Justice Department to help enforce the Voting Rights Act. As subsequent documents revealed, this was a complete fabrication, and it left Ross open to charges of perjury. The Justice Department got involved only months later, after prodding from the White House. When the case reached the Supreme Court in April 2019, the five Republican justices left little doubt that they would permit the Census Bureau to add the citizenship question. This in turn would reduce the voting strength in both Congress and the Electoral College of states inclined to support Democrats. As Trump's first term entered its second two years, the cynicism and antidemocratic ploys of the administration and its allies in Congress and the courts only deepened.

In a second Trump term, other government statistical and scientific agencies would be sitting ducks. The Bureau of Labor Statistics, a nonpolitical agency with an impeccable record, could be directed to cease collecting some forms of data that tend to reveal bad news (such as the income distribution) and devise new ones that tell good-news stories—for instance, counting in-kind benefits as income. Even under previous administrations, there have been minor efforts to rig census or BLS data.

For instance, Republican budget legislation passed in 2017 changed the way inflation is counted, to take into account the fact that people can substitute one product for another when a product becomes too expensive for their budget. That may be so, but as any consumer knows, Hamburger Helper is not sirloin steak, and cat food is not Chicken of the Sea. The gambit, using so-called chain weighting, was very controversial among economists, but it had the effect of reducing the stated rate of inflation, which saved the government money when it came to adjusting Social Security and other costs pegged to inflation, reduced worker cost-of-living raises, and allowed bragging rights about the low inflation rate.

Defunding the Opposition: A Politicized IRS. When Ronald Reagan took office in January 1981, the Heritage Foundation handed him a strategic playbook called *Mandate for Leadership* that ran to twenty volumes and more than 3,000 pages. One of the rightwing projects was a plan to "Defund the Left," a project relentlessly promoted by Richard Viguerie, a Republican fundraiser and strategist who at the time was the publisher of *Conservative Digest*. Viguerie had in mind withdrawing support from federally sponsored research projects that delved into areas of inquiry that either supported liberal scholars or contradicted Republican ideology and political goals, such as research into child poverty. For example, the Reagan administration drastically curtailed funding for the Institute for Research on Poverty at the University of Wisconsin. The administration also wasted little time in killing AmeriCorps's VISTA program, correctly perceiving that some federally subsidized VISTA volunteers were organizing local people to pursue objectives at odds with those of the administration.

Earlier, when Nixon became president in 1969, the big foundations had been seen as enemies. The Ford Foundation had underwritten policy proposals that became part of Lyndon Johnson's War on Poverty. Ford had compassionately but incautiously given temporary fellowships to senior staffers left jobless by the murder of Robert Kennedy. The center-left foundations were seen by Nixon as allies of the Democrats and liberal social engineering schemes. Nixon and the Republicans fired a shot across the foundations' bow by enacting rules that defined how much foundation money they had to give away every year and required them to pay taxes on some income. The foundations duly pulled in their horns and became more risk-averse about whom they funded.

Since then, nonprofits have become more aggressive about resisting the right. A more strategic autocratic administration could declare open war on the nonprofit sector. The typical nonprofit is tax-exempt under Section 501(c)(3) of the Internal Revenue Code. Tax-exempt status permits a nonprofit to accept gifts and grants for which the donor may take a tax deduction. The nonprofit is presumed to have a charitable or educational purpose, not a political one, except very incidentally.

Nonprofits with 501(c)(3) status include the Red Cross, the Boy Scouts, and your local symphony. But they also include Planned Parenthood, AARP, the NRA, the Economic Policy Institute, and the American Enterprise Institute. These are ostensibly charitable, nonpartisan research groups, but a great many of them have ideological goals and tacitly or overtly support one or the other of the major political parties. It just happens that AEI's worldview and political goals converge with those of the Republicans, and the EPI's, with those of the Democrats. (AEI also has about twenty times EPI's budget.) A closely related provision of the revenue code allows a group to organize under Section 501(c)(4). An organization with 501(c)(4) status is a tax-exempt nonprofit, but it may not accept tax-deductible gifts. In return, it is permitted to lobby or try to influence legislation.

Many groups organize as both C3 and C4 organizations with essentially the same officers and boards of directors, enabling the group both to take tax-deductible gifts and grants, and to engage in politics. At a meeting, the group will go through the motions of adjourning the C3 and convening the C4, but it is basically the same group. If you go to a clinic sponsored by Planned Parenthood, you will be visiting the C3. If you give money to Planned Parenthood to help its campaign to defend abortion rights and defeat antiabortion activists, you will be donating to the C4-status Planned Parenthood Action Fund. Both the left and the right engage in such manipulation. It seems a plain evasion, but it's legal and there are platoons of lawyers making sure that their clients play the C3/C4 game within the letter of the law.

However, the IRS could be directed to go after such nonprofits for technical violations of these maneuvers. In 2013, Republican members of Congress forced the early retirement of the IRS official in charge of nonprofit organizations, Lois Lerner, by alleging that her unit had disproportionately targeted conservative organizations for audits. An internal investigation subsequently found no abuses. An administration that wanted to systematically harass liberal groups could issue regulations tightening the rules in general. Liberal groups such as Planned Parenthood or the Center for American Progress are heavily reliant on tax-deductible gifts and grants. Rightwing think tanks like the American Enterprise Institute, by contrast, are drowning in corporate money. AEI could lose its tax-exempt status, and corporate America, flush from tax cuts, would go right on funding it. Thus, a general crackdown against all nonprofits could be ostensibly symmetrical but in practice more damaging to the left.

Liberal foundations and NGOs are also part of the progressive infrastructure and are vulnerable to rightwing official harassment. The Rockefeller Brothers Fund was a leader in underwriting and supporting the movement to encourage universities to divest from fossil fuel investments in their endowments. ExxonMobil worked hand in glove with a conservative Texas congressman, Lamar Smith, who chairs the House Committee on Science, Space, and Technology, to investigate and harass RBF. There were calls in rightwing circles for RBF to be indicted under racketeering statutes for interfering with the ability of oil companies to pursue their business. Even liberal foundations tend to have relatively moderate and risk-averse boards. It took unusual courage for RBF to stand up to this intimidation. A more competent and systematic far-right administration, given four more years, could seriously harm the progressive infrastructure and its financial supporters.

In September 2018, the chairman of the House Committee on Natural Resources, Rob Bishop, sent threatening letters to several mainstream environmental groups, alleging that they were doing the propaganda work of China and requesting them to register under the Foreign Agents Registration Act as agents of the Chinese, under penalty of fines and imprisonment. The letters based the allegation on selective examples of comments by the groups that had lauded some Chinese policy changes, while criticizing US policy. The letters went on to demand documents, in what was clearly a fishing expedition. No evidence was provided to support the contention that any of these groups had taken money from China. The letters were based mainly on innuendo, in best Joe McCarthy fashion.

The groups refused to comply. The Democratic takeover of the House a couple of months later shut down Bishop's committee. But Republicans still had the Senate. The real issue was not China. Rightwing Republican legislators are closely allied with extractive industries, which have long been the targets of environmental groups. It's not clear whether these actions by House committees were explicitly coordinated with the Trump White House. But in a second Trump administration, one might expect far more coherent and strategic harassment of environmental, consumer, and labor groups, many of which receive foundation funding. The letter sent under Rob Bishop's chairmanship began by noting that the committee was investigating "the potential manipulation of tax exempt 501 c 3 organizations by foreign entities." So, an attack on their tax status could dovetail with spurious claims of foreign influence, scaring off funders. At best, these harassing demands consume scarce time in groups whose resources are spread thin compared with those of the oil, gas, and coal companies.

A President above the Law. On several occasions, Trump or his aides have asserted that the president is literally above the law. During the transition Trump declared, "The law is totally on my side, meaning, the president can't have a conflict of interest." Attorney John Dowd told Axios that, by definition, the "President cannot obstruct justice because he is the chief law enforcement officer." (Nixon made the same claim when he asserted, to broad ridicule, "When the President does it, that means it's not illegal.") When district court judge James Robart blocked Trump's initial travel ban aimed at Muslim countries, Trump dismissed him as a "so-called judge." Trump political adviser Steve Miller then went on Fox News to declare that "an unelected judge does not have the right to remake the immigration laws and policies for the entire United States of America." Speaking on the Sunday talk shows, Miller repeatedly said, "There is no such thing as judicial supremacy."

Though most legal analysts predicted that Trump's selective ban on Muslim immigrants would ultimately be struck down as discriminatory against a particular religion, the Roberts court in June

2018 upheld the president's right to single out predominantly Muslim countries on national security grounds. When Trump asserted on the eve of the 2018 midterms that he had the authority to overturn the provision in the Fourteenth Amendment providing citizenship for anyone born in the United States, the assertion was ridiculed by most legal scholars. Trump contended that any offspring of someone who came to the United States illegally would not be covered by the Fourteenth Amendment. This eccentric view has been repeatedly rejected by the Supreme Court. But with the addition of another far-right justice or two to the Roberts court, it's not at all clear what the court might allow.

Trump has also called for summary justice in the case of "bad" people who he knows are guilty before they are charged, indicted, or tried. In a political speech to law enforcement officials in Brentwood, New York, he urged the officers not to be "too nice" to arrested suspects, and to slam them around. One such suspect, Freddie Gray, died of head injuries in the custody of Baltimore police, who had a long-standing practice of "rough rides," in which suspects were thrown in the back of police vans without seat belts and deliberately slammed to the walls and floor.

Under other recent presidents, the Justice Department was a force for the reform of abusive police practices. Several local police departments, after chronic abuses of basic rights of criminal suspects, reformed their practice only under court order, consent decrees, and hands-on Justice Department monitoring. Under Trump, the Justice Department has switched sides and become an ally of police-state tactics. After several notorious killings of black youths by Chicago police officers, Illinois attorney general Lisa Madigan and Chicago mayor

Rahm Emanuel signed a consent decree to begin the process of reform. The Trump Justice Department, which has significant powers to add teeth to such agreements, pointedly refused to help Chicago clean up its police practices. Madigan declared, "The Trump White House fundamentally does not agree with the need for constitutional policing."

Trump also felt free to try to intimidate the courts. He denied the legitimacy of an Indiana-born judge, saying that Gonzalo Curiel could not fairly rule in a lawsuit against Trump University because he was "Mexican." Trump referred to federal judges that blocked his anti-immigrant decrees as "so-called judges." When he disparaged the Ninth Circuit, one of the few remaining courts of appeal not dominated by rightwing appointees, as a hotbed of "Obama judges," Chief Justice Roberts, a Bush appointee and a hard-core conservative, felt compelled to object: "We do not have Obama judges or Trump judges, Bush judges or Clinton judges," said Roberts, seizing a high ground that he hadn't earned. "What we have is an extraordinary group of dedicated judges doing their level best to do equal right to those appearing before them."

If only. Trump shot right back:

Sorry Chief Justice John Roberts, but you do indeed have "Obama judges," and they have a much different point of view than the people who are charged with the safety of our country. It would be great if the 9th Circuit was indeed an "independent judiciary."

These contentions by the president, via tweets no less, undermine already dwindling faith in one of the few remaining trusted American institutions. As the Supreme Court is pulled by Trump appointments ever further to the hard right, it remains to be seen whether Roberts, sometimes naïvely described as the court's new center, will act on his professed regard for constitutional separation of powers, or whether ideology will drive him to continue in his role as enabler of antidemocratic behavior. In two key rulings in December 2018, not long after Trump's attack on him, Roberts joined the court's four liberals in sustaining key lower-court decisions that reined in rightwing policies. One decision blocked Republican governors from keeping Planned Parenthood out of Medicaid. Another sustained an appellate court order that blocked Trump's effort to deny asylum reviews to refugees who cross the border illegally and then turn themselves in. In February 2019, a third such ruling, this time by the full Supreme Court, with Roberts voting with the court's four liberals, overturned a Louisiana law whose practical effect banned most abortion providers in the state.

The Supreme Court is one of the institutions of the constitutional deep state beyond a president's control once a justice is nominated and confirmed for a lifetime term. Another such institution is the Federal Reserve. Given the Fed's power to create money, Congress made sure to insulate the Fed from short-term political control. Members of the Fed's board of governors serve fourteen-year terms, and the powerful chairman serves as chair for a fixed four-year term. When the Fed raised interest rates in late 2018, Trump threatened (by tweet, of course) to remove Chairman Jerome Powell. This threat demonstrated Trump's ignorance of both the law and the subtle art of seduction of the Fed. At the prospect of a Trump-Fed feud, the Dow promptly lost more than a thousand points. Trump's surrogates quickly told the media that the president, in fact, did understand that he did not have the power to fire the Fed chairman. Yet Powell may have gotten the message. Rate increases soon subsided, whether because of reduced inflation threats or presidential fulminations, or both.

One of the things that pleasantly surprised Trump watchers in his first two years was a potentially vicious dog that didn't bark—the use of a trumped-up national security crisis to rally support for the president. Trump did exaggerate several foreign threats, while he denied the very real threat of Russian meddling. But we were spared a full-blown fake national security crisis—until the Iran confrontation of May 2019. This was a manufactured crisis, reminiscent of George W. Bush's Iraq War. The more cornered Trump feels, the more we are at risk of such needless and potentially disastrous national security provocations.

Abusing the Presidential Power to Pardon. Trump's allies have suggested that if his confederates or family members were convicted of crimes, he could simply pardon one and all. When his former lawyer and fixer Michael Cohen was indicted, Trump used gangland language to condemn Cohen for "flipping" and cooperating with the special counsel. He lavishly praised his former campaign manager, Paul Manafort, for hanging tough—until Manafort also flipped. Trump told Fox News that flipping—cooperating with prosecutors in exchange for lesser sentences—"almost ought to be illegal." He then signaled that Manafort's subsequent lying to the special counsel put Manafort in line for a presidential pardon, and that Manafort should go right on stonewalling; Trump presumably would spare him prison time. Listening to all of this bravado, one almost forgot that the ultimate target of these investigations was Trump, and that Trump's proffer of a pardon to derail an ongoing investigation of himself was the epitome of impeachable obstruction of justice.

Trump's allies and lawyers have even suggested that he could pardon himself. In June 2018, Trump asserted in a tweet, "As has been stated by numerous legal scholars, I have the absolute right to pardon myself." He quickly added that this would not be necessary, because he had done nothing wrong. There are no such legal scholars, unless you count Rudy Giuliani, who quickly declared that the president "probably does" have the power to pardon himself. In fact, a legal memorandum on the question by the Justice Department Office of Legal Counsel written days before Nixon resigned, concludes, "Under the fundamental rule that no one can be a judge in his own case, the president cannot pardon himself."

What is seriously in contention is not whether a president can pardon himself—he cannot—but whether a sitting president can be the target of criminal prosecutions. Nixon was not prosecuted along with his senior aides but was named an unindicted coconspirator. That way of handling Nixon signaled that special prosecutor Leon Jaworski believed that a president could indeed be indicted, but in the context of a severe constitutional crisis he preferred to let the impeachment process play out. Subsequently, President Gerald Ford pardoned Nixon, reinforcing the view that Nixon could have been prosecuted. Special Counsel Mueller was following the same theory when he described Trump as "Individual-1" in the course of characterizing a criminal conspiracy with Michael Cohen.

Trump's promise of pardons to underlings as a way of discouraging them from sharing information with prosecutors is a flagrant obstruction of justice—interference with a criminal investigation of himself. But given that the appellate courts are increasingly in the hands of Trump loyalists, the realistic remedy would not be prosecution of Trump, but impeachment.

These are not just hypothetical concerns. Consider Trump's high-profile pardon of former Maricopa County sheriff Joe Arpaio. This was not just a random pardon of a far-right hero. Trump basically overturned a court ruling and condoned years of deliberate lawlessness by a lawman. For several years, Arpaio and his deputies had a regular practice of explicit racial profiling, detaining Hispanic-looking Arizonans not accused of any crime while they checked their immigration status. After four years of legal fencing, US district court judge G. Murray Snow in 2011 ordered Arpaio to cease racial profiling of people not accused of any crime. For five more years, Arpaio ridiculed and defied the court order. Finally, in 2016, Snow found that Arpaio had engaged in "multiple acts of misconduct, dishonesty and bad faith." Snow referred the cases of Arpaio and three deputies to the US Attorney's Office to be prosecuted for contempt of court. Arpaio was found guilty and sentenced to prison.

In pardoning Arpaio, a plainly political act overruling the courts, Trump asked at a political rally, "Was Sheriff Joe convicted for doing his job?" The implied answer was no, obviously he was convicted for defying the courts, dictator fashion. By pardoning Arpaio, Trump simply overrode the independent judicial branch of government for flagrantly political purposes. Other presidents have issued pardons long after the fact to help allies and donors, often when they were about to leave office. What was new about the Arpaio pardon was the in-your-face quality. And if Trump could pardon Arpaio, where would his abuse of the presidential power to pardon stop?

There is a good case to be made that the presidential pardon authority is not absolute. What if a president issued a pardon in exchange for a bribe? In a legal motion seeking to overturn the Arpaio pardon, the organization Protect Democracy pointed out that the original 2007 suit by Hispanic leaders accurately contended that Arpaio was violating the constitutional rights of Latino citizens. The legal motion contended that the pardon authority needs to be viewed by courts in the context of the other rights guaranteed in the Constitution.

Protect Democracy persuaded the Ninth Circuit Court of Appeals to appoint a special counsel to investigate whether the pardon of Arpaio should be vacated on the ground that it violated other constitutional rights more fundamental than the pardon authority. In a normal judicial era, the Supreme Court might agree with this line of reasoning. But the Roberts court has become a partisan instrument. And if Trump can pardon Arpaio, imagine what else he arguably might do. He might authorize illegal break-ins against political or media enemies, and then pardon those who followed his criminal orders. He could pardon anyone convicted of criminal acts in connection with his own election or his other actions as president, including the suppression of voting rights. Since the courts are largely captive, the only remedy is to make sure Trump is removed from office.

Private, Parallel Government and Political Use of the Military. When Trump took office, he briefly tried to bring with him a force of private security guards under his longtime private bodyguard, Keith Schiller, who would have had more authority than the Secret Service.

After some legal skirmishing, the Secret Service prevailed. Schiller was dispatched to be director of security for the Republican National Committee, but it was a close call.

This is, of course, just how autocrats behave. They have their own palace guards, hyperloyal only to themselves and beyond the reach of law. The ground has been softened for Trump to create other parallel forms of extralegal police authority. When the Justice Department has not given Trump the answer he wanted, he has turned to outside lawyers loyal only to himself, such as Rudy Giuliani.

Outsourcing of government functions has been a curse in recent years, and Trump has sought to build on it. In various dirty wars, the US government has outsourced combat operations to mercenary contractors such as Blackwater (now reorganized under private-equity ownership and known as Academi). This outsourcing does not save the government money; it adds costs. But when an operation goes badly wrong or civilians are massacred, the government can blame the contractor, whose soldiers are outside the constraints of the military justice system. US operations in Syria, which are conducted without any authorization from Congress, from the UN, or from NATO, have relied heavily on private military contractors. By the same token, prisons have been extensively outsourced, often with grotesque abuses of inmates.

It is an open secret that paramilitary vigilante groups operate on the US-Mexican border, sometimes in tacit or explicit cooperation with ICE. To the extent that ICE is subject to inconvenient legal constraints, Trump could outsource more border policing. In the run-up to the 2018 midterms, Trump committed several thousand regular military troops ostensibly to protect the southern US border against an imminent invasion by Central American refugees. The troops, essentially a campaign prop, were supposedly needed to reinforce the Border Patrol, which had not requested the help.

Normally, when there is a rare serious threat of civil disorder or insurrection, the president federalizes the National Guard. But the Posse Comitatus Act of 1878 prohibits the president from using the regular military to enforce domestic policy except under very narrow and well-specified circumstances. Trump has long hungered for the trappings of direct military power. He has been envious of large military parades of the kind used by dictators overseas, and he has tried and failed to get authorization for a massive display of military might on the streets of Washington. Suppose Trump called out the army to round up undocumented immigrants? Suppose he ordered mass prosecutions of those who protected them? Without courts standing in his way, we should be wary of new attempts by Trump to use the armed services for domestic political purposes.

Canceling Elections. The machinery of elections is handled by the states. But states controlled by Republicans coordinate closely with the White House and Republican congressional leaders. If a canceled or postponed election seems far-fetched, consider what almost happened in the Alabama special election that sent Democrat Doug Jones to the US Senate. Jones won 21,924 votes, a margin of 1.7 percent of the vote against the far-right former state supreme court chief justice Roy Moore. Sensing that Moore was in trouble because of credible allegations of sexual abuse, including with a minor, Senate majority leader Mitch McConnell consulted lawyers and pitched a plan to Alabama governor Kay Ivey to postpone the election.

Moore was the nominee because he had pulled off an upset against the incumbent in the Republican primary. After Senator Sessions resigned to become US attorney general, the governor had appointed state attorney general Luther Strange, a more mainstream conservative, to serve as senator, pending a special election. Moore, a darling of the right but a difficult sell in a general election, then defeated Strange in the Republican primary.

One McConnell scheme was to have Strange resign the seat, so that the governor could appoint someone else or postpone the election. However, Governor Ivey, a traditional Republican with little regard for Moore or for bending the law, rejected McConnell's scheming. But next time, a more corrupt and ideologically driven governor might go along with such a ploy.

There have been cases in which elections were rerun for legitimate reasons: Ballots were lost, destroyed, or purloined; people were found to have voted in the wrong district; or an election was literally too close to call. In September 2018, incumbent Georgia state representative Dan Gasaway persuaded a judge to order a rerun of the Republican primary (which he had lost by 67 votes) after presenting evidence that at least 67 people had voted in the wrong district. After massive fraud was revealed in the 2018 election for the Ninth Congressional District in North Carolina, the state election commission unanimously ordered a second election (see Chapter 4).

In those cases, the reruns were warranted. A second Trump administration, with the Justice Department aggressively becoming the instrument of rigged elections rather than fair ones, could come up with all manner of supposed cases of fraud and request do-overs, on terms that favored Republican candidates. The Congressional Research Service, in a 2004 legal opinion, found that in the case of a national emergency such as a terrorist attack, Congress has the constitutional authority to empower a president to reschedule an election. When Michael Cohen testified before the House Oversight Committee in late February, the single most alarming thing he said was this: "I fear that if he loses the election in 2020 that there will never be a peaceful transition of power, and this is why I agreed to appear before you today."

Many were inclined to dismiss Cohen's warning as hyperbole, coming from a serial fabulist who had gone from Trump's consummate henchman to his most severe critic. But consider this. The election of 2000 was effectively stolen, first by an inaccurate and partly rigged vote count in Florida, and then by a wholly partisan and extraconstitutional ruling by the Supreme Court in *Bush v. Gore* to halt an entirely legitimate and warranted statewide recount. For five weeks, until the court ruled on December 11, 2000, we did not know who the next president would be. If the 2020 election is close and Republicans bring charges of election fraud in several states, these appeals will ultimately find their way once again to the Supreme Court. Do we put this maneuver past Trump, who insisted in 2016 that he actually received 3 million more votes than were counted? Do we consider the Roberts court more honorable than the Rehnquist court?

Emergency Presidential Powers. In Chapter 2, assessing the long-term weakening of democratic constraints, I described the proliferation of statutes authorizing presidential declarations of emergency. In a second Trump administration, these could be used literally to turn the presidency into a dictatorship. For instance, the Communications

Act of 1934 was amended during World War II to allow the president to take control of "any facility or station for wire communication" based on his proclamation of a threat of war. This provision is still on the books. Trump could claim—accurately in this case—that social media were being used by a foreign power, and insert the government to take control. Such a move would actually be legal.

Under the International Emergency Economic Powers Act of 1977, the president has broad power to impose economic sanctions against foreign countries without the consent of Congress. This power has been used to target foreign governments, suspected terrorist organizations, and suspected drug traffickers (but not corporate tax evaders). After 9/11, President George W. Bush broadened its use further to target American citizens merely suspected of providing aid to suspected terrorists. It's only one more logical step for Trump to extend this authority to a general dragnet, for instance, of Americans suspected of helping immigrants who have entered the US illegally.

Even liberal courts have cut the president a very wide berth, and the current Supreme Court is among the most ideologically captive in our history. In his dissent in the 1944 Korematsu case, in which the Supreme Court upheld Franklin Roosevelt's incarceration of American citizens of Japanese dissent, Justice Robert Jackson wrote that each presidential emergency power "lies about like a loaded weapon, ready for the hand of any authority that can bring forward a plausible claim of an urgent need." There are far more such loaded guns today, and a president primed to claim urgent needs. If Trump's more outlandish claims—of refugee caravans amounting to acts of war—were taken literally, the executive power would be there to be abused.

A Close-Run Thing

The US was spared even worse, partly because Americans recoiled in the 2018 midterm elections against Trump's hate-mongering, but partly because of Trump's own impetuosity and short attention span. His inability to focus must drive many of his better-organized allies crazy. One observation by scholars who study the behavior of aspiring dictators is that they tend to learn by doing, in office. Former White House associate counsel Ian Bassin, now the director of the organization Protect Democracy, says, "Whether the autocrat is deliberate and strategic and Machiavellian in their planning, as Viktor Orbán has been in Hungary, or whether the autocrat is somewhat bumbling and instinctual as Donald Trump has been, you end up in the same place."

After the decisive Battle of Waterloo against Napoleon, the victorious Duke of Wellington described his victory as "the nearest run thing you ever saw in your life." The remark has often been rendered as "a close-run thing." If American democracy survives and flourishes once again, it will have been a close-run thing. Mercifully, the Democrats' impressive gains in the midterms of 2018 created a firebreak, a chance to contain and even oust Donald Trump, and to build to a resounding presidential win in 2020.

CHAPTER 4

≈

Suppression Meets Mobilization

A good deal of recent American politics can be understood as voter mobilization versus voter suppression. The suppression of the right to vote has taken a number of forms. Some of them are crude and ad hoc, such as reducing the number of Election Day polling places in precincts where blacks or Democrats are likely to vote, tampering with ballots and machines, and shortening the period for early or absentee voting. Others are more insidious and structural, such as mandating onerous ID requirements, excessively purging election rolls, gerrymandering districts, denying former felons the right to vote, and putting the federal government on the side of voter suppression rather than protection of the franchise.

Taken together, these tactics have denied millions of Americans their right to vote, to have their vote counted, and to have a decent chance of electing their preferred representative to office in an unrigged district. All of this created an undertow that gave the

Republicans a head start by millions of votes that might have been cast for Democrats, had they been permitted. In the House, gerrymandering gave Republicans a structural advantage of at least 20 House seats. The use of purges, excessive voter ID requirements, and kindred tactics cost Democrats at least 15 more.

How Mobilization (Sometimes) Beats Suppression

Against the background of intensifying voter suppression in more than a score of states, the Democratic gains in the 2018 midterms were miraculous, a tribute both to voter dismay at Trump and to massive organizing. Despite extensive gerrymandering, Democrats flipped 40 Republican seats to become the majority party in the House. They took 7 governorships (raising their total to 23) from the Republicans, including in Wisconsin, where voter suppression had been extreme. They won 360 state legislative seats from Republicans and increased the number of states where they held not only the governor but both legislative chambers from 7 to 14, while Republican "trifecta" control fell to 21 states. In North Carolina, Republicans lost their legislative supermajority, which had allowed them to commit innumerable antidemocratic abuses despite a Democratic governor. The 2018 gains suggest that Trump's strategy of fearmongering has its limits, given effective countermobilization.

It took an extraordinary upsurge of midyear turnout to achieve these gains. All told, the turnout rate, at 49.3 percent of eligible voters, was the highest in any midterm election in more than a century, significantly higher than the depressed rate of 37.6 percent in the previous (2014) midterms. Democratic House candidates received 63 million votes, only slightly less than Donald Trump received for president in 2016. There is no precedent for such a midterm turnout wave.

The 2018 midterms also broke a long-standing pattern in which turnout between the presidential year and the midterm year tends to fall more dramatically among identified Democrats than among identified Republicans. The decline between the presidential year of 2012 and the 2014 midterm election, for example, was just over 33 million among Democrats but only 22.6 million among Republicans. This pattern occurs partly because the Democratic base of minorities, young voters, and the poor tends to vote at lower numbers, especially in midterms.

In 2018, however, the pattern reversed. Turnout increased dramatically among Democrats and among the demographic groups most inclined to support Democrats. Young voters not only turned out in record numbers but also voted Democratic by a margin of more than 2 to 1. More affluent Democrats also turned out in record numbers. All told, more than 116 million people voted in 2018, compared to 83 million in the 2014 midterms,.

Looking back, it's clear that the low Democratic turnout in 2014 and 2016 was the result of both voter suppression and the relative lack of enthusiasm in 2016 for the Democratic candidate, Hillary Clinton. Turnout was depressed in the 2016 presidential year, relative to 2012 and 2008, both in states with strategies of voter suppression (such as photo ID laws and reduced polling places or hours) and also in states that work to maximize and ease voting. Conversely, turnout rose dramatically in 2018, not only in states that resorted to suppression but also in those that promoted exercise of the franchise.

Even so, turnout in 2018 was below the national average in the states where Republican governors, legislators, and local officials practiced systematic suppression: 43 percent in Louisiana, 41 percent in Mississippi, and 47 percent in Alabama. In Texas, one of the extreme suppressor states, where turnout increased by close to 4 million votes relative to 2014, it increased from a very low 2014 base to only 46 percent of eligible voters—still less than the national average.

Conversely, in states that did not block voting or that took steps to encourage it, turnout soared—to 64.5 percent in Oregon and 58.7 percent in Washington, both vote-by-mail states. Yet there were exceptions to this pattern. In Georgia, another state with extensive suppression, turnout was 55 percent. In North Carolina, another suppression state, turnout at 49.6 percent was right around the national average. And in the states that used stringent ID requirements, purges, poll closures, and other tactics to depress black voting, white turnout (as intended) exceeded black turnout.

With all the suppression, 2018 was a stunning success for the revival of activated citizenship. People participated and voted as if democracy itself were at stake—and it was. The voter mobilization in 2018 was the result of extensive on-the-ground work by dozens of groups like Indivisible. These groups started organizing not long after the shock of Trump's election. Indivisible, a loose federation of grassroots organizations following a basic template, spawned an astonishing 6,000 local groups committed to electing Democrats. Indivisible began when two former Democratic House staffers—Ezra Levin and Leah Greenberg, a married couple—decided to see what they could learn from the Tea Parties and wrote a playbook that soon went viral. And dozens of other new groups worked in candidate recruitment, training, and voter mobilization.

Even the Democratic Congressional Campaign Committee, normally risk-averse and typically interested in protecting incumbents or electing likely winners, behaved like an insurgent. The DCCC, as the official House Democratic fundraising body for candidates, had been humbled in previous elections and as recently as the spring of 2018, when several of its preferred candidates were defeated in primaries by upstarts with broad grassroots backing. This time, under the capable leadership of Representative Catherine Clark of Massachusetts, who headed candidate recruitment, the DCCC launched a Red to Blue project aimed at flipping Republican seats. It backed several long shots and welcomed insurgents. Red to Blue endorsed 104 candidates as worthy of financial support, mostly challengers—an unheard-of number for the DCCC. Its support helped challengers to succeed.

In addition, among the large Democratic field of presidential aspirants, several sought to build networks of support by helping to raise money for House and Senate candidates in the midterms. These several efforts, combined with a great deal of small-money fundraising by candidates and their supporters, meant that Democrats were financially competitive. Act Blue, the umbrella group for small-money Democratic donors, raised an astonishing $1.6 billion for all races, federal, state, and local. The average donation was $39.67. House Democratic candidates in the general election collected nearly $296 million in small donations, more than three times the $85 million collected by Republicans. All told, Democratic House candidates raised $923 million in the 2017–18 election cycle, compared to the Republicans' $612 million, according to reports filed with the

Federal Election Commission. The Senate spread was somewhat narrower, but still in the Democrats' favor, at $504 million to $396 million. This record contrasts with 2016 and 2014, when Republicans outspent Democrats for both House and Senate races.

These figures, however, do not capture independent outlays, which are typically far greater on the Republican side. Though the Koch brothers and other sources of immense independent-expenditure funding were active as usual, the predicted wave of "dark money," financing last-minute smear ads, was swamped by grassroots organizing—the traditional knocking on doors, manning phone banks, and undertaking efforts to get out the vote that are signs of a healthy democracy. In the 2020 presidential race, we can expect a new tide of dark money.

Much of the volunteer energy of the array of grassroots groups was female, as were a record number of newly recruited candidates and newly elected House members. Twenty-four, or more than half of the Democrats who flipped Republican House seats, were women. The 2018 election represented an even greater grassroots upsurge than the Obama army of 2008. And this mobilization will only grow between now and 2020.

Democrats made major gains not just in the suburbs, but deep in Trump country. Democrats flipped a seat in Oklahoma City that had been in Republican hands since 1974. They took a South Carolina district that had been redistricted in 2010 with the firm expectation that it would stay Republican. Despite the premise that America is now even more severely divided than ever between metro centers that back Democrats and rural areas that vote Republican, in 2018 not only were cities and their suburbs more intensively blue but there was a 5 percent swing back to Democrats in rural counties.

In Kansas, where Democrat Laura Kelly won a stunning upset against Kris Kobach in the governor's race, she not only ran well in cities but dramatically improved on Hillary Clinton's 2016 performance in rural areas. In small rural counties with fewer than 35,000 residents, Kelly received 35.8 percent of the vote, compared to just 23.5 for Clinton. If Kelly had done no better than Clinton in rural Kansas, she would have lost the election.

The story was the same in Montana, where Jon Tester, very much a progressive populist, held on to his seat by about 15,000 votes against Republican Matt Rosendale. In small rural counties, Tester received about 43 percent of the vote. Had he repeated Hillary Clinton's poor showing of 28 percent in rural Montana, he would have lost the election by about 20,000 votes. Tester's win, though narrow, was more impressive than it looked, because it was the first time he won with more than 50 percent of the vote. In his two previous elections, third-party candidates had helped Tester win with about 48 percent and 49 percent, respectively. And Tester won in a state that Trump had won overwhelmingly.

Similarly, in the hard-fought election for Wisconsin governor, Democrat Tony Evers rolled up big margins in Milwaukee and Madison. But he also improved on Hillary Clinton's record in rural counties. In rural counties with under 55,000 residents, Evers received 43 percent of the vote, compared to Hillary Clinton's 37.8 percent. Had he merely equaled Clinton's performance in rural Wisconsin, Evers would have lost to Republican Scott Walker. Evers was the state education superintendent. The Republican attack on public schools was another winning pocketbook issue for Democrats, not just in Wisconsin where Walker had declared war on teacher unions and promoted voucher schools but in more conservative states, such as Oklahoma. Activated teachers and parents, appalled by the state's dismal schools and the Republican legislature's refusal to fund them, were the key to Kendra Horn's surprise win in Oklahoma City.

In addition to the 40 Democrats who flipped Republican House seats in 2018, another 42 Democrats lost by just 8 points or less. Some of these were so far off the radar of national groups that they got hardly any financial support. These are potentially winnable next time as well. In a wave election, gerrymandering can backfire because that strategy tries to spread out expected Republican votes as broadly as possible to capture the maximum number of seats. But in a strong Democratic year, those predicted Republican votes are spread too thin. If there is a galvanizing Democratic candidate in 2020, Democrats could pick up at least another 30 House seats, restoring the sort of Democratic strength—270 House seats or more—that prevailed from most of the New Deal–Great Society era right through the 1970s.

The story of the 2018 midterms is all the more remarkable, given the appalling record of voter suppression. The gains would have been far greater, had it not been for extensive measures blocking the right to vote. The various tactics used by Republicans could fill several books. The worst is voter suppression based on race.

From the Rights Revolution Back to Jim Crow

For the first 200 years of the American Republic, our democracy was built on steadily extending the right to vote. The Voting Rights Act of 1965, the fruit of an extraordinary alliance between massive citizen protest and a repentant southerner determined to be a civil rights president, finally redeemed the promise of Lincoln. Until then, the black right to vote—explicitly guaranteed in the Fourteenth and Fifteenth Amendments—had been rendered hollow for a century by the most brutal forms of Jim Crow.

The reign of racial terror in the South depended, above all, on suppression of the vote. For a few decades after the Civil War, blacks in the South were able to vote and to hold office. But the federal guarantee of the black franchise ended with the so-called Compromise of 1877, a corrupt political deal in which electors in several southern states awarded a disputed presidential election to Rutherford B. Hayes in exchange for a promise to end the federal protections of Reconstruction. That deal led to a relentless wave of suppression of the black vote.

In the 1880s and 1890s, a brew of poll taxes, literacy tests, grandfather clauses (providing that you could vote only if your grandfather did), and state terrorism cut black voting rates in the Deep South to close to zero. In Louisiana the number of registered blacks fell from 130,000 in 1896 to 1,342 by 1904. In Alabama the number was cut from 180,000 to fewer than 3,000 in just three years. In several southern cities with biracial governing coalitions, violent coups ousted integrationist local governments. By 1901, the last black federal legislator from the South was out of office.

That exclusion persisted until the 1960s, even though several southern states had black populations in excess of 30 percent. In the same way that the tragically short-circuited First Reconstruction of Lincoln and the Radical Republicans in Congress literally required occupation of the South by the Union army to protect the black franchise, a century later racial suppression was still so fierce that the US Justice Department effectively had to play the same role of occupying army.

The Voting Rights Act gave the Justice Department the power to require states and other jurisdictions with a history of discrimination to submit all proposed changes in voting and representation systems for "preclearance" so that the Civil Rights Division could determine whether there was any scheme to weaken minority voting. In addition, Congress and more than two dozen states subsequently enacted other measures designed to enhance voting, such as the "Motor Voter" initiative (automatic registration at motor vehicle bureaus and other government agencies); same-day registration; greater ease of absentee voting, restoration of the franchise to former felons, and a host of other reforms. The Help America Vote Act, which was passed overwhelmingly in 2002 in response to the 2000 Florida fraud, sets national standards for voting machines, eases voter registration, specifies several acceptable forms of Election Day ID (not just a photo ID), allows a ballot to be cast provisionally if the voter claims to have been improperly dropped from the rolls, and provides federal funds to modernize state election systems.

By the late 1960s, a biracial, bipartisan, and modernized New South was coming to be seen as the new normal—the kind of South only imagined by Lincoln. With enactment of the Voting Rights Act, the black registration rate rose from under 10 percent in Mississippi in 1964 to almost 60 percent by 1968. Atlanta, which called itself the city "Too Busy to Hate," elected civil rights leader Andrew Young mayor in 1981, at a time when the electorate was still majority white. He was reelected in 1985 with more than 80 percent of the vote.

North Carolina became a model of bipartisan support for economic development initiatives under a string of progressive Democratic governors. In the 1970s and 1980s, and as late as the 1990s, racially moderate, economically forward-looking governors such as Jimmy Carter and Bill Clinton, even Democrat Ray Mabus in Mississippi, were seen as emblematic of the New South.

By 1976, the Mississippi delegation to the Democratic National Convention that nominated Carter for president was evenly split between blacks and whites, just twelve years after the party had refused to seat black delegates. An entire generation of southern governance portended black empowerment and racial reconciliation. The role of race finally seemed to be receding. A 2009 book by two respected political scientists, reviewing the landscape of the late twentieth century, was titled, *The Triumph of Voting Rights in the South*.

Yet this optimism proved woefully premature. The racist elements of the South were biding their time. The Second Reconstruction turned out to be an interlude. George Wallace, running as the candidate of racial resentment, won four southern states in the presidential election of 1968. Even more ominously, Wallace won broad support in the upper Midwest, in exactly the states where large numbers of white working-class voters defected to Trump almost half a century later. In five midwestern states, the Wallace vote was larger than the margin by which Richard Nixon defeated Hubert Humphrey.

Nixon and his strategists were quick to appreciate the potential of appealing to white southern racial resentment, which Nixon dubbed his Southern Strategy—playing to the white backlash against civil rights. It took more than three decades to fully execute, but by early in the twenty-first century, the South had gone from a single-party region dominated by racist Democrats, through an interlude of biracial moderate governing coalitions, and than back to a one-party racist region, this time dominated by Republicans. Indeed, by 2014, every single state of the old Confederacy had a Republican governor, all had majority-Republican legislatures, and the overwhelming majority of whites now voted Republican. Only in Virginia and Florida (both with an influx of northerners), North Carolina (where some biracial economic modernization had stuck), and idiosyncratic Louisiana were governorships effectively contestable. But North Carolina was fiercely divided and was one of the most extreme cases of a Republican-led strategy to maintain white supremacy by repressing black voting.

On paper, the Voting Rights Act of 1965 was regularly renewed and even strengthened by Congress, and signed by Democratic and Republican presidents alike. Originally set to expire in 1970, it was extended and expanded in 1970, 1975, 1982, 1992, and 2006 (when it was reauthorized for twenty-five years on an overwhelming vote in the House and a unanimous vote in the Senate), because of flagrant evidence of persistent efforts to deny or dilute the black franchise. Yet behind the façade of apparent progress was relentless skirmishing—"trench warfare," as constitutional scholar Randall Kennedy puts it, in which white southern officials played cat and mouse with the Justice Department. The number of voting changes submitted by states under Section 5 of the Voting Rights Act increased from 110 in 1970 to 1,357 in 1972. It wasn't quite the "massive resistance" promised by Virginia senator Harry Byrd after the 1954 Supreme Court ruling of *Brown v. Board of Education* ordering desegregation of public schools.

It was more like stealth resistance—which gradually became flagrant, thanks to Republican presidents and Republican courts.

In the early 1970s, the state of Mississippi resorted to a variety of subterfuges to hold down the black vote, including moving the location of polling places, requiring voters to reregister for each election, and revising the state's primary law to make sure that a black candidate could not win by gaining a plurality in a three-way contest. The Nixon administration, under Attorney General John Mitchell and the assistant attorney general in charge of civil rights, a Wisconsin lawyer with no civil rights background named Jerris Leonard, went along with all of these ploys. But in that era, the civil rights groups generally found redress in the courts, which kept ruling that these and kindred maneuvers violated the Voting Rights Act.

After four years of the Carter Justice Department vigorously enforcing voting rights, Ronald Reagan signaled an aggressive doubling down on the Southern Strategy. In Neshoba County, Mississippi, not a single black person had been permitted to vote before the Voting Rights Act of 1965. There, during the Freedom Summer of 1964, three civil rights workers—Michael Schwerner, Andrew Goodman, and James Chaney—were brutally murdered. By some mysterious coincidence, Ronald Reagan chose the Neshoba County Fair to kick off his general-election campaign for president on August 3, 1980, declaring, "I believe in states' rights." The signal was hard to miss.

Once elected, Reagan delivered. His Justice Department under Attorney General Ed Meese did not disappoint Reagan's white southern constituency. Southern officials resorted to a variety of tricks, ranging from enacting new voter ID rules, to relocating polling places, to manipulating legislative districts, in order to hold down black voting or to weaken its impact. Under Carter, these tactics had been challenged and overruled by the Justice Department. Under Reagan, the department was far more indulgent. By the early 1980s, the Supreme Court, now with a majority of Nixon and then Reagan appointees, began siding with the racist southern maneuvers.

Throughout the South, at-large elections had long been used to dilute black voting strength. In an at-large election, all of the electorate votes for the entire government body, such as a city or a county council or a school board. Thus, a jurisdiction that is 60 percent white can elect an all-white council, leaving the 40 percent who are black with no representation. In 1978, the US Commission on Civil Rights surveyed a sample of 75 localities with black majorities but no black elected officials. Most had shifted to at-large systems. In the Deep South, repeated civil rights investigations found that politics was heavily stratified racially. In many places, whites would simply never vote for a black.

In the 1970s, courts still tended to side with the Justice Department or private civil rights litigants in striking down these systems. That predisposition changed with the landmark 1980 case of *Mobile v. Bolden*, in which lower courts had held that Mobile's system of at-large voting was patently discriminatory. As a remedy, US District Court judge Virgil Pittman ordered Mobile to shift to a nine-member district system, as had been done in Birmingham and Montgomery. In Mobile, despite a population that was one-third black, there were no blacks on either the city council or the school board. The ruling was upheld by the Fifth Circuit, and the city appealed to the Supreme Court.

But on April 22, 1980, prefiguring worse to come, the high court, by a 6-to-3 vote, sided with the city government, laying out a new doctrine that would hobble voting-rights enforcement. The ruling held that in order to justify court-ordered remedies, the plaintiffs had to prove not just discriminatory effect but discriminatory intent. "Racially discriminatory motivation is a necessary ingredient of a Fifteenth Amendment violation," Justice Potter Stewart wrote for the majority. "The Amendment does not entail the right to have Negro candidates elected, but prohibits only purposefully discriminatory denial." The intent of the city fathers was all too obvious to anyone who cared to examine it, as Thurgood Marshall pointed out in his dissent. But under Stewart's logic, racist officials could get away with tactics to reduce black voting and representation, as long as they covered their tracks. The court had changed since the heyday of civil rights. Nixon had named four new justices—Warren Burger, Lewis Powell, William Rehnquist, and Harry Blackmun—who all voted with the 6–3 majority.

It did not take long for racist southern officials to act on the invitation that the court had offered. The forays became more audacious, and for the most part the Reagan administration turned a blind eye or worked flagrantly on behalf of the new wave of voter suppression.

In 1984 in Perry County, Alabama, where absentee ballots were beginning to increase the number of black officeholders, Jeff Sessions, later attorney general and at the time the local US attorney, rounded up black poll workers and had state troopers drive them 160 miles away to be fingerprinted and interrogated by a grand jury. All were eventually acquitted of trumped-up charges of voter fraud, but intimidation like this worked to hold down black voting. Despite the nominal protections of the Voting Rights Act, exercise of the franchise was far less than secure when the federal government was on the wrong side.

With the election of Bill Clinton in 1992 and Barack Obama in 2008, the US Department of Justice once again intervened on the side of voting rights, though it was increasingly undercut by conservative courts. Even so, until 2013, the reversion to a racialized, one-party South was accomplished more via racial politics than via voter suppression. Blacks were not a majority in any of the southern states, and Republicans had become the party of whites. The GOP delivered low taxes, scant public services that would be consumed by blacks, de facto segregated schools, and a policing and criminal justice system designed to keep blacks in their place. The party complemented these tactics with voter suppression ploys when it could get away with them. Depending on whether the president was Republican or Democrat, the Justice Department sided either with voting rights or with racist subterfuges, while the courts steadily became more indulgent of racial voter suppression.

The Cynical Consequences of *Shelby County v. Holder*

The dramatic reversal came in the *Shelby County v. Holder* ruling of 2013, one of the most disingenuous decisions ever delivered by the US Supreme Court. Shelby is the Alabama county between Birmingham and Montgomery that was the epicenter of the voting-rights marches of the 1960s. The county government filed suit after the Obama Justice Department rejected a transparent scheme in which officials redistricted the town council in the hamlet of Calera, adding white neighborhoods so that the town's lone black council member, Ed Montgomery, would lose his seat. After a year of negotiation between the Justice Department and the town, the remedy was a revised system ensuring that blacks, who were about 15 percent of the population, would likely regain at least one seat. The county sued.

In a 5–4 vote, the Supreme Court concluded that the South had changed and that preclearance was a dire and no longer necessary intrusion on federalism. Seldom have factual assertions on a Supreme Court ruling been so instantly refuted by events. The decision was not even a day old before southern states and localities resurrected racist voting schemes that been overruled by the Justice Department.

In his majority decision, Chief Justice Roberts declared, "Any racial discrimination in voting is too much, but our country has changed in the past 50 years." He added, "When taking such extraordinary steps as subjecting state legislation to pre-clearance in Washington and applying that regime only to disfavored states, Congress must ensure that the legislation it passes speaks to current conditions. The coverage formula, unchanged for forty years, plainly does not do so and therefore we have no choice but to find that it violates the Constitution."

Roberts, as clerk to Chief Justice William Rehnquist, had been at the center of the earlier voting-rights disputes of the Reagan era, and he knew this history of suppression efforts intimately. Given the record of extensive maneuvers by southern states to thwart the intent of the Voting Rights Act, Roberts must have known that he was attributing to improved behavior the effects of the Act itself. The court's four liberals were scathing in dissent. Ruth Bader Ginsburg wrote, presciently and commonsensically, "Throwing out pre-clearance when it has worked and is continuing to work is like throwing away your umbrella in a rainstorm because you're not getting wet."

With the Voting Rights Act thus gutted, southern legislatures got busy. In Texas, legislators resuscitated a scheme that the Justice Department had rejected as discriminatory. The law, which limited permissible forms of photo ID, was designed to favor whites but restrict blacks. Under the bill, rammed through the Republican legislature barely two hours after the Shelby ruling, gun licenses were accepted as valid forms of voter ID, but not college ID cards.

Three weeks later, the North Carolina state senate passed a bill eliminating from the list of acceptable forms of voter identification student IDs from public universities, out-of-state driver's licenses, and public employee ID cards. As the bill worked its way through the legislative process, it became more flagrantly restrictive, shortening early-voting periods, expanding purges of the rolls, narrowing provisional voting, and eliminating state-supported preregistration drives for high school students. In 2014, Thom Tillis, the Speaker of the North Carolina House who had pushed the bill through the legislature, ran for the US Senate, narrowly defeating Democrat Kay Hagan by 48,000 votes. His margin was far less than the number of citizens who had been prevented from voting by North Carolina's new restrictions. His election was effectively stolen.

The 2016 presidential election was the first to be held without the protection of the Voting Rights Act. The damage was massive, and not just in the South. All told, according to a comprehensive study by the Brennan Center, twenty-four states controlled by Republicans have introduced new forms of voting restrictions since 2010. Of these, thirteen states have added more restrictive voter ID requirements, eleven have made it more difficult for citizens to register, and seven have cut back early voting. In 2016, fourteen states had new voting restrictions in place for the first time in a presidential election. In Alabama, public housing IDs were dropped from the list of acceptable forms of ID, even though they are issued by a government agency.

Purges of voter rolls were an especially devious weapon. Typically, purge laws allow election officials to drop a citizen for failing to vote in recent elections. The official is required to send a postcard advising the citizen to reregister or be purged, but often the voter has moved or does not receive the card. A citizen who has previously voted and is unaware of this policy may thus show up at a polling place and be turned away because of not being listed as a registered voter. According to voting scholar Carol Anderson of Emory University, in Florida 182,000 voters were purged; in Indiana, 481,000; and in Ohio, over 2 million. The purged voters were disproportionately poor, black, and Hispanic.

In two of the most closely fought states in 2018—Georgia and Florida—the Democrat would very likely have won races for governor in Georgia and for governor and senator in Florida, but for purges. The Georgia election was all the more scandalous because the secretary of state, Brian Kemp, who was in charge of election administration, was also the candidate for governor. Kemp had run the table on all forms of voter suppression.

In 2017, with Kemp's guidance, the Georgia legislature enacted "exact match" legislation, voiding registration if an initial or a hyphen in a person's name failed to match state records. This tactic caused some 53,000 voters, disproportionately minority, to be put into a limbo status called "pending." It is up to citizens to correct even trivial discrepancies, of which they may not be aware, or they risk removal from the rolls. Between 2012 and 2016, Georgia also conducted one of the country's most aggressive purges, removing some 1.5 million voters from the rolls. Georgia also selectively closed polling places or shortened their hours in predominantly black areas. In the 2014 midterms, black turnout in Georgia was depressed by 41 percent. In 2018, spurred by a charismatic black candidate for governor who had a real shot at winning, Stacey Abrams, turnout rose to over 49 percent, a record for a midterm election, but not quite enough to vote her in. It could well have been far more but for various forms of suppression.

The Fraud of Fraudulent Voting

When Trump took office, he doubled down on voter suppression. He claimed, on the basis of no evidence whatever, that between 3 and 5 million ineligible voters had fraudulently cast ballots for Hillary Clinton. A thoroughly discredited theme of Republicans has been that fraudulent voting is epidemic in America, and that strict ID requirements and regular purges of the rolls are necessary to combat it. Despite extensive efforts to uncover actual examples of such fraud, neither Republican operatives nor the press could find them. A comprehensive study by the *Washington Post* in 2014 found just thirty-one credible instances of impersonation fraud out of more than a billion ballots cast between 2000 and 2014. Several academic studies yielded similar results. So rare were cases of ineligible voters showing up to vote (often in innocent error about whether they are eligible) that when Republicans actually found a live case, especially a black case, they threw the book at the offender.

In Texas, Crystal Mason, an African American mother of three, waited in line in 2016 to vote for Hillary Clinton. When she tried to vote, her name was not on the register, so she cast a provisional ballot. She was not aware that because of a previous conviction for tax evasion, she was ineligible to vote under the Texas law that bars former felons from voting. Ferocious prosecutors charged Mason with voter fraud, to make an example of her, and in September 2018 she began serving a five-year prison term. In Houston, two black women were also sentenced to prison time for voter fraud. One of them, Olivia Reynolds, was ineligible to vote because of a bad-check conviction back in the 1980s that she had long forgotten about. In North Carolina, Republican prosecutors in Alamance County found twelve former felons who had mistakenly sought to register and vote. They were charged with violating that state's ban, which can result in a two-year prison term, even though they had not been told by parole officers or voting registrars that former felons were not eligible to vote.

It's worth pausing a moment to reflect on the extreme double standard. Black citizens get hard prison time for innocently casting a ballot in error. White officials flagrantly and deceptively deny millions of people the right to vote. But there is no federal or state crime called voter suppression, and no case of any official ever being punished for it, much less doing jail time.

In May 2017, Trump created a presidential commission on electoral fraud nominally headed by Vice President Mike Pence but actually run by one of the more crackpot exponents of the claim of massive voter fraud, Kansas secretary of state Kris Kobach. When it comes to suppressing the vote, Kobach is one of the worst offenders. In 2015, Kobach persuaded the Kansas legislature to give him powers of criminal prosecution to identify cases of fraudulent voting. He turned up exactly one case, a sixty-six-year-old (white) entrepreneur named Lincoln Wilson who lived near the Kansas-Colorado border, owned a vacation home in Colorado, and had voted in local elections in both states. Wilson was duly prosecuted, but unlike the black women in Texas who were made to do serious prison time, Wilson was let off with a misdemeanor and a $6,000 fine.

Not only did Kobach use all available techniques to repress the black vote in Kansas, but he came up with a scheme to hold down voting nationwide, via a computer program called Crosscheck. The program, implemented in 2005, was expanded by Kobach's mission-ary efforts to twenty-nine Republican-controlled states. The premise is that there is massive voting by people who cast ballots in more than one state. The program uses a database of names and dates of birth, which is notorious for false positives, based on common last names. In 2017, Crosscheck, administered by Kobach's office, reviewed 98 million voter registration records from twenty-eight states and advised other states of upwards of 7 million "potentially duplicate registrants." Virtually all of the accused voters proved to be innocent.

With the creation of Trump's Pence-Kobach panel, the conten-tion of widespread illegal voting now had the resources and prestige of a presidential commission. But in one of the more embarrassing and revealing episodes of the Trump presidency, the Pence-Kobach commission blew up. In July 2017, Kobach demanded extensive vot-ing records from every state—a move that was widely understood to be part of a broader campaign of voter suppression. Many states, including several with Republican secretaries of state, refused to provide the files.

The commission then produced an amateurish study, relying heavily on seriously flawed claims by the Heritage Foundation, and found no evidence of more than minuscule wrongdoing. Even though the commission's members had been carefully selected to support the fable of massive voter fraud, several began taking issue with both the commission's methods and its false premise. Trump, sensing a fiasco in the making, abruptly shut the commission down in January 2018. In that fall's election, Kobach attempted to parlay his service as Kansas secretary of state into a run for governor and was soundly defeated by Democrat Laura Kelly, who overcame a Republican registration advantage of 44 to 25 percent of voters. Not all is the matter with Kansas.

In a charming turnabout, the 2018 election did at last yield a major case of ballot fraud—and it was the work of Republicans. In North Carolina's Ninth Congressional District, Republican operatives circulated absentee ballots door-to-door. They had the voter leave blank the line for Congress and then helpfully selected the Republican candidate, Mark Harris; or if the citizen voted for the Democrat, Dan McCready, they failed to turn in the ballot. Harris ostensibly won the election by 904 votes. The election was voided by the state's board of elections, which consists of four Republicans, four Democrats, and one independent. Republicans were less than sympathetic to Harris, because his operatives had pulled the same caper against his primary opponent. In Bladen County Harris won a suspicious 96 percent of the unusually large number of absentee ballots. This Republican ballot stuffing was the only documented case of voter fraud in the 2018 election.

Extreme Gerrymandering

After Barack Obama's victory in 2008, Republican strategists turned their attention to the 2010 state elections, spending tens of millions of dollars on a stealth campaign to take over state legislatures so that they could gerrymander congressional districts after the 2010 census. Gerrymandering had been used by both parties since the dawn of the republic, but new computer technology permitted precise targeting. The extreme gerrymandering of 2010–12 was unprecedented, as were its successes.

Under a program called REDMAP, computer experts devised a system in which an algorithm would enable computers to try an infinite number of possible map configurations until they maximized the likely number of Republican seats. Thanks to this strategy, computer-aided extreme gerrymandering enabled Republicans to flip partisan control of one or both chambers in several key state legislatures, including those of New York, Pennsylvania, Ohio, North Carolina, Michigan, and Wisconsin. This in turn allowed Republicans to redraw both congressional and state legislative districts.

As a result of the gerrymandering of congressional districts that followed, Republicans kept control of the US House by 33 seats after the 2012 election, even though Obama was reelected president by 3.5 million popular votes. In Pennsylvania, Democratic candidates for Congress won 51 percent of the popular vote, but Republicans gained

13 of the House seats to the Democrats' 5. In Ohio, Republicans with 52 percent of the votes, captured three-quarters of the state's seats in Congress. In Michigan, Trump won by just 11,000 votes, but Republicans took most of the gerrymandered House seats. In recent elections, Republican House seats have exceeded the Republican share of the popular vote nationally by about 4 percentage points.

However, in a major wave election with a big swing to Democrats, gerrymandering can backfire because the gerrymandered map spreads likely Republican voters too thin and overestimates districts that are presumed safe. The Republican strategy is to pack Democratic voters into as few districts as possible, and then have Republicans take the remainder with margins of something like 60–40 or a little less. But such margins are safe only in a normal year. By my count, at least 15 of the seats flipped by Democrats in 2018 were in districts that had been gerrymandered to be safely Republican but succumbed to the Democratic wave.

Given the intensified use of various forms of voter suppression, coupled with extreme gerrymandering, the citizen mobilization of 2018 is all the more astounding. It's possible to get a sense of how much more might have been achieved by looking at states that don't use voter suppression and at states that have measures to reduce barriers to voting, such as same-day registration and expanded early voting. In Pennsylvania, where gerrymandered districts were revised by court order, Democrats picked up 4 House seats. They gained 3 in New York and 4 in New Jersey. In California they ran the table in once heavily Republican Orange County, gaining a total of 5 seats statewide. But even more heartening is the fact that Democrats were able to pick up seats in states with severe voter suppression and gerrymandering, including 2 in Texas and 2 in Florida. In 2020, with several states expanding access to voting, plus the restoration of voting rights for former felons that was ordered in Florida by ballot initiative in 2018, the picture should be even brighter.

Despite *Shelby County v. Holder*, it remains to be seen how extreme suppression would have to be in order for the courts to intervene. Even some Republican judges have been offended by some of the crude tactics used to hold down black voting. In a 2016 lawsuit challenging several Republican suppression tactics in North Carolina, a three-judge panel of the US Circuit Court of Appeals struck down five key provisions of North Carolina law. These included its voter ID requirements, a rollback of the early-voting period from seventeen days to ten, elimination of same-day registration, preregistration of some teenagers, and its ban on counting votes cast in the wrong precinct. The court upheld the ruling of the district court judge, who had found that North Carolina had targeted blacks "with almost surgical precision." Voting-rights advocates were heartened when the Supreme Court, in a one-sentence notice by Chief Justice Roberts, declined to hear the state's appeal but indicated that this was not a ruling on the merits of the case. The revised voting rules created by the legislature retained many provisions designed to hold down black voting, and litigation continues. Elsewhere, courts have blocked some of the worst excesses in voter suppression, but they have let many others stand.

Several lawsuits are still moving forward. It is unlikely that the current Supreme Court would disallow even the most grotesque partisan gerrymandering schemes, though with Democrats having taken control of one or both houses in more state legislatures and further gains possible in 2020, the year of the census, politics should help remedy at least some of the extreme cases.

As the 2020 election approached, however, Republicans doubled down on voter suppression with new depths of cynicism. In Tennessee, Republican lawmakers have promoted new restrictions on voter registration efforts with criminal and civil penalties for minor technical omissions. In Florida, where voters overwhelmingly approved a constitutional amendment restoring the voting rights of former felons, the Republican governor and legislature sought to require payment of fines as a condition of voting. The playbook of the Jim Crow era keeps being modernized, and the struggle to protect the franchise is never-ending.

The Continuing Mobilization

Thanks to the 2018 electoral miracle, there is now a massive infrastructure of citizen organizing and voter mobilization on the progressive side. It is not going away. The ongoing drama of Trump's efforts to survive, as Democrats deepen their investigations and use their House majority to lay out a governing agenda, will only intensify citizen interest in politics.

Donald Trump was not on the ballot in 2018, but he did everything he could to make the midterm elections a referendum on himself, literally defining the outcome as a plebiscite on his presidency. Speaking at a Springfield, Missouri, campaign rally, he declared:

> You've got to get out. Can't be complacent. It's fragile. You've got
> to get out. You know, a poll came out, they said, "Everybody's

going out in 2020, because they want to vote for you, they want to vote for the president. But they're not maybe coming out in 2018."

Get out in 2018, because you're voting for me in 2018. You're voting for me. You're voting for me.

Trump's strategy worked all too well—for Democrats. Normally, a president with approval ratings that peaked in the low forties would think twice about inserting himself into his party's midterms, and the results suggest the deeper Republican vulnerability in 2020, if Trump is on the ballot. Even if he is not, Democrats and progressives have found an energy and a resolve that has been missing in many recent elections.

The dangers of Trump's unstable personality are so great that it would be too much to call these gains a silver lining of the Trump years. But the energy is welcome, and it is likely to continue to build. Against large odds, the 2018 midterms represented the victory of mobilization over suppression.

CHAPTER 5

≈

The Two Faces of Corruption

Corruption has been the hallmark of the Trump presidency. His personal corruption is legion, from his use of foreign policy to promote his personal business interests to his efforts to profit domestically from the presidency. His personal intervention into the decision of where to relocate FBI headquarters perfectly sums up his modus operandi. Trump overruled a long-standing plan to move the offices to a suburban location, out of concern that the current HQ, a prime parcel of land across the street from his Trump International Hotel on Pennsylvania Avenue, might fall into the hands of another developer. Meanwhile, representatives of forty special-interest groups and eleven foreign governments seeking to curry favor with his administration made sure to stay at one of his hotels in his first year alone.

Russians with close ties to the Kremlin have long financed Trump's businesses when he could not get any other funding. The

Chinese did special favors to cut red tape so that Trump's daughter could obtain patent and trademark benefits, granting Trump family businesses thirty-eight special trademarks in all. The Saudi regime has extensive business dealings with Trump's son-in-law, Jared Kushner, which helps explain Trump's indulgence toward that barbaric kingdom. US foreign policy is twisted in order to reward leaders who serve the president's financial interests.

There are many explanations for Trump's romance with Vladimir Putin, including Putin's help with the 2016 election, but one surely is that Putin serves as a role model in his fusion of autocrat, plutocrat, and kleptocrat. The kind of corruption that Trump aspires to is a system in which people get very rich to the extent that they are loyal to the tyrant, and the dictator uses the immense power of the state to reward himself, his family, and his allies in the ostensibly private sector that is reliant on political favors. This model is all too familiar from corrupt dictatorships the world over. It replaces democracy with oligarchy.

Trump's personal corruption has lost its capacity to shock. When the New York State attorney general, Barbara Underwood, closed down the Trump Foundation in late 2018, declaring that Trump had used it as "little more than a checkbook to serve Mr. Trump's business and political interests," coordinating its outlays with the presidential campaign in "a shocking pattern of illegality," the story was a one-day blip that barely made the front pages.

Every new story about Trump's conflicts of interests just feeds the general cynicism. If Trump is impeached, an open-and-shut case is his serial violations of the Constitution's emoluments clause, which explicitly prohibits an officer of the United States from personally profiting from his office.

Several of Trump's cabinet members have been at least as corrupt as Trump himself. EPA administrator Scott Pruitt spent hundreds of thousands of dollars of government money on personal travel, used his wife to disguise several bouts of self-dealing trading on his official duties, and deployed government staff for personal errands. Wilbur Ross, as commerce secretary and a leading official on trade policy, continued to maintain partial ownership of a Chinese state-owned company, an auto parts company with a direct interest in department policy decisions, and, most egregiously Navigator Holdings, a shipping company linked to Russian oligarchs. According to investigative reporting by *Forbes* magazine, Ross shorted the stock just before an exposé of his holding was published, thus finding a way to profit from his own corruption.

A whole second tier of Trump administration corruption involves senior regulators who came from the industries that they regulated and altered policies to benefit their former (and very likely future) colleagues. These included the heads of the FDA, the FCC, the SEC, and the FTC, as well as scores of subcabinet officials. Indeed, the norm was to pick regulators from the regulated industry.

It would take an entire book to detail all of the corruption displayed by the Trump administration. There is a big difference between Trump and other recent presidents when it comes to direct conflicts of interest. Barack Obama was a model of probity. There were very few personal scandals during his administration, and no cases, like those of Scott Pruitt or Ryan Zinke, of a cabinet member needing to resign because of conflicts.

Yet voters accurately sensed that in other recent administrations, where the corruption was neither so flagrant nor so grotesque, something was nonetheless rotten. As corporate interests increasingly corrupted Democrats as well as Republicans, the terms of economic engagement were turned against the citizenry. Long before Donald Trump appropriated the slogan, Elizabeth Warren declared, "The system is rigged" against ordinary people.

In many agencies, such as those regulating the environment and labor, Democratic presidents did a good job of appointing public-minded officials. Yet in other parts of government, revolving doors between the regulator and the regulated were all too common in both Democratic and Republican administrations, especially when it came to the deregulation or the nonregulation of finance. Ordinary voters accurately grasped that someone had the inside track with government, and it was someone else. All of this increased voter cynicism and paved the way for a demagogue posing as a total outsider.

Envelopes, Small and Large

In Greece, there is a venerable custom known as the *fakelaki*, the "little envelope." If you want a permit for a building or a registration for your car, you pass a little envelope of cash to the right official. Otherwise, the process might take forever. If you need surgery and want a skilled doctor to treat you in a decent hospital, a *fakelaki* is required. The practice is all too familiar in much of the world. In the Middle East, the customary bribe is known as *baksheesh*. In Mexico, it's called the *mordita*—the "bite." When Greece's indignant, northern European minders put that small, suffering land through a brutal wringer of austerity and imposed their version of reform, one of the things that most annoyed the rigid Dutch and German officials from the European Commission was that a member nation of the EU could openly tolerate petty corruption.

In the United States, we do not have to slip an envelope of cash to the motor vehicle clerk or the surgeon, but a far deeper corruption is endemic to the system. Grand corruption, on a scale vastly more damaging and far less transparent than petty bribes, is the norm today in the United States. The idea of a system in which the rules are fair and all comers are treated alike has gotten away from us, in favor of money doing the talking.

What sort of corruption? The financial collapse of 2008 is best understood as a wholesale, system-wide case of corruption. The biggest and most reputable banks created financial products that were *designed to be fraudulent*. These included mortgages with no prospect of being repaid, securities backed by no assets, deliberate strategies of making bets against customers, and a great deal more. Regulators did not take the trouble to learn how these worked, much less to assess their true risks to the system. Far too many regulators were members of the same club as the bankers, as they moved back and forth between Wall Street and the government. They had no reason to shut down the casino.

Private bribery, disguised via several layers of lucrative quid pro quos, is even more insidious than explicit kickbacks to public contractors or straightforward payoffs. The corruption of credit-rating companies, which bestowed triple-A ratings on securities that were designed to fail, in exchange for lucrative fees, was almost impossible for ordinary citizens to detect. If a credit-rating company expected to keep the business of corrupt big banks, it had to turn a blind eye to their fake books. The experts at the SEC, who were supposed to be alert to this kind of systemic conflict of interest, had also been corrupted and left the credit-rating companies to their own devices.

Politicians go to jail occasionally for outright bribes. But in the financial collapse, leading bankers pulled off the greatest bank robbery ever, and nobody went to jail. The difference between the opaque activities of the most prestigious banks and the more straightforward Ponzi scheme created by Bernard Madoff, the sole outlier who did end up in prison, was simplicity and scale. Madoff invented fake financial transactions. His frauds were transparent once investigators got wise to them, and they were not large enough to sink the entire economy. The frauds perpetrated by the largest and most prestigious investment banks were byzantine and systemic. Even Madoff got away with his scam for decades because the SEC displayed a studied incuriosity, despite tips from credible whistle-blowers.

Wall Street's biggest banks could get away with these frauds because their friends in Washington had changed the rules in their favor. Some regulations that could have prevented the collapse were not enforced; others were repealed. New abuses that demanded scrutiny, such as the invention of credit default swaps and mortgages virtually designed to default got a free pass. When it all blew up, it was not Wall Street that suffered. Indeed, nearly a trillion dollars in direct public funds went to bail Wall Street out, complemented by more than $4 trillion in emergency Federal Reserve credit creation. But upwards of 10 million Americans lost their homes.

So complicit were Democrats in the defense of Wall Street that in February 2009, when a rightwing populist TV commentator, Rick Santelli of CNBC—speaking from the floor of a financial exchange, of all places—went on a rant blaming the financial collapse on low-income borrowers and their Democratic champions (rather than on the creators of fraudulent subprime mortgages), his call for a new Tea Party found a large audience. Anger about the collapse helped the right more than it helped the left. A new Democratic president, ostensibly elected to clean up a near-depression caused by Republicans and their laissez-faire ideology, managed to shore up a corrupt financial system—and lose 63 House seats in his first midterm. Had Democrats immediately demanded that the big banks be broken up rather than propped up, they and not the far right could have been the champions of popular anger.

In earlier financial scandals, the Justice Department's criminal division had set up special task forces. These sought information from other agencies, such as the IRS, the SEC, and the bank regulatory agencies. They worked closely with state attorneys general and local US attorneys' offices, most notably in the Southern District of New York, which has expertise in going after financial crimes. In the case of the far less consequential savings and loan scandal of the 1980s—under the Reagan administration no less—prosecution was aggressive, and more than a thousand S&L executives were prosecuted, several hundred doing prison time for fraud.

But after the collapse of 2008, it took two years for the Obama Justice Department to even create a task force. The close Wall Street allies around Obama persuaded him and his attorney general, Eric Holder, that the big banks were too weak to withstand criminal prosecution of their senior executives, even though those executives were personally responsible for the creation and execution of fraudulent schemes that had cost innocent investors and home owners trillions. Instead of pursuing the prosecution of individual bank executives, Holder agreed to settlements of criminal cases, in which the corporations—that is, their shareholders—paid fines that could be deducted from taxable income as a cost of doing business. No senior executive faced personal criminal prosecution.

Top financial officials under both Bill Clinton and Barack Obama (in many cases the same people) came from Wall Street and returned to Wall Street. What's corrupt about this pattern is that people with this career trajectory hardly ever make tough regulators, because they are looking to their next job. Throughout the financial crisis, their advice to Obama was to bail out rather than clean out the big failed banks. Such an approach has negative economic as well as political consequences. It's hardly accidental that the dissenters from these policies—Fed officials Daniel Tarullo and Sarah Bloom Raskin; FDIC chair Sheila Bair; and economic adviser Jared Bernstein—neither came from Wall Street nor returned to Wall Street.

But the A-team—the most senior and influential people whom Obama appointed—were all part of the Robert Rubin crowd, with views to match. Peter Orzag, Rubin's protégé and prime designer of Obama's budget-balance policy, later re-joined his mentor at Citigroup as a senior executive. Michael Froman, who was Rubin's chief of staff at the Clinton Treasury and then was with Rubin as a senior executive at Citigroup, was Obama's chief of trade policy and foreign economic policy generally. Post-Obama, Froman found work as vice chairman and president for strategic growth at Mastercard.

Jack Lew, yet another Rubin acolyte, served in the Clinton administration, then followed Rubin to Citigroup, and later returned to government as budget director and then treasury secretary under

Obama. Lew subsequently went back to Wall Street as partner at the private-equity firm Lindsay Goldberg. Former treasury secretary Timothy Geithner, prime architect of the financial bailout, got a seven-figure job as managing director and president of another private-equity firm, Warburg Pincus. (Geithner subsequently coauthored a book on lessons of the financial crisis—with Republicans Ben Bernanke and Hank Paulson—a perfect illustration of the bipartisan Wall Street clique.)

Private equity is among the worst sources of financial abuse. Private-equity firms enjoy a blanket exemption from disclosures to the SEC, epitomizing the failure to regulate finance and the systemic abuses that result. They borrow money that is tax-deductible to buy up companies in retail, health care, media, and other sectors. The debt must be serviced by the cash flow of the company. They often bleed these companies dry, in order to pay themselves special dividends, cutting wages, laying off workers, and stinting on investments that the company needs to survive. If the company goes broke, the private-equity owner can declare bankruptcy, having already made back its actual investment many times over. More than 11 million Americans now work for companies owned by private equity.

When Sears Roebuck went bankrupt in 2018, the main culprit was its hedge fund owner, Eddie Lampert, who acquired Sears in 2005, borrowing billions of dollars for the purchase—debt that was put on Sears's own balance sheet. Over more than a decade, Lampert sold off Sears real estate, compelling the company to bear the cost of rent, paid himself special dividends that came out of Sears's operating budget, billed the company for management fees, and sold off Sears's most profitable divisions and brands. Lampert became a billionaire many times over, while Sears itself headed for Chapter 11. After the company went bankrupt, Lampert managed to keep control of the remains.

Lampert got his start at Goldman Sachs, as a protégé of Robert Rubin. The story of private-equity abuse ending in bankruptcy has been repeated many times over, from Toys "R" Us to the A&P chain. Any Democratic Party worthy of its name would be exposing private-equity scams and fighting for reform legislation to shut them down. There is no constructive need for private equity to exist, other than to enrich predators. Until a small loophole in the Roosevelt-era Investment Company Act (which was intended to enable small family investment firms to avoid SEC disclosures) was widened in the 1980s, private equity did not exist, and it should be shut down now.

But leading Democrats are among private-equity executives, and a campaign to shut down the industry would run head-on into the political and financial influence of Wall Street Democrats. Besides Geithner's involvement in private equity, Deval Patrick, the former liberal governor of Massachusetts, is a principal at Bain Capital, an influential private-equity firm. Some of the leading private-equity moguls, such as David Rubenstein, are prominent Democrats, and Hillary Clinton was a major defender of the sector.

Corrupted capitalism and corrupted politics feed on each other. When the electorate concludes, with weary cynicism, "They all do it," not only do government and democratic politics—the indispensable instruments for housebreaking capitalism—lose credibility and legitimacy, but so does the Democratic Party as a counterweight to the insecurity of the market. A disgusted public then turns to a leader who paradoxically epitomizes the double corruption, because he is a perceived outsider who promises to burn down the barn. Challenging

Trump's flagrant fakery will not be enough. A revived Democratic insurgency needs to be a credible challenger of both corruptions.

Corruption: A Brief History of an American Scourge

There is a huge literature in political science on the breakdown of trust in large institutions as one key indicator of the danger to democracy. But too little attention is paid to role of the imbalance of economic rewards in that breakdown. In 1958, when the National Election Study first asked whether people trusted the federal government to do the right thing all or most of the time, 73 percent of respondents reported that they did. That support peaked in 1962, at 78 percent. By 2018, confidence had fallen to less than 20 percent.

To be sure, in the intervening years government's credibility suffered from the assassinations of the 1960s, Vietnam, Watergate, the Iraq War, the Monica Lewinsky mess, and a lot more. But it took a prolonged economic slide in the security and prospects of ordinary people for government legitimacy to collapse. In the post–World War II era, government was not without its blemishes, from the rampages of Senator Joe McCarthy to an unpopular stalemated war in Korea. But it is more than a coincidence that in the 1950s and 1960s, when government enjoyed broad credibility, the postwar social contract still held and government was accurately perceived as delivering a fair deal for ordinary people.

Democracy, it turns out, can survive a fair amount of corruption, as long as the benefits are delivered with rough economic justice. What it cannot survive for long is corruption that serves primarily elites.

The founders of the American Republic were obsessed with two civic ills. The better known of the two was tyranny. They dealt with this risk by devising separation of powers and other ingenious checks and balances. They abhorred not just unchecked executive power but the passions of direct popular rule, and they made sure that they were creating a republic rather than a democracy, to be governed by an aristocracy of talent.

The founders' less appreciated but equally fervent concern was corruption. The men who created the republic had a very straightforward conception of corruption: the use of public office for private gain. Corruption, they feared, could undermine republican government just as surely as tyranny might. This concern is expressed repeatedly in the *Federalist Papers*, and it is reflected in several constitutional provisions. In *Federalist 10*, James Madison writes that leaders may "by corruption . . . betray the interests of the people." Alexander Hamilton, in *Federalist 75*, warns that "an avaricious man might be tempted to betray the interests of the state to the acquisition of wealth." The Articles of Confederation explicitly prohibited any officeholder from accepting "any present, emolument, office or title of any kind." Similar language was carried over into the emoluments clause of the Constitution in 1787.

The founders, for the most part classically educated men of high principle, saw corruption as emblematic of all that they abhorred in the rule of European monarchs. They saw the British Crown eroding the independence of Parliament with bribes, patronage, and special favors. Patents and royal monopolies granted by the king to courtiers epitomized the blend of political and economic corruption. When the Patriots dumped tea into Boston Harbor in December 1773 after secretly boarding the ships of the British East India Company, they were protesting not just the tax on tea but the royal monopoly that allowed the company to charge exorbitant prices.

The founders observed corruption in the sale of cheap land both before and after America gained its independence. With so much real estate being seized from native tribes and resold to settlers or land speculation companies, opportunities were rife for officials to profit from bribes, kickbacks, and a share of land deals. Thomas Jefferson, with mixed success, fought to contain absentee speculators so that cheap land could go to yeoman farmers.

The fledgling banking system was also a notorious opportunity for corruption. In many states, the surest way to get a banking charter, literally a license to print money, was to put the right officials on your board and give them a cut. When Hamilton, as Washington's treasury secretary, organized America's first central bank, the Jeffersonian Republicans were worried about both the concentrated financial power and the potential for corrupt insider dealings.

Viewers of the hit musical *Hamilton*, or readers of the Ron Chernow biography on which it is based, may recall how Alexander Hamilton was blackmailed and ruined politically. While living in Philadelphia as treasury secretary, Hamilton had a sexual liaison with a woman, Maria Reynolds, who pretended to be estranged from her husband. In a classic confidence game, the husband soon showed up, feigned outrage, and demanded payment to keep silent.

Hamilton duly paid the blackmail over several years, and he kept meticulous records of it. When his political enemies got hold of the records years later, they claimed that these payments represented financial speculations on Hamilton's part, attempting to profit from privileged information. Hamilton, seeking to clear his name, truth-fully but naïvely admitted that they, in fact, were blackmail payments to avoid exposure in the country's first political sex scandal. What is remarkable, and revealing of the extreme sensitivity to political corruption in the early republic, is that Hamilton assumed that disclosure of marital infidelity and botched hush-money payments would be less damaging to his career than disclosure of insider trading.

In the nineteenth century, corruption coexisted with a sense of broad popular possibility. The federal and state governments provided funds for public improvements such as canals and later railroads. Legislators were often cut in on deals that involved massive transfers of public funds or public lands. Yet, pervasive corruption was not sufficient to discredit the basic premise of American democracy. The expanded public works and the broad availability of cheap land for (white) settlers meant that much of the public outlay, however corrupted, did manage to trickle down to ordinary Americans. The rough-and-tumble democracy of the Jacksonian era was far from the high-minded deliberation envisioned by the classically educated Federalists at Independence Hall, but it delivered for the common people.

In the period between the Civil War and the Progressive Era, ineffectual presidencies, stolen elections, and corrupted alliances between politicians and robber baron capitalists coexisted with populist demands for radical reform of both the economy and the polity. It took thirty-five years after the Civil War for some of this reform to come to pass in the accidental presidency of Theodore Roosevelt beginning in 1901, and thirty-two more years for it to reach full flowering under his distant cousin, Franklin.

After half a century of deepening economic concentration and the political corruption that it bred, the republic had come full circle to the Jeffersonian understanding that democracy cannot coexist with massive concentrated wealth. Yet, under Teddy Roosevelt and Woodrow Wilson, a lot of progressivism was essentially technocratic. Many elite progressive reformers feared the rabble, just as the founders had. They sought to apply scientific methods to what were plainly political questions. Corrupt big-city machines, by contrast, were sometimes closer to the people. The journalist and civic reformer Lincoln Steffens tells an emblematic story on himself in his famous autobiography, published in 1931. Early in his career, he is trying to gain a better understanding of raucous machine politics, and he arranges an interview with a political boss from Boston's West End named Martin Lomasney. Boss Lomasney is of the "bucket of coal and Christmas turkey in return for votes" school of urban politics. Steffens is preaching high-minded reform, but Lomasney is having none of it. "There has got to be in every ward someone that any bloke can come to—no matter what he's done—and get help," he explains to Steffens. "Help, you understand. None of your law and your justice, but help." In New York, the Tammany philosopher and boss George Washington Plunkitt termed this form of on-the-ground redistribution, with the machine taking its cut, "honest graft."

During the Progressive Era, the goals of the uptown civic reformers only occasionally came together with those of the coarse practical populists. That alliance awaited the New Deal. After 1933, some urban machines were part of the Roosevelt coalition, but Social Security checks were not subject to bribery. People at risk of losing their homes got mortgages refinanced by the Home Owners' Loan Corporation because of their situation, not their connections with ward heelers. Slots in Civilian Conservation Corps camps were available to one and all.

The Roosevelt administration finally compelled capitalism to clean up its act, damping down both the economic and the political corruption. The New Deal at last brought together both sides of Steffens's argument with Lomasney. The reformers got long-sought improvements in law and justice, and the people got practical help.

In our own time, that alliance has been sundered. Today, government is not just corrupted; it has ceased delivering enough to regular people. The voters are increasingly wary not just of corrupt politicians, but of politics itself.

Rigged Rules and Lost Faith in Democracy

More than a decade ago, the political scientist Jacob Hacker presciently wrote of "the great risk shift." He was referring to the fact that risks that had been borne by government or by paternalistic employers in the era of the postwar social contract have been shifted back to workers and their families. These include the risk of the loss of a good job, the risk of poverty in old age due to collapsing pension systems, the risk of needless illness or medical bankruptcy because insurance fails to cover lots of conditions. But beyond these risks, ordinary Americans face rules that have been rigged to their disadvantage.

The rigged rules of the game affect all of us—as workers, consumers, students, parents, debtors, patients, and citizens. In literally every area of economic life, those rules have shifted in favor of the wealthy and the powerful, thanks to an alliance between corporate elites and their allies in government. Some Democrats have sometimes opposed these shifts, but not strenuously or consistently enough as a party to be a clear and credible tribune of the people.

Unreliable Jobs. Most ordinary people earn their living from their jobs. To hear some economists tell it, the degradation of American jobs and resulting precariousness of economic life is driven mainly by technology and by globalization. That's mostly a myth. What has really occurred is politically driven changes in the rules—to the advantage of employers at the expense of wage earners.

Take the case of "gig" work. Employers are increasingly defining jobs as contract work. But a worker defined as an independent contactor loses most rights and benefits. The company pays no share of Social Security or Medicare taxes; the workers have no retirement or unemployment benefits, no opportunity to join a union, a much higher hurdle to overcome to complain about various forms of discrimination, and no sense whatever of reciprocal employer loyalty. In reality, most jobs in the so-called gig economy could be regular payroll jobs—if the government were serious about enforcing the laws against payroll fraud. Under the Fair Labor Standards Act, if an employer dictates the terms of employment, then the worker must be considered a regular employee. Yet many large employers get away with defining such employees as contract workers.

For instance, FedEx and UPS provide essentially the same delivery service. But UPS categorizes its workers as regular payroll employees. Most are also members of a union. Over at FedEx, the workers use FedEx computers, drive FedEx trucks, and wear FedEx uniforms. For all intents and purposes they are regular workers. But FedEx gets away with classifying them as contractors—which means no benefits, few protections, and no chance to unionize. With tougher rules and better enforcement, FedEx workers would be regular employees.

Federal, state, and local governments, as well as the labor movement, have been fighting a series of skirmishes with Uber and Lyft. These companies contend that they are merely sophisticated ride-matching services. The reality is that they tightly define the term of employment; under the law they should be considered employers. With better regulation, Uber and Lyft drivers could enjoy legal protections as employees, including minimum-wage protection, as well as the right to have the employer pay the customary share of Social Security, Medicare, and unemployment taxes.

The Covert Theft of Rights. Most American workers don't realize how many rights have been stolen from them under an innocent-sounding law called the Federal Arbitration Act and its interpretation by rightwing courts. When we think of arbitration, most of us imagine a genuinely neutral third party impartially resolving a dispute so that the two sides can avoid the hassle and expense of going to court. In practice, arbitration is a rigged process increasingly used by employers to deny rights to both workers and consumers.

Today, most large employers require new employees, as a condition of getting the job, to sign a contract that waives their rights to sue for employer violation of a broad range of rights that have been legislated by Congress. These include the right to sue for race or sex discrimination, or theft of wages, or hazardous working conditions, as well as a flat ban on class actions. Instead, the new employee agrees that any such complaints will be submitted to binding arbitration, with the arbitrator chosen and paid by the employer. Workers seldom win these cases. In reality, the Arbitration Act was never intended by Congress to give employers a mechanism for reversing a broad array of laws directly legislated by Congress to protect workers. Corporations use a similar set of fine-print clauses and mandatory arbitration to deny consumers a whole other set of rights of redress. Despite the plain intent of Congress, far-right courts have creatively held that that law basically allows employers to use arbitration as they please.

To turn the rules of the game further against working people, employers became much more ferocious about attacking or avoiding unions. Ronald Reagan signaled open season on unions when he fired striking air traffic controllers and broke their union. Democratic presidents, beginning with Jimmy Carter, did not make the revival of unions any sort of priority. The rights of the Wagner Act—to organize or join a union free from the fear of employer retribution—survived mainly on paper.

A Collapsing Retirement System. The pension system has also been brutally turned against working people. Until the late 1970s, about half of all jobs came with a pension. A true pension provides a guaranteed income as long as the retiree lives, often with adjustments for inflation. The usual formula is based on the worker's years of service, and on the worker's pay in his or her final few years on the job. Typically, retired workers received pensions equal to 70–80 percent of their paychecks.

After the economic turbulence of the 1970s, most large employers shifted to retirement systems that place all the risk on the workers. A 401(k) plan is not a pension; it is simply tax-deferred savings. As wages have lagged behind the cost of living, workers simply don't save enough, despite the tax breaks and, in some cases, an employer match. The typical employee on the eve of retirement has 401(k) savings sufficient to finance only a few years of retirement, against a life expectancy that exceeds fifteen years. With a true pension, the check comes as long as you live. With a 401(k), you can burn through your savings and have nothing.

More and more Americans are holding jobs well into their seventies and eighties not because they love their work but because they can't afford to retire. By contrast, the affluent professional class can afford to retire, yet many keep working because their work is fulfilling. It's one more hidden class divide that requires exposure, explanation—and remediation.

Burdening the Young with Debt. The rules have also been rigged when it comes to college education. As late as the 1970s, when the country was a lot poorer on average, state budgets covered about 75 percent of the costs of public universities, making them essentially free to students. In that era, more generous federal Pell Grants subsidized costs for very-low-income students. Free public higher education, dating back to the land grant colleges of the Lincoln era, provided a crucial rung on the economic ladder for children of the working and middle classes. Today, the government share is down to about 15 percent, and even the cost of attending a public university often requires a young graduate to be encumbered with debt. This is a classic case of how the two parties tacitly colluded in an outcome that turned the economic rules brutally against the children of the non-rich.

State governments relentlessly enacted tax cuts; they partly made up the difference by reducing state support for public universities, shifting costs to tuition and fees. The federal government helpfully provided a guaranteed student loan program, run by private, for-profit companies. By 2018, the accumulated debt was $1.4 trillion. The debt burden resulted in a precipitous decline in the home ownership rate of people in their thirties, whose large debts disqualified them from obtaining mortgages. In 2004, the home ownership rate for people aged thirty-four or younger was about 43 percent. By 2017, this proportion had declined to 35 percent.

Alas, this travesty was the work of both parties. Though Republican-led states took the lead in shifting public university costs from state budgets to students, there is no significant difference today in the share of public funding in states governed mostly by Democrats. In-state tuition at the state university is just as high (and the government share just as low) in "blue" Massachusetts as it is in "red" Texas. UCLA, a flagship research university in heavily Democratic California, gets just 7 percent of its budget from the state. And the for-profit, government-guaranteed student loan program exploded steadily under Republican and Democratic presidents alike, while the fraction of tuition covered by Pell Grants fell. The Obama administration, to its credit, did introduce a direct loan program with lower interest rates, but this program was not available for refinancing existing debts.

Unaffordable Housing. Like employment, retirement, and education, affordable housing has become a vanishing part of the American dream. Historically, the rule of thumb was that you could afford a house that cost about two and a half times your income. With an $80,000 income, about the median for couples, you could purchase a $200,000 house. But try finding a $200,000 house. In most large cities and metro areas today, the median family income cannot come close to purchasing the median-priced house. In Los Angeles, the median house costs over nine times the median income. In Seattle, Denver, Boston, and New York, the figure is over five times the median income. Like the other aspects of the vanishing social contract, affordable housing should have been a priority for Democrats. But the default was all too bipartisan.

What happened? First, American metro areas ran out of cheap development land, and real estate became more expensive because of dwindling supply and increasing demand. But here, public policy might have made a constructive difference. For a time, government and nonprofit developers created affordable rental housing that was intended to be treated as "social" housing immune to market pressures to bid up prices and rents. By analogy, Central Park would be worth a king's ransom if it were chopped into parcels and sold to the highest bidder. But mercifully, it is not for sale.

In the postwar era, government spent hundreds of billions in direct outlays and tax breaks to create affordable rental housing. Government built direct public housing and also subsidized nonprofit housing. In Parkchester, the project in the Bronx where I was born, the Metropolitan Life Insurance Company was given huge tax breaks in order to build and manage affordable apartments. MetLife developed sister properties at Stuyvesant Town and Peter Cooper Village in Manhattan. All became oases of moderate-income housing as surrounding market rents soared. Later, in the federal housing programs of the 1970s, the government not only gave developers tax breaks but also subsidized low-interest mortgages to create low-rent apartments under HUD's Section 236 program. Government also subsidized rentals by issuing housing vouchers.

All of these programs shared one huge flaw: the housing was not permanent social housing. As real estate values soared, selling off these properties became irresistible. Buildings subsidized under the government's Section 236 program were required to have low rents for only thirty years. Most have now been converted to market rentals, and their tenants have been evicted. Stuyvesant Town and Peter Cooper Village were sold to speculators and have been converted to market-rate condos. A lot of public housing has been demolished and used for development land. Housing vouchers were handy while landlords waited out the lean years, but in cities with hot housing markets, owners evict renters with vouchers and charge whatever the market will bear.

What's left of government's affordable housing policy is deals in which developers agree to keep perhaps 10 or 15 percent of units affordable, in exchange for government approval, plus some tax breaks. That formula doesn't begin to meet the need. The norm is that rent is supposed to consume not more than one-fourth of net household income. But today, the majority of families in the bottom 20 percent of households spend more than half their incomes on rent—exacerbating the squeeze on all the other necessities of life. Even in the second quintile, which reaches well into the working middle class, the median renter family spends close to 30 percent of its income on rent. What we need is a social housing sector, which could be a mix of different forms of ownership, but with these features in common: it would be insulated from market pressures, would not be permitted to be sold to the highest bidder, and would provide affordable housing in perpetuity.

Bad policy also harmed owner-occupied housing, which at its peak accounted for about two-thirds of all housing in the US. Until the subprime collapse, with its cynical targeting of Americans of modest means, good home ownership programs demonstrated that families could become successful home owners well down the income ladder. But the 2008 collapse blew that dream away, causing more than 10 million foreclosures and setting back at least a generation of growth in home ownership among blacks, who were just starting to recover from systematic discrimination. The collapse also cut home ownership rates among moderate-income whites and left in its wake a mortgage industry obsessive about credit scores, further depressing housing opportunity for the nonrich. To add insult to injury, private-equity speculators bought up foreclosed homes to be short-term rentals as they waited for markets to recover, often competing with local groups seeking to restore owner occupancy and stabilize neighborhoods.

Most citizens are not expert in the finer points of housing policy. They just know that it has become harder to afford a place to live, and that neither political party seems to be looking out for their interests.

Health Insecurity. The Affordable Care Act did reduce the number of uninsured. But it did so at great economic and political cost. One of the reasons why health care is so expensive is that the medical sector is riddled with middlemen, each taking a cut. The ACA did not change that; it merely had government pick up the tab. The program was such a confusing mess that it was far less popular than more straightforward government programs, such as Medicare and Social Security. As a public-private mélange, it put the government in the position of reaping the animus both for its sheer complexity and for some of the games played by private insurers.

While it nominally increases insurance coverage, the ACA tolerates and even exacerbates an epidemic of underinsurance. The "gold" policies, which have low deductibles and low copays, tend to be very expensive and beyond the reach of many people who need them. But the lower-cost "bronze" policies have very high deductibles and high copays, with the result that many people don't get the care they need. Even though they are insured, they can't afford to see a doctor. A poll conducted by the Kaiser Foundation and the *New York Times* found that about 20 percent of *insured* people had severe problems paying their medical bills. Of these, 63 percent reported that they had used all or some of their savings, 42 percent had worked an additional job or worked more hours, 14 percent had moved or taken in a roommate, and 11 percent had turned to charity.

The rising out-of-pocket costs in the insurance provided under the Affordable Care Act mirror what has been occurring with employer-provided insurance. As costs keep escalating, corporations cap their own exposure by increasing the premium share paid by employees, raising deductibles and copays, and limiting patient choice of doctors and hospitals via more intensely "managed" care. Once again, the result is that people who are nominally insured go without needed care. ·

And almost a decade after passage of the ACA, there are still 28 million uninsured Americans—an increase of 3.2 million since 2016. With the diversion of the "free-care" financial pool for hospitals and community clinics to help bear the costs of the ACA, these uninsured Americans are likely to get even worse care than they did before the ACA was passed. Meanwhile, the Medicaid cost squeeze is leading many states to limit what Medicaid will cover, and there is de facto rationing even in states with comprehensive coverage, such as Massachusetts, because very low reimbursement rates lead many doctors to refuse to take Medicaid patients.

As in the case of housing, few Americans grasp this squeeze in all of its convoluted dynamics. But they do get that it is becoming harder and harder to afford needed medical care.

Monopolies and Price Gouging. The rigging of the rules of patents, trademarks, and copyrights has intensified under Democratic and Republican presidents alike. Antitrust enforcement collapsed under both parties. Sectors such as the pharmaceutical industry are allowed to charge astronomical prices because of the interplay of extended patent laws designed for their benefit, weakened antitrust enforcement, and the industry capture of the primary regulator, the FDA. Giant platform monopolies such as Google, Facebook, and Amazon are allowed to dominate, acquire, or crush potential rivals—and to invade privacy—because government has failed to regulate them. The Democratic Party's alliance with Silicon Valley reinforced that regulatory lapse.

The doctrine that corporations are citizens and that money is speech intensified the systemic corruption. Republicans took more advantage than Democrats of the unlimited capacity of the wealthy to spend, but that capacity pushed many Democrats into greater reliance on large donors. Many of these donors were liberal on race, feminism, immigration, and LGBT rights; hardly any had progressive views on regulation, unions, wages, or the economy generally. They promoted the catastrophic blend of left on social issues, right on economics. The new rich of Silicon Valley, mostly Democrats and huge donors, were even more libertarian on economic policy—the government couldn't possibly understand, much less regulate, what they do—and even more left on cultural issues.

Connecting the Dots

Too few Americans today have a political understanding of these deep forms of economic corruption. But they experience them viscerally in their daily lives. People live the effects of deep corruption whenever they waste time, money, and denial of needed care while trying to navigate the health insurance system; whenever they pay an inflated bill for cable or internet or cell phone service; whenever they find that their job is at risk because they put illness or family needs ahead of going to work, or simply because a new parent firm acquired the company where they work; whenever they find that the price of attending college or sending a child to college is astronomical debt; whenever they have to strap themselves to afford housing in a jurisdiction with halfway decent schools.

All of these frustrations, small and large, are the consequence of corrupted systems, in which a few people get very rich because the system has failed to insist on fair play for everyone else. Democrats as well as Republicans tolerated a privatized health system financed largely by government, with webs of middlemen adding cost and complexity. Both parties abandoned affordable college and created an insane system of private college debt guaranteed by government. Both promoted voucher and charter schools in which entrepreneurs get rich at taxpayer expense while the quality of public schools suffers.

The next Democratic candidate needs to connect the dots between these daily forms of economic frustration and narrate the deeper corruption that afflicts that American political economy. The nominee needs a deeply held, well-informed, and coherent view of what ails American capitalism, not a scattershot set of poll-tested slogans. The role of progressive leadership is to help citizens to connect the hazy perception of generalized corruption of America's political and economic life to the palpable frustrations of their own lives—and to political remedy. Leadership needs to offer a drastically different politics that places the blame in the right place and offers radical reform that serves ordinary people. A cleaner political system and a fairer economy go together because with cleaner politics, fewer politicians are on the take. The rot in American plutocracy has penetrated so deeply that only drastic reform can clean it out.

Trump, paradoxically, has set the stage for a new, politically robust era of reform by taking corruption to a grotesque extreme. But if progressive leadership is not crystal clear in identifying a corrupted capitalist system and its political clients as the overarching problem, then issues of identity and race will crowd out the deeper concerns that potentially unite working Americans of all races and backgrounds. The Democrats could lose not only the opportunity, but the election. Getting this right is the most urgent challenge for Democrats in 2020.

CHAPTER 6

≈≋

Overcoming the Racial Fault Line

In August 2017, I experienced a few days of abrupt fame from a totally unexpected quarter. My wife and I were on vacation in western Massachusetts. An odd email came across my computer screen from an intern at the White House who worked for Trump's chief political strategist, Steve Bannon. According to the message, Mr. Bannon had read a column of mine on China and trade policy and wanted to invite me to the White House to discuss it.

I was aware that Bannon fancied himself a trade hawk and sometimes looked for allies on the progressive side. I phoned and told the assistant that I was not interested in coming to the White House on my vacation but that I'd be happy to speak to Bannon by phone. The result was a call that I recorded and quoted, in which Bannon said several incautious things about his boss. (I published the interview, and he was fired the next day.) But when I turned the conversation to

Bannon's alliance with the racist far right, the most revealing thing he said was this: "The Democrats—the longer they talk about identity politics, I got 'em. I want them to talk about racism every day. If the left is focused on race and identity, and we go with economic nationalism, we can crush the Democrats."

This was clearly the Bannon-Trump strategy: to racialize grievances and hope that Democrats would take the bait. The more that Democrats made the election about identity, the more they risked driving away downwardly mobile white voters who were sick of hearing more concern for illegal immigrants (some of whom were taking their jobs) than for the lost economic prospects of good, law-abiding American citizens. Trump, meanwhile, could rally a much uglier racial sense of white identity. To an appalling degree, the strategy worked for Trump in 2016.

The challenge for Democrats in 2020 is to keep the emphasis on economics—not to duck realities of racism or gender discrimination, but to focus the election on all that unites rather than divides. There is definitely a strategy and a narrative that accomplishes this goal. More on this in a moment. Given all of the cross-pressures of race in a large candidate field and Trump's skill at exploiting them, this balancing act will be no mean feat.

Despite his bizarre performance as president, Trump has been darkly brilliant at wielding symbols of fear to create an us-versus-them politics, where the "us" is patriotic and implicitly white Americans, and the "them" is blacks, Muslims, Mexicans, terrorists, caravans of refugees, and gender minorities. But a hard look at the trajectory of the US economy in recent decades indicates that the real us versus them is working America of all races versus the financial and corporate elite. It takes a pocketbook progressive, black or white, to narrate that reality and win broad support.

Some of the best polling and political science research demonstrates why pocketbook populism is a winning message for Democrats. In a survey conducted on behalf of the Center for American Progress, pollster Guy Molyneux tested the following message:

> We need to take back our government so that it works for all Americans, not just billionaires and special interests. The size of government is less important than who it works for. Instead of giving tax breaks and subsidies to big corporations, we should create jobs, improve education, lift wages, and help people retire with dignity. And we should get big money out of politics, so that our government is accountable to the people.

By 64 to 36 percent, white working-class respondents reported they would vote for a candidate with that message over a conservative candidate promising to cut government waste and "revive the American dream by curbing big government."

In a spring 2018 survey of voters, pollster Stan Greenberg found that by a margin of 92 to 6, respondents agreed with the statement "Health care costs are out of control," and 64 percent agreed with "My wages aren't keeping up with the rising cost of living," compared to 31 percent who disagreed. By large margins, people in every major demographic group felt their wages were not keeping pace, including African Americans, Hispanics, millennials, women, and white working-class voters generally.

Trump cultivated white Americans who have big grievances

about their falling status. But on the economic issues, he delivered only for elites. In 2020, this will be the main vulnerability of both Trump and his party. Republicans thought their 2017 tax cut would be a big winner in 2018, but polling and focus groups found that the more voters learned about it, the less they liked it. Republicans quietly shelved the tax cut in their talking points.

The powerful thing about bread-and-butter issues such as decent pensions, good day care, comprehensive health care, higher minimum wages, affordable college, or protection from rapacious mortgage companies is that they disproportionately help both black voters and white working-class voters, bridging rather than dividing on the basis of race. That reality alone suggests why pocketbook issues are the necessary bridge for Democrats.

The more subtle challenge is to hone a politics and a language that doesn't leave out race but emphasizes commonalities. The pro-democracy group Demos Action has sponsored a pioneering project called the Race-Class Narrative. The idea was to find themes and ways of talking about them that bridged race and class issues. Demos worked with the pollster Celinda Lake and the linguistic scholar Anat Shenker-Osorio to test various ways of framing issues with the potential to unite or divide. Using panels of 1,500 people divided into "base" voters already sympathetic to racial and economic justice, "opposition" voters inclined to scapegoat minorities, and "persuadables" with ambivalent feelings about both sets of issues, the Demos message testing demonstrates that language that mentions both race and class in an inclusive way does better than language that just mentions pocketbook issues and tries to waltz around race. Consider these two messages:

- To make life better for working people we need to invest in education, create better-paying jobs, and make health care more affordable for people struggling to make ends meet.
- To make life better for working people we need to invest in education, create better-paying jobs, and make health care more affordable
  for white, black, and brown people struggling to make ends meet.

The first message, seemingly a winner, did not do as well with
"persuadable" voters as the second. This finding was repeated over
and over, with a variety of messages on several subjects. The Demos
report concluded:

Conservatives villainize African Americans, and increasingly
Muslims and immigrants, as criminal and undeserving in order
to diminish the social solidarity and support for collective action
that are the foundation of a progressive agenda. Pointing out
this strategic racism and tying it to the class war that wealthy
reactionaries are winning helps connect the experiences of
targeted people of color and the experiences of economically
anxious white people. It provides a way for people of all races
to understand our noxious racial environment and makes clear
that white people will gain more from cross-racial solidarity
than from siding with billionaires.

The goal here is not just to spotlight clever campaign messaging,
but to build genuine bonds of cross-race empathy and consciousness
as the durable basis for a long-term progressive coalition. Demos has
shared its findings with candidates, and they are available on its web-

site. In the pressures of a prolonged campaign, however, it remains to be seen how widely this kind of unifying language will be used.

The circumstances for this sort of unity politics are more propitious than they sometimes seem. The power of Trump's appeal to tribalism to the exclusion of other issues is fading. In the off-year Virginia elections of November 2017 that foreshadowed the gains of 2018, Democrats won seats in the state legislature that had been written off for decades. One such winner was Danica Roem of Manassas, who defeated a twenty-five-year incumbent. Roem is transgender. But her campaign was all about improving Virginia's congested roads. Her gender evidently did not scare off thousands of crossover Republican voters. In 2018, voters in Arizona, which had last sent a Democrat to the Senate in 1976, elected Kyrsten Sinema, who is bisexual. The subject of her sexuality barely came up. Maybe, just maybe, if we keep the focus on real issues, America can grow beyond the hate stoked by Donald Trump.

Lessons of the 2018 Midterms

Democrats did well in the 2018 midterms by keeping the focus on pocketbook issues while not ducking race. This strategy worked both in hard-core Trump territory and in swing districts. Though Trump sought to use fearmongering, deploying the image of an immigrant caravan invading America's southern border, for the most part Democrats kept the focus on the frayed pocketbooks of working Americans. Even more impressively, many citizens who had voted for Trump or for Republican members of Congress in 2016 did not take the bait either.

The heartening story of the 2018 midterms was not just the overall Democratic gains, but where and how Democrats won. About two-thirds of the Democrats who flipped Republican seats won as pocketbook populists, supporting either Medicare for all or Medicare at age fifty-five, expanded Social Security benefits, controls on prescription drug prices, a higher minimum wage, and relief of college debt. These themes worked well to bridge potential divisions of race and ethnicity, both within the Democratic coalition and in the country as a whole.

The role of race in 2018 was the opposite of what Trump and Bannon intended. Millions of former Trump backers voted for black candidates. In Newt Gingrich's old district, Georgia's Sixth, which is just 13 percent African American, a black woman, Lucy McBath narrowly won the seat, which Republicans had held since 1978. Her seventeen-year-old son, Jordan, was murdered in 2013 at a gas station by a racist white man for playing music too loudly. Yet McBath won in the Atlanta suburbs, incredibly enough, calling for Medicare for everyone over age fifty-five, a higher minimum wage—and gun control.

In other unlikely places, where the usual suspects would counsel centrist moderation, Democrats flipped Republican seats, advocating Medicare for all. These included Jason Crow in the Denver suburbs, Colin Allred in Dallas, Antonio Delgado in upstate New York, and Sharice Davids in Kansas. Davids is Native American and openly lesbian. Her district, suburban Kansas City, is 83 percent white. Former Rhodes Scholar Delgado, who is African American, ousted John Faso in a district that is just 4 percent black and that had backed Trump.

In former Republican House Speaker Dennis Hastert's old district in the exurbs west of Chicago, in the race for a seat that was not even considered in play, a thirty-two-year-old African American nurse named Lauren Underwood won a stunning upset. The district is just 3 percent black. The incumbent, Randy Hultgren, had used coded language calling Underwood an outsider, even though she was born in Naperville, in the heart of the district. The tactic backfired. Colin Allred, a former NFL player and civil rights lawyer, who is black, won a huge upset to gain his Dallas seat, ousting Pete Sessions. The district is just 11 percent African American.

How did these candidates do it? Here is a passage from Colin Allred's basic speech:

> I believe Medicare and Social Security are promises we've made to our seniors that should be honored; Pete Sessions voted for a tax law that gives a trillion dollars in handouts to corporate special interests, while threatening Social Security and Medicare. I believe you should be able to get healthcare regardless of whether or not you have a pre-existing condition; Pete Sessions voted to let insurance companies deny coverage to people with pre-existing conditions and to impose an age tax on older Americans.

Many white voters were willing to look past Allred's race to his message. The fact that white southerners and other nonurban white voters in 2018 were willing to vote for black economic progressives tells us that America is ready to move beyond Trump's message of tribal hate, and that pocketbook issues are the key part of a winning strategy. In all, eight African American candidates picked up seats formerly held by Republicans, all of them in majority-white districts, all running as pocketbook progressives. Even in the suburbs, where Trump managed to alienate large numbers of Republican voters, "moderate" Democrats were quite progressive when it came to the issues.

That's the hopeful news. But the dynamics of protracted primary contests for the presidential nomination are different from those of a single congressional race. In a House or Senate race, a candidate can tailor the campaign to local constituents, and find the discipline to stay on message. In the contest for a presidential nomination that spreads over a year, with as many as two dozen Democratic contenders, rivals send multiple, often contradictory messages. Candidates and their surrogates are tempted not just to contradict the messages of one another, but to caricature them, with the press, social media, interest groups, and Republicans egging them on.

As horrific as Trump is, there is only one of him. Despite his impulsivity, he and his handlers will have an easier time staying on message than a large flotilla of fractious Democrats. And as heartening as the 2018 results were, they continued to display chasms of division on race and class. Aggregating the votes in all congressional races, white men without college degrees voted for Republicans by a staggering margin of 42 points—only moderately better than the comparable 49-point chasm of the 2016 election. Yet that shift represents an improvement of 17 percent (42 divided by 7) and is just the beginning of what's possible. These voters are the historic constituency of the Democratic Party, and with the right message, more of them can be won back.

Beyond the Tribal Trap

Against the evidence of the potential of a cross-race coalition based on common economic interests, there is a three-way argument among strategists and pundits about how Democrats can best position themselves for 2020. Contrary to a strategy of class uplift, some counsel doubling down on race and identity; others urge centrism and civility. Neither of those strategies is likely to work as well as racially inclusive pocketbook populism to produce a victory in 2020, much less a governing majority.

Some commentators and activists have pointed to the fact that the electorate will soon be "majority minority." After the 2018 midterms, Steve Phillips, who heads the organization Democracy in Color, called on Democrats to "mobilize and call forth a new American majority in a country that gets browner by the hour and will be even more diverse by November 2020." Presumably, Democrats can win by appealing to a "rising electorate" made up of ethnic minorities, young people, LGBT voters, unmarried women, and well-educated professionals, all of whom tend to vote heavily for Democrats. The hope is that massive black and Latino turnout can offset the racist appeal of Trump among whites. It's an idealized and enlarged version of the coalition that elected Barack Obama.

It's certainly true that Democrats need to maximize turnout among a rainbow of diverse ethnic groups. Yet it's a stretch to think that Democrats can win by stressing identity and ignoring the potential bond between black, Hispanic, and white working-class voters. That view overstates the demographic shifts, understates the need for a cross-race coalition of the nonrich, and misses the opportunity for a broader mobilization suggested by the Demos Action research.

Some 28 percent of the electorate is considered nonwhite by the Census Bureau, but that figure includes people with Hispanic surnames whose families have been here for centuries and who may not identify as people of color. It also includes various subcategories of Asians, not all of whom support Democrats. As the Pew Research Center has demonstrated, by the third generation, about two-thirds of Hispanics have intermarried and increasingly identify as whites. In earlier times, the category of whiteness expanded, as Italians, Irish, and Jews "became" white. So the dream of a majority-minority America, now projected to be achieved by about the 2050s, may keep receding for a while.

As Jamelle Bouie, now a columnist for the *New York Times*, wrote in a 2014 essay, "Ethnic identity is fluid. It shifts and changes with the circumstances of society. Right now, we think of Latinos and Asians as separate from the white mainstream. But there's no guarantee that will be true in the future. Indeed, if it isn't, we could have a politics similar to the one we have now."

Even if the so-called rising electorate turns out in 2020 at far higher rates than it did in 2016 (and let's hope it does), it's a mistake—empirically, tactically, and *ethically*—to write off the white working class as beyond redemption. White working-class voters, defined as non-college-educated whites, are distributed with great electoral efficiency, and they are concentrated in the very states that tipped the election to Trump in 2016. In Ohio, Indiana, Iowa, Michigan, Missouri, and Wisconsin, as well as western Pennsylvania, the white working class exceeded 50 percent of the electorate. In counties of several states where traditionally Democratic support collapsed, the figure was 60 percent. The point isn't just that a progressive coalition tactically needs the votes of white working-class people, whose horizons have been so diminished by three decades of plutocracy and who are primed to blame other ethnic groups. It's that their lives also matter, and that common interests need emphasis and cultivation.

A Democrat needs not just to win in 2020, but to win a Roosevelt-scale mandate to govern. If a Democrat won by stitching together a coalition that ignored working-class whites as hopelessly biased and lost to Trump, the victory would be narrow and the country even more bitterly divided. A Democratic Party that turned its back on a major portion of the working class in favor of a coalition of minorities, the poor, and the socially liberal rich would not be worthy of the name.

The majority-minority analysis also overlooks the fact that the Obama coalition of 2008 included lots of working-class whites. In that campaign, Obama was an ambiguous figure. People read into him their own hopes. But he definitely campaigned as an outsider and an anti-establishment insurgent. That stance was sufficient for a lot of working-class whites, who were tired of being ignored and disrespected by the usual politicians, so they voted for Obama, his race notwithstanding. But when the economy continued delivering one assault after another and Obama's designated successor, Hillary Clinton, turned out to be the epitome of an insider, their frustrations found a paladin in Donald Trump.

Obama bent over backward not to talk about race. Far from signifying a postracial America, however, Obama's very existence activated latent racism on the part of many whites, for whom it was an affront to see a black man and a black first family in the White House. At the same time, Obama gave insufficient attention to the plutocratic assault on working Americans of all races, and thus he left his inept would-be successor, Hillary Clinton, vulnerable to both a white working-class backlash and a black sense of letdown. The perfect storm of 2016 intensified latent tribal politics.

The 2018 midterms pointed to a very different road, prefiguring what will be possible in 2020. Yet a reversion to the politics of 2016 remains a threat. The *New York Times* columnist Thomas Edsall has repeatedly called attention to the perils of "the deepening racialization of American politics." In a recent column, Edsall warned, "Heading into the 2020 election, President Trump is prepared for the second time in a row to run a racist campaign." At the same time, Edsall cautioned, Democrats are "doubling down" on racially liberal multiculturalism. The need to maximize minority turnout while retaining or recruiting more working-class whites remains "the continuing Democratic quandary."

For many African America leaders, lectures by white critics admonishing practitioners of "identity politics" are just another form of affront. Kamala Harris, speaking at Netroots Nation in August 2018, declared,

> I have a problem, guys, with that phrase, "identity politics." Because let's be clear, when people say that, it's a pejorative. That phrase is used to divide, and it is used to distract. Its purpose is to minimize and marginalize issues that impact all of us. It is used to try and shut us up. These issues that they're trying to diminish and demean, are the very issues that will define our identity as Americans.

Harris may be overdoing the emphasis on identity in her own campaign, but she has an important point. The truly toxic identity politics are the politics of division practiced by Bannon and Trump.

Yet most of the criticism of identity politics has been directed not at Trump but at African Americans and other groups that have long suffered vicious discrimination. As the party of racial and economic uplift, the Democrats need to hone a subtle politics of both/and—both economic populism and antiracism. It's rather easier to be the party of hate.

Connecting Black Lives to All Lives

The Obama years and their appalling aftermath heightened black consciousness and produced a whiplash of hope followed by despair. The election of Trump, who was determined to expunge everything that Obama had accomplished, added to the sense of outrage. Ta-Nehisi Coates spoke for a lot of black Americans when he wrote:

> Before Barack Obama, niggers could be manufactured out of Sister Souljahs, Willie Hortons, and Dusky Sallys. But Donald Trump arrived in the wake of something more potent—an entire nigger presidency with nigger health care, nigger climate accords, and nigger justice reform, all of which could be targeted for destruction or redemption, thus reifying the idea of being white.

Half a century after the great civil rights acts, a century and a half after Lincoln, and a decade after Barack Obama was elected president, young black men are still at risk of being murdered by police for the crime of driving while black or just walking down the street while black. Despite some modest reforms, mass incarceration persists. The prisons are still littered with black men who've grown old for convictions as teens, sent up for drug offenses that have now been reduced to misdemeanors or dropped entirely in many states.

Thanks to stand-your-ground laws promoted by the far right and duly enacted by several state legislatures, angry whites are literally able to shoot blacks with impunity. In countless jurisdictions, black teenagers find themselves with outstanding bench warrants for minor infractions that cascade into fines they cannot afford to pay. In chance encounters with cops, these teens are subject to summary arrest. Even in the Obama era, several young African Americans fleeing such arrests were killed by police. All of this occurred before Donald Trump did his best to expunge Barack Obama.

Race will remain a potentially divisive issue for Democrats, and there will be incidents that keep rubbing wounds raw. In December 2018, a long-planned women's march broke into two rival groups. Two of the leaders, who are black, commented that Jews needed to look more deeply at their own racism. One of these leaders, Tamika Mallory, is an admirer of an open anti-Semite, Louis Farrakhan. An early Jewish leader of the women's march, Vanessa Wruble, felt she was pushed out of the organization because of her religion.

The potential for racial ghosts to emerge without warning was demonstrated again in February 2019, when it was revealed that Ralph Northam, Virginia's moderate Democratic governor, had a 1985 yearbook entry that contained a photo of one person in blackface and another dressed as a Klansman. Northam admitted, then denied, that he had been the one in blackface. It didn't help that Northam's reported student nickname was "Coonman."

The ethnic fault lines in the Democratic coalition were stressed yet again when a freshman member of the House, Ilhan Omar, who is Somali American, as well as Muslim, criticized the excessive influence of the Israeli lobby. In two tweets, she glibly attributed that influence to campaign money, evoking odious stereotypes. Omar's accusation prompted near-universal condemnation, followed by an abject apology by Omar—leaving the impression that there are bright lines when it comes to anti-Semitism, but more blurry lines when it comes to racism.

As William Faulkner famously wrote, "The past is never dead. It's not even past."

To show their good faith with black citizens, Democratic candidates have been pressed by relatively marginal groups to support massive outlays for financial reparations. While white America surely owes the descendants of slaves significant compensatory policies, polls show that nearly 90 percent of white voters oppose large-scale reparations.

Embrace of the reparations movement could well alienate far more voters than it mobilizes, and provide a 2016-style cudgel for Republicans. In the age of social media, it's a fairly short step from the demands of an obscure group to a center-stage controversy. When a *New York Times* reporter cited growing support among African Americans for reparations and asked several Democratic candidates where they stood, Kamala Harris, Elizabeth Warren, and Julian Castro all chose their words very carefully. "We must confront the dark history of slavery and government-sanctioned discrimination in this country that has had many consequences, including undermining the ability of black families to build wealth in America for generations," Warren told the *New York Times*. "We need systemic, structural changes to address that."

Warren did say that she would support a commission on reparations. But it was sufficient for the *Times* to run a news story under the inflated headline "2020 Democrats Embrace Race-Conscious Policies, including Reparations." The *Times* story flatly asserted that Warren "said she supported reparations for black Americans impacted by slavery—a policy that experts say could cost several trillion dollars, and one that Barack Obama, Hillary Clinton, Bernie Sanders and many top Democrats have not supported." But a reparations policy costing several trillion dollars is not what Warren called for.

Not to be outdone, the *Washington Post* then ran several more stories repeating the *Times*' characterization of Democrats and reparations. Reparations then dominated the news cycle as a highly divisive and somewhat inflated controversy spotlighting Democrats' vulnerability on race. This media frenzy was not the work of some Russian fake-news trolling operation, as happened in 2016, but of America's two most serious newspapers.

Race and Rhetoric

In the era of Trump, black voters—the most loyal segment of the Democratic base—are demanding both respect and tangible commitments to back it up. Honoring those legitimate demands while not playing into the Trump/Bannon trap will require both integrity and finesse. For instance, the term "white privilege" may sound extreme to whites whose circumstances are far from privileged, and who can point to policies of affirmative action for minorities. But white privilege is still the lived experience of most blacks, who correctly observe that Caucasians needn't be anxious about driving while white. To break through this dance of dueling racial complaints, the resentment of privilege needs to be redirected against the truly privileged in America—namely, the economic super-elite.

One candidate who does this particularly well is Elizabeth Warren. Speaking at the 2018 annual gathering of Netroots Nation, Warren framed the challenge as broad class unity:

> In Trump's story, the reason why working families keep getting the short end of the stick isn't because of the decisions he and his pals are making in Washington every day. No, according to Trump, the problem is other working people, people who are black, or brown, people born somewhere else. . . .
>
> It all adds up to the same thing—the politics of division. They want us pointing our fingers at each other so that we won't notice that their hands are in our pockets. That stops here. That stops now. We say, no, you will not divide us.

This language is an elegant call for unity against Trump, around common issues of class. One might also interpret it as a warning to candidates, left or right, who would make race the paramount issue.

Here is one more Warren speech, worth quoting at some length because it is such a powerful example of how a white leader can talk about race in a way that is credible to blacks and also unites whites and blacks around the reality that the rules are rigged against working families of all races. Addressing the December 2018 graduating class at Morgan State University, a historically black college in Baltimore, Warren spoke movingly about the role of home ownership in building wealth for the white middle class and the brutal history of redlining against black neighborhoods, much of it actually required by the federal government. Then she said this, emphasizing both the history of discrimination against blacks and injuries common to working people of all races:

Finally, during the 1960s, redlining was banned. And over the next twenty-five years or so, black families started building more wealth. The black-white wealth gap began to shrink. And that might have been the end of the story.

But in the 1990s, as more black families were buying homes and building wealth, big banks and sleazy mortgage lenders saw an opportunity. They targeted communities of color for the worst of the worst mortgages. And bank regulators, the guys who are supposed to work for the American people, looked the other way. The results were catastrophic. Black homeownership rates are now lower than they were when housing discrimination was legal. Today, the black-white wealth gap is bigger than it was back in the 1960s. . . .

I'm not a person of color. And I haven't lived your life or experienced anything like the subtle prejudice, or more overt harm, that you may have experienced just because of the color of your skin. Rules matter, and our government—not just individuals within the government, but the government itself—has systematically discriminated against Black people in this country.

Ultimately subprime mortgages spread far beyond communities of color, and it eventually wrecked our economy. During the crash of 2008, millions of people—black, white, Latino and

Asian—lost their homes. Millions lost their jobs. Millions lost their savings—millions, tens of millions, but not the people at the top. The bank CEOs just kept raking in the money.

Two sets of rules: one for the wealthy and the well-connected. And one for everybody else. Two sets of rules: one for white families. And one for everybody else. That's how a rigged system works. And that's what we need to change.

In short, abuses by Wall Street devastated home owners generally; they particularly targeted blacks. The nonrich of both races were sucker punched by the banks and need to appreciate their true enemy. Warren, in subsequent speeches, went on to address such issues as day care, maternal health, and student debt, always taking care to point out that inadequate policies harmed working families generally and families of color disproportionately. Whether or not Warren is the nominee, she is a good model for how to talk about class, race, and common interests. And there are other role models, both black and white.

Andrew Gillum, both an African American and a flat-out economic progressive, lost his race for Florida governor by only a point, speaking a common language of economic uplift—a better performance than that of any recent Florida Democratic candidate for governor regardless of race. Gillum brilliantly demonstrated how it was possible both to talk about race and to talk beyond race. He did not flinch from calling out the racism of his opponent. In the first debate against Republican Ron DeSantis, Gillum said,

First of all, he's got neo-Nazis helping him out in the state. He has spoken at racist conferences. He's accepted a contribution and would not return it from someone who referred to the former president of the United States as a Muslim n-i-g-g-e-r. When asked to return that money, he said no. He's using that money to now fund negative ads.

Now, I'm not calling Mr. Desantis a racist. I'm simply saying the racists believe he's a racist.

Yet most of what Gillum put forth in his campaign was about economic injustice. Stacey Abrams in neighboring Georgia, a black gubernatorial candidate of exceptional charm, charisma, and broad appeal, lost by the same narrow margin. Both Gillum and Abrams would likely have won, but for voter suppression. Both unmistakably represented black uplift, not only by their presence but by what they had to say. Both, however, offered wide appeals beyond race, by challenging the economic status quo.

Yet Warren's own DNA/Native American misstep, ironically, provides further evidence that divisive pressures will continue. The journal *Critical Ethnic Studies*, an icon of the cultural far left, published a syllabus of articles on Warren and the sin of "cultural appropriation." Here is an extract, which is followed in the text by links to dozens of articles, many by Native American scholars.

In October 2018, US Senator Elizabeth Warren released the results of a DNA test in an effort to prove her claims to Native American ancestry. Far from resolving the question of her supposed Cherokee and Delaware heritage, her actions distracted from urgent issues facing Indigenous communities and undermined Indigenous sovereignty by equating "biology" with culture, "race" with citizenship. In response, Indigenous scholars, activists, and the Cherokee Nation itself, rebuked the dangerous connection between DNA testing and Indigeneity.

The syllabus project aims to contextualize the history of colonialism erasing and assimilating Indigenous populations through the regulation of blood—found in the contemporary iteration of DNA testing. It collects some of the responses from Indian Country in the wake of Warren's misguided political gamble.

This language could not have served rightwing purposes better had Steven Bannon ghostwritten it. In fact, Warren demonstrated conclusively that her assertion of Native American ancestry in two obscure documents unearthed by Republican opponents was never used to advance her career; she took the DNA test only to prove that she had not been lying. In an era of 23andMe and Ancestry.com, most of us believe it is entirely legitimate for Americans to be curious about their ethnic roots. The Warren DNA affair is a purely political canard, but one in which the exquisite sensitivities of the cultural left will be exploited by the cynical right.

Many of the writers of these articles, presumably, are far less interested in electing a progressive Democratic president than they are in using Warren as an object lesson in their narrative of cultural appropriation and pressuring politicians to adopt their framing. Very few voters have even heard of *Critical Ethnic Studies*. However, activists in the cultural left wing of the Democratic Party, in order to keep faith with Native Americans as a constituency, are influenced by such demands.

In late 2018, the Trump administration came up with the diabolically clever ploy of having the Department of Health & Human Services consider a regulation requiring transgender people to keep, for official purposes, the gender that they were assigned at birth. Medical experts and rights activists alike protested that the ruling made no medical sense. But that was not its rationale. The political purpose was to agitate the transgender community to elevate the issue in the political debate and force others in the progressive community to demand repeal of the regulation. (And the transgender community had every right to object and to seek allies.) That reaction, in turn, would give more prominence to an issue that riles up Trump's base and give pause to some political moderates.

Trump will keep coming up with divisive traps like this one. The immigration issue suggests how Trump is sometimes crazy like a fox. For most of 2018, Trump's obsession with his wall and supposed caravans of invading migrants seemed a political loser except with his hardest-core base. Despite his claims, the statistics showed that illegal migration from Mexico has been steadily dropping. But in early 2019, the facts on the ground and the politics both shifted in Trump's favor. Swollen flows of refugees from Central America's northern triangle indeed created a crisis on the US-Mexican border. Trump and immigration hardliners were not wrong when they contended that the humane policy required by treaty commitments, of admitting refugees with a well-founded fear of persecution, encouraged more people to come. Trump's policies of separating children from families, setting up tent cities, and denying entry to bona fide refugees were indeed barbaric. Polls seemed to show that most Americans did not support Trump's views or his remedies on refugees. But with the emergence of a genuine crisis and the plain reality that American are not prepared to admit unlimited numbers of the world's economic refugees, the border issue was no longer such an easy winner for liberals.

The publicity given to social and cultural issues has the potential to divide Democrats and mislead the broader public—especially if Democrats fail to keep the focus on pocketbook issues with the potential to unite. The hopeful news is that more and more Democratic candidates, black and white, seem to be finding their way to narrative language that emphasizes commonality more than difference. There is also good news in the increasing prevalence of habitats where a multiethnic coalition is rooted in the common politics of class uplift.

If you visit a local of the hotel and restaurant workers union in a large city with a strong local, you will find people from dozens of different ethnic backgrounds working together to demand and get middle-class wages. In New York, a room cleaner in a hotel with a union contract makes upwards of $50 an hour. You will never view a more genuinely diverse scene of interracial solidarity than Local 6 in New York. One can see the same multiethnic struggles for solidarity and uplift in unions such as the SEIU (Service Employees International Union) and organizations like the worker center movement, where young workers of many ethnic backgrounds look beyond race to find a common political identity in their common economic struggle. Democratic candidates would do well to spotlight such efforts and successes.

Social scientists observe that race is a "social construct," with shifting definitions of membership. The same is true of class. Pollsters typically define white working-class as white non-college-educated, but that is just a demographic shorthand that lumps together different people with different values. Those values also shift over time and are responsive to leadership, both cynical and noble.

Some lower-income whites self-identify on the basis of race more than others do. At a union hall, white workers tend to appreciate that they have more in common with black coworkers than with white billionaires. Most African Americans consider themselves working-class. Black workers are likely to identify more with white coworkers than with black corporate executives. Steve Bannon's effort was to get downwardly mobile white people to identify *tribally* on the basis of race. Conversely, a successful Democrat will work to alter the social constructs of class and race, so that "working family"[*] becomes a unifying concept that embraces multiple ethnic identities—and becomes a stronger force in American politics and American life than race or class alone.

The admirable work done by Demos Action, and the language modeled by candidates such as Warren and Gillum, using a narrative that unites race and economics, shows what's possible. The risk, in the heat of a protracted primary contest, is that candidates, goaded by social media, interest groups, their opponents, and the press, turn to language that is more inflammatory and divisive.

---

[*] The Working Families Party, which began in New York and is now active in several states, is a group devoted to building broad, grassroots, multiracial alliances to elect progressive candidates and to offset the corporate influence in the Democratic Party. The new Democratic members of the New York State Senate, who took back control from the Republicans in 2019, all benefited from the endorsement and grassroots activism of the Working Families Party. The eight successful candidates endorsed by the WFP included blacks, whites, and Latinos. A majority of the New York City Council had WFP endorsements.

The Moderation Muddle

In addition to those who urge Democrats to double down on identity, another set of commentators argues that America is really at bottom a country of moderates, and that Democrats should try to win by seeking the center. The group Third Way, representing corporate Democrats, makes creative use of polling to argue that it's a mistake for Democrats to run to the left, on either identity or economics.

For instance, Third Way makes a big deal out of the fact that standard polling asking how people identify shows that more Americans characterize themselves as moderates or conservatives than as liberals. But a deeper look reveals that the majority of voters are substantive progressives. In fact, the percentage of Democrats who now identify as liberal rather than moderate has risen steadily in the past decade. By 2018 more than half of all Democrats considered themselves liberal.

But more to the point, a large majority of Democrats are substantively progressive on the issues, once we go beyond superficial labels. Fully 70 percent support Medicare for all—a figure that includes 82 percent of self-identified Democrats and even 52 percent of Republicans, as well as a majority of independents. Large majorities also support making higher education debt-free. Pew found that 58 percent of Americans supported a $15 minimum wage. According to Gallup, 62 percent of Americans approve of unions—a fifteen-year high. Gallup also found broad majority support for a large infrastructure program.

Third Way also circulated a paper purporting to show that most of the Democrats who won primaries in 2018 were moderates. Steven

Rattner, a wealthy private-equity mogul, appearing at a preelection debate with progressives in October 2018, contended,

> Guarantee a $15 an hour income to all? That would cost around the order of $680 billion annually. Expand Social Security? That sounds pretty good, until Americans understand that the trust fund is on track to go broke in 2034 and jeopardize the benefits that we've already promised. Make public colleges and universities tuition-free? It's a great goal for the underprivileged, but if any of my kids were to go to a public institution, I have no idea why they should get a free ride.

If you unpack these arguments, they're pretty much what you'd expect from an investment banker, and a good illustration of the toxic influence of Wall Street Democrats on their party. For people who don't enjoy Rattner-scale wealth, $15 an hour barely makes ends meet. The $680 billion estimated cost would not be borne by taxpayers, of course; it would be paid by corporations that have made off with the lion's share of the nation's rising wealth and income.

By the same token, the real story of Social Security against the backdrop of collapsing private pension plans is its inadequacy, not its fiscal costs. If we raised the ceiling on income subject to taxation, and expanded it to include income from dividends and capital gains on people in Rattner's income class, tens of millions of ordinary Americans might get a little more in their Social Security checks.

Rattner's argument against free public universities is the most insidious of all. He makes it sound as if this is a bad idea because his children don't need the help. But of course 99 percent of the students at public universities are not in Rattner's income bracket, and most do need the help. The idea of free higher education is far from radical. For more than a century, public universities charged little or no tuition. We dealt with the slight leakage of the public benefit to rich people by having a progressive income tax. We need to revert to both policies now.

It's unbelievable that a professed Democrat can argue that a $15 minimum wage, expanded Social Security, and free public higher education are too leftwing for the Democrats. The corporate Democrats in groups like Third Way are basically moderate Republicans. If they simply joined the Republican Party, the caliber of both parties would improve.

Both before and after the 2018 election, Third Way spun the results as a victory for moderate Democrats. They pointed to centrists who had won and progressives who had lost. This debating tactic reminds me of a favorite caveat of the late sociologist Daniel Bell: "'For example' is not an argument." Third Way can cherry-pick cases of Democrats who picked up House seats running as centrists, and I can match their examples with many more cases of Democrats who won as economic progressives. But the battle of examples misses the point. The fact is that many Democrats *did* win as progressives, and in unlikely places. And if Democrats can run and win as progressives, that's what they should do—because this is the only strategy that has the potential of bridging over racial splits, of bringing back Trump voters, and of galvanizing a large majority.

The other problem with the counsel of centrism is that the potential Democratic electorate is not likely to be mobilized by an appeal for a new moderation. It's true that there are some districts, especially traditionally Republican suburban ones, where Democrats prevailed in the 2018 midterms because swing voters were fed up with Trump's fearmongering. At the same time, the Democrats who made big gains in the heart of Trump country did so as economic progressives.

In the December 2018 fight over the Speakership, corporate Democrats in the House associated with strategist and famed "triangulator" Mark Penn concocted one bogus bipartisan alliance of convenience after another in the quest to replace the progressive Nancy Pelosi with a more centrist House Speaker. They were faced down by the overwhelming majority of the House Democratic Caucus, who saw through the ploy. It was subsequently revealed that Penn had quietly paid a visit to President Trump, his more natural ally.

Some commentators, defining class only in terms of the poor, have insisted that class politics cannot work in America. Social critic Mark Lilla, in an influential critique of identity politics, contended that class consciousness has far less effect on Americans than leftists would like to believe, adding that if solidarity "is based solely on economic resentment, it will be shared only by those who feel disadvantaged, and will disappear as soon as their fortune improves in an economic upturn." That sweeping conclusion misreads both the economics and the history, and the multiple opportunities for political leadership and definition of common class interests (see Roosevelt, Franklin). The broad, tacit sense that all the gains have gone to the top is deeply felt, not just by the "disadvantaged" but also by the broad workaday middle class. And as the history of the past forty years shows, the fortunes of the bottom 70 percent—not merely the disadvantaged—seldom improve more than trivially in the next upturn.

Many commentators keep insisting, ad nauseam, that the Democrats need to choose between aligning themselves with the grass-roots move toward the economic left and winning elections. In an emblematic January 2019 piece expressing that conventional wisdom, staff writer Jonathan Martin of the *New York Times* wrote:

> After a 2018 midterm election that energized the left, perhaps the most consequential political question facing the Democratic Party is whether liberals will insist on imposing policy litmus tests on 2020 presidential hopefuls, or whether voters will rally behind the candidate most capable of defeating the president even if that Democrat is imperfect on some issues.
>
> Will candidates sprint to the left on issues and risk hurting themselves with intraparty policy fights and in the general election? Or will they keep the focus squarely on Mr. Trump and possibly disappoint liberals by not being bolder on policy?

This view, so prevalent in the Washington media echo chamber, has it exactly backward. The Democratic nominee needs to articulate all the ways that plutocratic rule is destroying the livelihoods of working Americans—not out of a sense of litmus tests or ideological purity *but to win the election*. A strong pocketbook theme is the key to rallying voters, bringing back white working-class voters to Democrats, bridging schisms of race, and defeating Trump.

The latent support for a positive economic message and program has been evident for decades. In 2004, when Democratic presidential candidate John Kerry booted a winnable election, activists in Florida qualified a ballot initiative raising that state's minimum wage by one dollar, from $5.15 to $6.15. The campaign was led by the federation of community organizers called ACORN (Association of Community Organizations for Reform Now), with help from unions. Kerry was asked to come down and campaign for it. He declined.

In this quintessential swing state, which George W. Bush carried on Election Day, the minimum-wage initiative won overwhelmingly, with 71 percent of the vote. It carried *every single Florida county*, including some very conservative counties where the sort of working people who later voted for Donald Trump care about their paychecks. Even for the 93 percent of Floridians who did not stand to personally benefit, the initiative had powerful symbolic resonance because it delivered something tangible for working people.

The minimum-wage initiative won by 3 million votes. It received about 2 million votes more than Kerry did, and a million votes more than Bush did. If Kerry had accepted the invitation to go out on street corners and campaign for the minimum-wage hike as a signature issue, he might have been elected president.

Even in seemingly conservative parts of America, there is a latent receptivity to a progressive economic message articulated by a galvanizing candidate. In 2018, that appeal was demonstrated in the most unlikely places. Arkansas and Missouri passed ballot initiatives to increase the minimum wage. In Idaho, Nebraska, and Utah, all conventionally red states, the voters approved initiatives to expand Medicaid coverage. Education emerged as the sleeper issue in Oklahoma, leading to the election of one member of the House who campaigned on better schools, and almost to the election of a second. In a ballot initiative in supposedly conservative Missouri, voters by a 2-to-1 margin overturned a right-to-work measure enacted by the legislature that made it harder to organize or join a union. This outcome is all the more remarkable because after decades of union bashing, the percentage of unionized workers in Missouri is down to just 9 percent. But people who suffer economic distress know in their bones that stronger unions could be good for them.

The Road to 2020—Including the Potholes

It's too early to tell whether Trump will be forced out of office, but between ongoing congressional investigations and findings of the special counsel, Trump will be on the defensive except among his most hard-core supporters (for whom Trump could indeed shoot someone in the middle of Fifth Avenue, as he boasted, and it would be just fine). But they are far from a national majority.

These revelations will also be awkward for the Republican Party. Trump's strategy in 2018, of doubling down on hard-core hate and division, worked to rally his base, but it was lethal in the suburbs and painful for many business leaders in his coalition. As investigations produce more and more damaging detail, the latent splits in the Republican coalition will only widen.

There are those who think that Vice President Pence would be a formidable opponent, should Trump be forced out of office. I beg to differ. This is a politician who took the job only because he was about to lose a reelection campaign for governor of Indiana—quite a feat for a Republican incumbent in a deep red state. Pence is an ordinary far-right Christian fundamentalist politician. He has little of Trump's feral charisma or his demonic intuitive genius as brash tactician. Indeed, if Trump were to leave office, it's far from clear that Pence would even be the nominee. Trump's departure would set in motion a free-for-all between Pence, Tea Party candidates claiming to be Trump's true heir, and anti-Trump moderates like former Ohio governor John Kasich or former Arizona senator Jeff Flake or freshman senator Mitt Romney hoping to take back their party. Even if he remains, Pence's Republican critics are likely to speak up more forcefully. The Republican schisms would only widen.

In addition, Trump's economic record will be vulnerable, especially in the hands of a skilled opponent. For his hard-core base, Trump's fulminations produced a lot of psychic income, but not much more. The tilt of the economy to major metropolitan areas only intensified under Trump. Researcher Anthony Orlando, who teaches finance at California Polytechnic State University, reviewed a variety of studies and found that "the larger the Trump electorate [in a particular county that voted for Trump], the worse the county's economic performance." The small cities and rural areas of America that had good reason to resent their diminished prospects got precious little help from Trump. A skilled Democratic progressive can connect these dots. The antidote to faux populism has to be true populism—not in the sense of cheap class-warfare rhetoric but in the sense of a narrative and program that credibly puts the government and the economy back on the side of working families.

A Democratic candidate who runs on progressive kitchen-table economics and cross-race unity is better positioned to defeat Trump or a faux-populist successor than is either an identity-politics Democrat or a centrist conciliator. The Democratic gains in 2018 suggest that the electoral map can include all of the winnable states that Hillary Clinton lost in 2016—Pennsylvania, Ohio, Michigan, Wisconsin, Iowa, and Florida. In 2018, Florida voters passed a ballot measure restoring the right to vote for 1.4 million former felons. Had they been able to vote in 2018, Florida almost surely would have elected Democrats as senator and governor, and this reform also bodes well for 2020. An effective Democrat would also have a shot at winning back North Carolina and Indiana (both of which Obama carried in 2008), and Arizona as well, and by 2024, perhaps also Texas and Georgia.

A strong Democratic presidential win would increase the Democratic majority in House. The Senate, currently 53–47 Republican, is a steeper climb. But in the same way that Democrats were unlucky in 2018 in terms of which Senate seats were up for election, the luck of the draw favors Democrats in 2020. If the Democrat is elected president, three Senate seats need to change hands to bring the Senate to 50–50, in which case the vice president breaks the tie and control reverts to the Democrats. In 2020, seven potentially vulnerable Republicans are defending seats, and just one seriously vulnerable Democrat. So Democrats would need to win at least four of the possible seven to take back a Senate majority.

The Republicans are Martha McSally of Arizona, Cory Gardner of Colorado, Joni Ernst of Iowa, Susan Collins of Maine, Steve Daines of Montana, Thom Tillis of North Carolina, and John Cornyn of Texas. Gardner, Ernst, and Tillis all were elected by narrow margins. McSally was appointed to fill a vacancy in 2018, a year when a Democrat was handily elected to fill Arizona's other seat. Montana is a Democratic-trending state that has a streak of electing Democratic senators and governors. Collins lost a lot of support in Maine because of her flip-flops on the Brett Kavanaugh confirmation. There will also be an open seat in Tennessee. In early 2019, polls were showing that even Mitch McConnell, up for reelection in Kentucky, is vulnerable. The vulnerable Democrat is Doug Jones of Alabama. But in a good Democratic year with a strong presidential candidate leading the ticket, at least four or five net Democratic pickups are quite possible, leading to Democratic control of the Senate.

To complete this exercise, we need to assume that democracy will hold and that there will be a reasonably free election in 2020. Yes, there will be voter suppression in some states, but as 2018 showed, that undertow can be overcome with sufficient mobilization. The 2018 elections also produced several reforms at the state level. In Michigan, Missouri, Colorado, and Utah, ballot initiatives passed to create nonpartisan redistricting commissions. In Nevada and Michigan, automatic voter registration passed. In Maryland, same-day voter registration was approved. Maine provided the first test of ranked-choice voting, which flipped its Second District House seat from Republican to Democrat.[*]

The progressive wing of the Democratic Party provided most of the energy in 2018 and is well mobilized for 2020. One indicator

---

[*] With ranked-choice voting, the voter can list second- and third-choice candidates. If no candidate wins a majority on the initial ballot, the candidate who came in last is dropped, and his or her votes are redistributed until someone wins a majority. In this system, votes more accurately reflect preferences. The system prevents third-party or independent candidates from functioning as "spoilers" and tipping the election to a candidate whom most voters opposed. In Maine, Republican Bruce Poliquin initially won a plurality, but Democrat Jared Golden was the second choice of most voters who had backed the independent. When those votes were redistributed, the Democrat won.

is that even centrist Democratic politicians have sought to rebrand themselves as progressives. New York senator Kirsten Gillibrand, who began her career as a darling of the financial industry and an opponent of progressive economic policies, now supports a tax on financial transactions, a federal jobs guarantee, public banking through the post office, and several other progressive causes. This repositioning is testament to the plain fact that both the grassroots energy and the center of gravity in the party today are well to the left and nobody can expect to be nominated without playing to that enlarged base. The conversion may be sincere, or it may be opportunistic posturing. But even if Gillibrand is a weather vane, as her critics contend, her stance tells a lot about where the wind is blowing.

This is not the place to handicap the entire field, which will keep changing by the week. When I was the junior man on the *Washington Post* national staff, I drew the assignment of covering the presidential announcement of Jimmy Carter in December 1974. At that point, he had 2 percent national name recognition, and few other reporters showed up for his press conference. The *Post* put my story on the shipping page. As late as January 1976, as the election year dawned, Carter was the choice of just 4 percent of polled Democrats. But in a fragmented field, Carter went on to win the Iowa caucuses a month later, and eventually the nomination and election.

The abrupt emergence of Pete Buttigieg in March and April 2019 shows how this dynamic can work. A fresh face, who seems a decent and principled person, can come out of nowhere; the media publicity feeds on itself, donations flow, volunteers materialize, crowds gather, and suddenly a thirty-seven-year-old gay mayor of a small city is a serious contender.

Despite the grassroots energy and the unmistakable shift of the party toward economic populism, the progressive wing of the party (and thus the party itself) faces four big risks in 2020.

One risk is an embarrassment of riches. Several progressive candidates will be in the race for the Democratic nomination, depending on how you count. Given the logic of primary and caucus contests, it's conceivable that this group of candidates could fragment the progressive vote, and perhaps open the door to a more centrist nominee. There is a related risk that in a huge field, of as many as twenty candidates, it becomes impossible to stage serious debates on the issues. In the 2016 Republican contest we saw the kind of circus that a large field can generate. The risk is that the most outrageous or sensationalist or personally compelling candidate breaks out of the pack. Mercifully, there are no Democratic Trumps, but in a field this large, almost anything can happen.

A second risk is that if a candidate such as Elizabeth Warren or Bernie Sanders were to win the Democratic nomination, a lot of nominally Democratic money and support from the corporate wing of the party would back the Republican, either tacitly or overtly. There could well be an intensified push for a business-oriented "moderate" to run as an independent. In a three-way race, it's not clear who would lose more votes to such a candidate, but a progressive Democrat would likely do better in a straight two-way race.

The third risk, as noted, is that race becomes highly divisive, once again enabling the Republican candidate to stir up white voters on the basis of racial backlash, and thus to evade responsibility on the pocketbook issues where Trump has proved to be a total fake. The southern primaries, in which the Democratic electorate is heavily

African American, are relatively early in the season. South Carolina, closely followed by Alabama, Louisiana, Texas, Florida, and North Carolina, all have their primaries in March. One could imagine a kind of reverse dog whistle, in which black candidates play to their natural voting base, and race comes to the fore at the expense of broader party unity. There is the related risk of what some have termed "rainbow neoliberalism," in which an identity-politics candidate is a close ally of Wall Street and tries to use cultural radicalism to disguise a corporate agenda that undermines the promise of pocketbook populism. This would repeat the disaster of 2016, only worse, given the even higher stakes.

Under the current Democratic rules, candidates in state primaries and caucuses are awarded delegates proportionally. There is no longer a winner-take-all rule. With a very large field, the lack of a winner-take-all rule increases the final risk—that the nominee will not be decided until the August convention. That drawn-out decision process, in turn, leaves Democrats to pummel each other for more than a year instead of concentrating their fire on Trump.

Yet another possibility is that two of the leading candidates, who together may have 50 percent of the delegates, join forces before the convention balloting begins and run as a ticket. This could produce an earlier winner but also a fraught ideological anomaly—and not for the first time. Liberals in 1960 were appalled when John Kennedy selected Lyndon Johnson as his running mate, and the 1932 ticket of FDR and "Cactus Jack" Garner as his running mate was even weirder.

Two other important caveats: Ideas are unusually important in this election—ideas about how to make the rules of American capitalism work once again for ordinary people, on every front from labor policy to financial regulation, debt relief for students, trade, tax reform, and a major green infrastructure program. But ideas do not run for president. Candidates do. And the eventual Democratic nominee may or may not the one with the most winning policy ideas. Moreover, the most powerful ideas candidate may or may not be the most effective personal challenger to Trump or his successor. The whole package has to work.

One also has to imagine each of the leading contenders in the general election against Donald Trump. If he survives, Trump will wage a campaign that is at least as reckless, bullying, and mendacious as the one he ran against Hillary Clinton. This time, he will have the power of the presidency to time crises and do other stunts, as well as the support of far-right websites, media, and ostensibly independent dirty tricks. The Trump TV spots that have already been circulated are reminiscent of Leni Riefenstahl's *Triumph of the Will*. Bots, trolls, fake websites, and foreign meddling will also be in play. Voters will need to think hard about which possible Democratic candidate has the tenacity, ingenuity, charm, and grit to stand up to all of this and turn it against Trump.

It remains to be seen whether the Democrats' reckoning with race and class will produce a new unity, as prefigured by the 2018 midterms, or a train wreck. The combination of high-stakes primaries, interest groups, social media, and the press looking for a new morning line—all easily exploited by Republicans—suggests trouble. To take a more optimistic view, we can hope that the entire Democratic field will grasp the stakes and refrain from playing into Trump's narrative.

The Democratic race will be in flux until at least spring 2020, and maybe until the August convention. The nominee could be any of several contenders. But if a progressive Democrat can be nominated and elected president, what then? Even with a majority in both houses of Congress, what would it take for that president to govern, and to govern successfully?

CHAPTER 7

≋

The View from 2021

I have suggested in this book that there is a path to electing a progressive Democrat, as well as an urgency. But winning the election is not enough. The new president needs to be able to govern. I hope to persuade you that there is also a path, albeit a narrower one, to a successful progressive presidency.

The election of a president always seems momentous. This time, the stakes are even higher than usual. The new president must not only reverse the slide into despotism and restore American democracy. She must begin the process of reclaiming a decent economy for ordinary Americans, and the affirmative role of government in bringing about that economic rejuvenation.* Simultaneously, the president

---

* For the sake of grammatical simplicity (and audacity), let's assume that the next president will be a woman and use "she," rather than the awkward "he or she" or the incorrect "they." This is not a pitch for any single candidate.

needs not only to be a strong partisan leader with a clear agenda but to restore a sense of procedural fair play. She must revive America's role in the world as a beacon of decency, while protecting America and the world from terrorism and nuclear war. And she has to begin the process of damping down the racial hatred cultivated by her predecessor. With time fast running out, the new president needs to rouse Americans to a massive commitment to save the habitability of the planet. And I haven't even gotten to a score of major second-tier issues, from trade to taxes to immigration reform.

None of this would be easy under the best of circumstances. And the circumstances in 2021 will be arduous. Republicans will do everything possible to make the new president fail.

Can a Progressive President Succeed?

Most recent Democratic presidents did not realize their major goals. The one who clearly succeeded was Franklin Roosevelt. The New Deal got the US partway out of the Great Depression, and World War II did the rest. Roosevelt's lasting legacy was a managed form of capitalism that harnessed business and finance in a broad public interest, demonstrated the promise of government, empowered labor, and created an economy of broad prosperity.* But his successor, Harry Truman, was hobbled both by the Republican capture of Congress

---

* Roosevelt's main failure was his acceptance of a New Deal for white people, as the price of southern support in Congress. In some cases, such as housing policy, the New Deal actually intensified segregation. Civil rights were made to wait.

in 1946 and by racists in his own party. (The anti-union Taft-Hartley Act of 1947 was passed over Truman's veto, thanks to the support of Dixiecrats who feared that unions would promote integration.)

John Kennedy was assassinated before his promise could be realized. Lyndon Johnson was on the way to becoming a second FDR, achieving broad success with his Great Society and civil rights efforts, until he squandered much of it with the Vietnam War, dividing his own party and opening the way to half a century of mostly Republican rule. Clinton and Obama both managed to be reelected, but both lost their congressional majorities just two years into their first terms. And to the extent that they succeeded, it was often on Republican terrain—cutting back social supports, sponsoring financial deregulation, promoting budget austerity, supporting a corporate version of trade. This is not an auspicious history.

So, the new president will need to learn from the missteps of her predecessors—not only to succeed, but to succeed as a progressive. Is all of this possible? Barely. Is it necessary? Supremely. The costs of failure would be catastrophic.

History's one great exception to the pattern of a new president losing House seats in the first midterm was FDR. He won by a landslide in 1932 and then picked up more legislative seats in 1934— a net gain of 8 in the House and 9 in the Senate. Beginning with his first 100 days, Roosevelt gained popular support because ordinary people correctly perceived that he was working on their behalf. He went on to win an even bigger victory in 1936. The only recent president to avert the usual midterm losses was George W. Bush in 2002. Bush used the attacks of September 11, 2001, to rally the citizenry in a time of real crisis, and then doubled down with a fake crisis via his Iraq War.

For once, the luck of the draw will be on the Democrats' side in the 2022 midterms. There are between five and nine vulnerable Republican Senate seats, and no seriously vulnerable Democrats. So if the new Democratic president delivers, the Democrats could well increase their House and Senate majority, FDR style. Four of the vulnerable Republican senators facing reelection are Richard Burr in North Carolina, Rob Portman in Ohio, Pat Toomey in Pennsylvania, and Ron Johnson in Wisconsin. There is likely to be a very competitive open seat in Iowa, assuming the retirement of Chuck Grassley, who will be eighty-nine. In neighboring Kansas, which elected a Democratic governor in 2018, Pat Roberts has already announced his retirement. In a good Democratic year, Todd Young in Indiana, Marco Rubio in Florida, and Roy Blunt in Missouri could also be vulnerable. But the Democrats will need to earn those victories with a presidency that is convincing in its first two years.

If Republicans hold the Senate in 2020 and 2022, the road to Democratic success is much steeper. Republican obstructionism might begin with a refusal to confirm major presidential nominees, as well as court appointees. The new presidency would start, and end, with continuing gridlock. The next president should be prepared for scorched-earth tactics such as these, and worse.

There are antidotes to such tactics. First, obviously, the Democrat needs to rally the citizenry and win in 2020 by a convincing margin. A president who wins big is likely to have sufficient coattails to bring along a Democratic Senate majority, which is essential for passing legislation and confirming executive and judicial nominees. The stronger a popular mandate the president has, the harder it is politically for Republicans to pursue a strategy of total obstruction without further marginalizing themselves.

Second, the new president needs to pursue policies and themes that broaden and deepen support. As Lincoln famously said, "In this age, in this country, public sentiment is everything. With it, nothing can fail; without it, nothing can succeed." A great president has the power to be transformative in shaping public opinion, and to build popular support in office rather than suffering an abbreviated honeymoon.

The political scientist James MacGregor Burns distinguishes between transformative presidents and transactional ones. Bill Clinton was a transactional president. Barack Obama hoped to be transformative on the issue of tolerance but ended up being transactional on key pocketbook issues. Clinton, elected with just 43 percent of the vote, never built on his mandate and ended up with one of the worst midterm losses ever—54 seats—until Obama beat Clinton's record by losing 63 seats.

The new president needs to use her incumbency to solidify and expand the initial base of support. She can do this by being strategic, selective, and thematic in the legislation that is proposed and, one hopes, enacted. Straightforward legislation that delivers concrete and visible benefits has two virtues: It restores public support for the premise and promise of affirmative government with Democrats as custodians of that bargain. And it forces Republicans to take awkward votes that either embarrass or divide them.

One hopeful sign is that several Democratic contenders are thinking big, with such proposals as universal health care and childcare, substantial investments in infrastructure, and wealth and income taxes on the very rich to pay for those programs. Not only are the proposals good policy and galvanizing politics, but the surprising general support for them has demonstrated that transformative ideas long dismissed as fringe are, in fact, mainstream.

A Few Big Themes

Rather than squandering the initial honeymoon on multiple issues, the new president needs to focus on a few big themes that will be hard for Republicans to oppose without embarrassing themselves—themes that both teach lessons and provide practical help.

Reclaiming Nationalism. One emblematic strategy is to take the nationalism issue away from Trump and the Republicans and to define a new progressive nationalism—built on the kind of economy that Americans work for and deserve, as Americans. Globally, we need a form of nationalism, stripped of foreign policy adventures, that restores America's role as a beacon of liberty, common purpose, and broadly shared prosperity—but that does not sacrifice America's broad economic well-being to a cosmopolitanism that serves mainly elites. Domestically, we need a nationalism that builds on all that defines and unites us as Americans.

As a number of scholars have pointed out, great progressive presidents have embraced a positive form of nationalism—the government helping the entire nation, and invoking our common destiny as Americans. Benign nationalism is too constructive a force to allow Trump to spoil it. The American constitutional founding was an act of nationalism—of shared identity, values, and common purpose, embodied in the newly defined American nation. Although many commentators in the Trump era have associated nationalism with the far right, scholars of American history know better.

In an authoritative book on the subject, historian Gary Gerstle demonstrates that there are two basic strands of American nationalism: civic and racial. The more rightwing brand of nationalism, which Trump sought to rekindle, defines the American nation racially. In the twentieth century, progressives cultivated a "new nationalism," a term coined in 1909 by the progressive journalist Herbert Croly and embraced by Teddy Roosevelt. "Other liberal presidents," Gerstle writes, "would follow in Roosevelt's steps, arguing that a welfare state, the protection of labor's right to organize, and limitations on industrialists' power were now necessary to fulfill the nation's civic mission." It is the task of the new president to reclaim the vision of civic nationalism, both because this is necessary in its own right, and to defeat racialized nationalism.

As the Oxford political philosopher David Miller writes, "Where the citizens of a state are also compatriots, the mutual trust that this engenders makes it more likely that they will be able to solve collective action problems, to support redistributive forms of justice, and to practice deliberative forms of democracy." The political historian John Judis points out that the welfare state was built on a sense of a common national identity—and it helped reinforce a common sense of national purpose. Judis adds that failed states are often the consequence of rival national identities, such as Iraq, Syria, and Nigeria. To the extent that Trump tries to use identity to divide, progressives need to promote a sense of shared destiny to unite. Judis concludes,

"Nationalist sentiments can be the basis of social generosity or of bigoted exclusion."

Make America Great Again. Never was there a slogan more belied by policies supposedly pursued in its service. To make America truly great again, we might start with policies that pay decent wages for decent work and rebuild domestic industry—and do so via massive public investment in public needs. A $15 national minimum wage, as House Democrats have shown, is broadly popular, signals real help for working people, and usefully embarrasses Republicans.

America needs a public infrastructure program, to modernize decaying public systems, create millions of well-paying blue-collar jobs, and serve as a down payment on a transition to a sustainable green economy. According to the American Society of Civil Engineers, which is far from a radical group, the cost of deferred maintenance in our basic public systems is about $4.3 trillion. That includes water and sewer systems, electricity grids, public buildings, roads and bridges, and mass transit. Beyond that sum, climate change requires new public investments to protect coastal areas against storm surges, as well as new outlays to replace carbon-based systems with renewable ones. To take an Acela train, one of the few bits of presentable public twentieth-century technology, from Boston to Washington, is to pass through a living museum of nineteenth-century infrastructure. The express train from New York to Chicago was faster in 1906 than it is today.* The contrast with, say, Germany—a country with

---

* Eighteen hours for the 20th Century Limited in 1906, versus nineteen hours and ten minutes for Amtrak's current Lake Shore Limited.

about our level of average GDP per capita—is appalling. Japan, as a far poorer nation, had high-speed "bullet trains" beginning in the 1960s that still beat anything America has half a century later.

If you take a close look at our great bridges, tunnels, and water and power systems—from the Golden Gate to the George Washington Bridge, and from the Hoover Dam to the Tennessee Valley Authority (TVA)—you can appreciate that we are still living off the public legacy of the New Deal from nearly a century ago. In that era, a much poorer America found the money—during a deep depression—for serious investment in public works. That investment, in turn, helped pull the country out of the Depression, and built popular support for the premise that we could do great things in common.

We need to be spending at least $500 billion a year for a decade. We can get part of that money by repealing the Republican tax act, which costs $1.6 trillion over a decade. We can get some of it by restoring traditional tax rates on the richest Americans. In the booming postwar era, the top marginal rate on very high incomes was at least 77 percent until 1964, and 60 percent as recently as 1982. That rate could be restored, while Social Security taxes on working people could be cut. We could get some of the needed investment funds via new, very-long-term infrastructure bonds or a public infrastructure bank.

In the context of today's conventional budget discourse, $500 billion sounds like an astronomical sum. It is actually only 2 percent of the GDP, and the investment would be repaid in improved productivity, innovation, and jobs. Because the benefits of both job creation and public works projects would be broadly diffused throughout the country, to red and blue states alike, such expenditure would be hard for Republicans to oppose frontally.

A serious public investment program would also force the government to redefine trade policy to serve America's interests rather than to function as a vague and self-defeating commitment to corporate globalism. There is a very simple principle here. Money generated by American taxes and American debt should create American jobs and American industries. In trying to sell a corporate version of globalism to the world, recent trade deals limited our ability to use buy-American policies. When it comes to public infrastructure created by public tax and debt, we need to reclaim "Buy American."

World War II functioned as a massive program not just of good jobs, but of creating new industries and new technologies, virtually all made in America. An infrastructure program at proper scale could do likewise. Politically and ideologically, it would provide a vivid contrast with Republican versions of growth programs based on tax cuts and trickle-down theory, and infrastructure programs based on privatization. It would also serve as a defensible form of economic nationalism that would take the trade issue away from the right. Trump postured tough on trade, but in the end he delivered little of benefit to the US, and his actual policies were an incoherent stew.

A Bill of Rights for America's Young. There has been a lot of talk about student debt relief or free public higher education. These are worthy ideas, but they need to be nested in a broader narrative about what America has been doing to its young. The under-35 generation, except for those with wealthy parents who can pay to give them a head start, is the stunted generation. Most nonrich college graduates begin with debt even before they become productive citizens. Such financial burden is unprecedented in the American experience unless we go back to the colonial era of indentured servitude.

This generation also faces unaffordable home ownership. Their parents' generation also face downward mobility, but many are protected because they became home owners while housing was still affordable. So, people in their fifties through their eighties have a lot of net worth stashed in their houses. The combination of student debt and high housing costs has pushed down the home ownership rate among young adults to low levels not seen since the 1930s. And given supply and demand and the scarcity of affordable rentals, young adults also pay astronomical costs in rent. More are doubling and tripling up, and more are moving back in with their parents.

To make matters worse, this generation is less likely than their parents' generation to have reliable payroll jobs, and less likely to have employer-provided pensions or health insurance. Young adults are often told a fable that many of them internalize, at least for a while: I may not be able to afford a house, but I need to move around a lot for my job anyway. I don't have my own room, but it's fine to take my laptop to Starbucks. I can't afford a car, but it's cooler, greener, and a better source of exercise to take my bike. This fable of downward mobility as a superior lifestyle may be plausible at age twenty-five, but it is not so attractive at thirty-five, when one hopes to start a family.

Much of this generational stunting has been depoliticized, in the sense that many young adults either fault themselves or attribute their economic slide to technology and the new economy, and try to cope by making themselves more attractive to employers. This is another facet of the ideology of ultramarketization, which holds that we are all competing against each other, all of the time. Yet the shift of the terms of engagement against the young mainly reflects political choices that were made, or not made. A new president needs to repoliticize the stunting of the young, to narrate the life experience of struggling young adults and connect it to politics.

With a different politics and different policies, America could indeed make public higher education free once again, as it was for the first century of our great public universities. We could offer partial debt relief for those already in debt, based on income. Senator Sanders has proposed a very good model in his College for All Act. Tuition at public universities now totals about $70 billion a year. Sanders's bill would have the federal government cover $47 billion of that amount via grants to the states, on condition that states cover the rest. He would pay for this—and a lot more—with a small tax on Wall Street transactions, which could raise an estimated hundreds of billions a year.

A "Bill of Rights for the Young" could package affordable college with affordable starter housing, as well as improvements in retirement plans and health security. Young people not only turned out in record numbers in 2018; they also voted Democratic by a margin of better than 2 to 1. A candidate and a president who ran and governed as champion of the young would win their lifelong political affection and affiliation.

Real Health Security. The issue that galvanized voters in 2018 turned out to be health care. The Republicans' effort to kill the Affordable Care Act backfired, as did their stealth attack on Medicaid. Yet tens of millions of Americans are still uninsured, and tens of millions more are underinsured. Attempting to achieve single-payer health insurance in one fell swoop is probably a bridge too far. But there are several strategies for drastically increasing coverage under Medicare that logically lead to eventual Medicare for all and build political support along the way.

Here are three variants: (1) a public option that would allow anyone dissatisfied with private health insurance to buy into Medicare, at affordable rates (this option would help stabilize Medicare's finances, since younger people are less likely than older people to incur costly medical bills); (2) an optional Medicare buy-in, at age fifty or fifty-five; or (3) simply expanding Medicare automatically to everyone over fifty. The big virtue of these approaches is that they are very straightforward and easy to grasp, unlike the Affordable Care Act, which was a complex stew of public and private provision that confused the public, initially hurt the Democrats, and only slowly won grudging voter support as better than nothing.

Another variant, to address the health insecurity of the young, would be to give everyone under age thirty a Medicare card. Then the logic of gradually expanding Medicare to everyone would be inexorable. Eventually, Medicaid and the Children's Health Insurance Program would be folded into Medicare, as would be the current privatized Medicare drug benefit. There is a core principle here: *simpler is better and public is better.*

Since prescription drug costs are a major source of pocketbook distress, a comprehensive drug reform bill is also a good idea. Such legislation could include giving Medicare and Medicaid the same right that is now used by the Department of Veterans' Affairs to negotiate bulk pricing discounts, as well as changes in the excessive terms of patent protection so that more drugs would reach generic status a lot sooner. Elizabeth Warren, citing extensive abuses in the generic-

drug industry, has proposed a bill authorizing the government to produce generic drugs. Bills such as these both deliver tangible, practical
help and put Republicans on the side of defending unpopular special
interests.

Spreading the Growth Around. One of the most important findings of economic development research is the degree of regional concentration of recent economic expansion. Most of the recovery from
the 2008 recession was heavily concentrated in a handful of large
metro areas. Smaller cities and rural regions were left behind. A 2018
Brookings Institution study found that since 2008, the number of
jobs in large metro areas had increased by 9 percent, while they had
remained flat in small towns and decreased by 4 percent in rural
areas remote from large metro areas.

These were the areas that voted heavily for Trump. Experts disagree on what precisely accounts for intensified regional concentration of growth. But some likely suspects include the fact that tech
industries tend to cluster where there are other tech industries and
thick pools of skilled specialists, while traditional smaller manufacturing cities have been given up for global supply chains and cheaper
foreign workers. But things don't have to be that way.

America urgently needs a national policy to spread the new economy around. The conservative/Republican version is to institute spe-
cially targeted tax breaks. These have been around for decades, with
such names as "enterprise zones" and "opportunity zones." For the
most part they don't work, functioning mainly as tax giveaways.

In past eras, the government did work to spread economic development. The TVA, initially a combination flood control and electri-

fication initiative, became an economic development catalyst for an entire region. Likewise the great dams and public power systems of the Pacific Northwest.

The city of Chattanooga, where the TVA legacy lives on, has a municipal internet system run by the local public power company, the Electric Power Board of Chattanooga. It is among the nation's cheapest and fastest, offering broadband service at one gigabit per second. Citizens of Chattanooga now pay just $70 a month for combined cable and internet service, which forces commercial competitors to hold down their prices. FDR, back in the day, referred to this public option strategy as "yardstick competition": use public options to lower prices, expand choices, and keep private companies from engaging in price gouging. The logic still applies.

In this case, Chattanooga's ultra-high-speed internet not only benefits citizens as consumers but serves as an economic development tool to attract companies that need very-high-speed and reliable internet service. Chattanooga, though far from the coastal tech zones, has become a tech hub. As part of an infrastructure and regional development plan, the federal government could make available grants to localities that desire public, high-speed internet. Such a measure would also reinforce the meta-lesson that public is often simpler and better. Before Chattanooga could successfully implement its municipal internet service, it had to defeat a lawsuit brought by Comcast and win the support of the FCC. Yet, commercial rivals have been able to limit cheap, high-speed public internet to the city; in the suburbs, commercially provided web service is still slow and expensive. This battle demonstrates the importance of the ground rules of capitalism, in which innovation serves either the broad public or elite special interests. A transformative president, as narrator, can tell stories like this one and use them to shift public sentiment.

The Berkeley sociologist Arlie Hochschild, renowned for her deep look at Trump country before Trump was elected, in her 2016 book *Strangers in Their Own Land*, wrote a fascinating article in 2018 titled "Silicon Holler." Hochschild reported on a small pilot project created by some tech executives and promoted by Silicon Valley's progressive congressman, Ro Khanna. The idea is that rather than exporting coding jobs to Bangalore, why not export them to places like Kentucky and West Virginia, so that despairing young people can aspire to $50-an-hour jobs writing code rather than minimum-wage jobs at Walmart. Khanna also called for an $80 billion program to extend high-speed internet to rural America. Rural access to high-speed internet would not only be good for growth; it would provide lots of on-the-ground good jobs. Unless we believe that kids in Appalachia are hopelessly dumb, the missing ingredients are subsidized training and a commitment by tech companies and/or government to diffuse the jobs. A pool of technical talent, in turn, can seed and attract entrepreneurs.

Young people in left-behind places are rightly skeptical of paying scarce money for training that doesn't lead to jobs. So the two missing links in a successful Silicon Holler program are a generous stipend that not only covers the cost of the training but pays people to take the course, plus a guarantee to locate jobs. In the pilot program described by Hochschild, the stipend is $400 a week. The training is provided by a company called Interapt, subsidized by a $2.7 million grant from the Appalachian Regional Commission, a deep-state entity that Trump's budget proposed to defund. Successful graduates of the training program, now earning $40,000–$60,000 a year, had previously been in minimum-wage jobs at places like Super 8, Little Caesars, and convenience stores.

A program like this beats Trump posing in front of a coal mine or bashing General Motors, since it provides real hope and real help. Under the aegis of a Democratic president, it demonstrates the kind of practical gains that government can deliver.

Let's not write off rural America. Politically, some liberal analysts bemoan the structure of the Senate as a kind of permanent gerrymander written into the Constitution, in which smaller, rural states, generally conservative, have the same number of senators—two—that larger, more urbanized, and typically Democratic states have. The Senate, presumably, is close to a lost cause, giving Congress a structurally conservative tilt. But think again. There was a time when most rural states in the Midwest, the Mountain West, and the West voted for progressive Democrats. This political alignment had everything to do with the federal role in regional economic development.

In the mid-twentieth century, among our greatest Democratic senators were progressives from Washington, Montana, Idaho, Utah, North and South Dakota, Iowa, Oklahoma, Missouri, and Tennessee, as well as less surprising states, like Michigan, Wisconsin, and Minnesota[*]—a belt that extended from Washington State all the way

---

[*] These included Warren Magnuson of Washington; Frank Church of Idaho; Mike Mansfield of Montana; Frank Moss of Utah; Byron Dorgan of North Dakota; George McGovern of South Dakota; William Proxmire and Gaylord Nelson of Wisconsin; Philip Hart of Michigan; Hubert Humphrey, Walter Mondale, and Paul Wellstone of Minnesota; Dick Clark and Tom Harkin of Iowa; Fred Harris of Oklahoma; Tom Eagleton of Missouri; and Albert Gore Sr. and Estes Kefauver of Tennessee.

to Appalachia. Republicans began taking these seats during the Reagan revolution of 1980. Yet a swing back of rural voters to Democrats began in the 2018 midterms. According to data from Catalist, rural America gave Republicans a 35-point advantage over Democrats in 2016, but only 28 points in 2018. The main shift was in younger rural voters, age eighteen through twenty-nine. They voted for Republicans by 17 points in 2016 but supported Democrats by 8 points in 2018—a remarkable and encouraging swing of 25 points. This trend could intensify, given the right messages and policies.

A High-Wage Economy. We need to return to an economy that pays a living wage for all. As I've suggested, that goal can be accomplished through a mix of policies that include a law that raises the minimum wage, a massive green infrastructure program, a very different trade strategy, and policies that restore the capacity to organize effective unions. Government, which is also the source of most of the paychecks for people who work in human services, can commit to a national policy to regularize such jobs and careers, and provide that nobody who works taking care of the old, the sick, or the young shall be paid less than $35,000 a year. And there are a lot of such people in Trump country.

Beyond these emblematic and easy-to-grasp commitments are a set of more complex policies that are necessary to put government back on the side of working Americans. These other areas are more challenging to accomplish politically, because the details are technical, and thus vulnerable to special-interest lobbying well out of the public spotlight. Yet they are as urgently needed as the easier-to-narrate policies.

Reclaiming Government's Capacity to Regulate Capitalism

The flip side of empowering and decently compensating labor is restoring salutary constraints on a predatory financial industry. Making these connections will require narrative skill from the educator in chief, of the sort that Franklin Roosevelt displayed in his fireside chats and great speeches. You don't win support for reregulating finance by calling for a return to the Glass-Steagall Act, whose details are obscure, but by calling out the economic royalists, as FDR did with such verve, and then political support for the needed policy specifics follows.

Making Finance Servant Rather than Master. We need a suite of policies to limit the reign of speculative finance. These include restoring a financial sector simple and transparent enough to regulate, and sufficiently dispersed that one big bank failure does not cascade throughout the system and take it down. Few of the financial innovations added to the economy since the 1980s made the financial economy more efficient, and that was not the real goal. Mainly, they allowed new forms of exotic securities that make their originators and traders astronomically rich, and pass along the risk to everyone else. The result was the collapse of 2008.

In contrast to the radical reforms after 1929, the reign of finance continues. The biggest banks are now more concentrated, with more market share than they had before the collapse. New forms of securitized loans and exotic securities are proliferating again. Despite the Dodd-Frank Act, which has been steadily weakened by nonenforcement and by legislative changes, the financial economy continues to be parasitic on the real economy.

Hedge funds and private-equity firms, most of which extract value rather than adding it, are growing relative to the rest of the economy. They take advantage of what was once a small loophole in the Roosevelt-era securities laws, and create a large sector basically immune to government oversight. That loophole needs to be closed, so that hedge funds and private-equity companies are subject to the same rules as ordinary mutual funds and publicly traded companies. Otherwise, more and more economic activity will gravitate to hedge funds and private equity, in a kind of Gresham's law in which the less regulated part of the financial economy displaces the more regulated part.

A hedge fund and private-equity reform act would begin by closing the loophole that excuses such firms from making the usual disclosures required by the securities laws. Another straightforward reform would limit the tax deductibility of debt financing that exceeded a set ratio. This tax deduction cap would drastically limit the game of "leveraging up" to take over companies and then crippling them by saddling them with the costs of debt service. Reforms could also limit the ability of private-equity owners to pay themselves exorbitant "special dividends" and management fees. Bankruptcy reform could limit the use of the bankruptcy code to allow private-equity firm and hedge fund owners to shed debts, shut down worker pension funds, and slash jobs, while keeping control. The price of running a company into the ground by withdrawing too much capital should, at the very least, be losing control. And conflicts of interest on the part of private-equity firm and hedge fund owners should be spelled out and made illegal.

In the corporate sector, stock buybacks are setting new records. When a corporation buys back its own shares, this is nothing but a strategy for pumping up the share value and enriching insiders whose compensation is tied to the stock price. It is a confession that the company does not know what real uses of capital to invest in. Legislation proposed by Ro Khanna and Bernie Sanders would simply prohibit buybacks.

Reducing Abuses of Economic Concentration. As a result of a wave of mergers and acquisitions, economic concentration today is at a post-Depression peak. In industry after industry, two or three companies control most of the market, giving them the power to crush or buy out potential competitors. According to a study by the Open Markets Institute, industries in which just two companies control more than half of market share include pharmacies, car rentals, private prisons, hardware stores, mattress manufacturers, optical companies, airline booking systems, and of course smartphones, where two companies have almost 100 percent market share. Despite a proliferation of labels, two corporations brew most of our beer. Thanks to recent mergers, cable companies, airlines, and pharmaceutical companies are not far behind, and in some regional retail markets a single provider is dominant.

Under both Democrats and Republicans, the antitrust agencies (the Justice Department and the Federal Trade Commission) have simply stopped challenging most mergers. The premise is that these mergers increase economic efficiency and reduce prices in the long run. Actual research has demonstrated that this is not the case. The whole point of a merger is pricing power and the sidelining of potential rivals. Yet, since the 1980s the antitrust authorities have generally permitted already-dominant players to buy out innovators.

This modus operandi has only worsened with the platform economy. Facebook, with over 50 percent market share, made seventy-three acquisitions over a decade, including potential major rivals Instagram and WhatsApp. Google bought YouTube, the Android operating system, and the popular Waze GPS navigation company, as well as DoubleClick, to entrench its dominance of internet advertising. Google's core strategy has been to buy out any company that might challenge its dominance as a search engine. Amazon has been notorious in either acquiring or stealing the business model of companies that offer internet product marketing where Amazon is dominant. All told, over the past decade, Amazon, Apple, Google, Facebook, and Microsoft have bought 436 rival companies, without any regulatory challenge. Monopoly power in the platform sector is built on the collapse of antitrust.

Hyperconcentration of the big platform companies combines traditional antitrust abuses with novel ones peculiar to the internet. Facebook, Amazon, and Google acquire massive amounts of information on the buying habits of their users. Their real product is the tabulation, use, and sale of this data. That's worrisome enough as a privacy invasion, but it is also anticompetitive. When a company that relies on Amazon to sell products is also a competitor with Amazon's own product line, Amazon not only knows more about the customer base than the upstart does but can selectively underprice the upstart to drive it out of business or into a shotgun merger. The proof that these practices are abusive is the astronomical profits made by the large platform companies. In a genuinely competitive sector, those excess profits would be competed away.

Though some of the abuses are novel, most have counterparts in the original monopolistic behaviors that led Congress to enact the first antitrust laws in 1890 and 1914. When Facebook or Google buys up potential rivals, or when pharmacy companies combine to reduce consumer choice and increase pricing power, that's old-fashioned monopoly. Likewise when Google and Facebook together control 80 percent of internet ads. That dominance gives them the power to take too much of the share of profits generated by content providers.

When Apple makes it very difficult for you to use non-Apple products, thus raising its power to charge exorbitant prices for must-have accessories, that's known as a "tying arrangement"—also illegal under antitrust laws. And when Amazon uses privileged information against competitors that rely on its platform to reach customers, the possible remedy is a variation on a centuries-old concept known as "common carriage." Namely, you can be the provider of either the network or the commerce that relies on the network—but not both. The power of Facebook, Google, and Amazon to traffic in users' personal data should also be drastically limited.

Another familiar antitrust abuse is known as "monopsony"—domination of a market by one buyer. In the case of Amazon, consumers seem to benefit from its discount prices, but those discounts come at the expense of Amazon's price pressure on suppliers, and when the dust settles, Amazon has made monopoly profits at the expense of other vendors, which in turn squeeze wages of their workers.

Seemingly, it will be a challenge for our new president to move public opinion by making a big deal of such anticompetitive abuses. Yet Facebook grows more resented by the day. And even though consumers love their smartphones, there is now pushback against

Apple's price gouging as the cost of a new phone breaks the $1,000 barrier. Consumers also wonder whether Alexa and Siri are spying on them, as ads keep popping up on our computer screens with eerie precision. Here again there is a role for the next president as narrator in chief, and connector of dots, and the resurrection of antitrust is a key part of a corporate reform agenda.

Happily, a new generation of antitrust scholars has devised a set of strategies for modernizing the application of traditional antitrust laws and concepts to the new predatory practices of the internet age. Lina Khan, a young scholar who has been both at Yale and at the FTC, wrote a pathbreaking law journal article on how to revive antitrust and adapt it to the platform economy. People like Khan are in the wings as the senior officials of the next progressive administration. Some of this needed reform can be accomplished by more aggressive enforcement rather than by new law. There will be massive industry resistance, and it will take presidential leadership to persuade the public and Congress of the need to act.

Making Corporations Great Again. There was a time in America when corporations looked to more than just maximizing profits for insiders at the expense of workers and communities. That was the very era that many Trump supporters remember as great. The era was also good for corporations themselves, since they were not obsessed with their quarterly earnings reports as a way of pleasing the financial market and they could plan for the long term.

To return to a more social corporation, a good place to start would be the Accountable Capitalism Act, introduced in late 2018 by Senator Elizabeth Warren. The bill would require all corporations worth over a billion dollars to get federal charters. The charters, among other things, require company directors to consider stakeholders such as workers, communities, customers, and suppliers in their decisions, and not just shareholders. Employees would elect 40 percent of directors. Corporate political activity, including donations, would have to be approved by 75 percent of shareholders and 75 percent of directors. Executives compensated with stock would have to wait five years before cashing it in—a disincentive against manipulation of the share price. Much of this is nothing more radical than the co-determination and stakeholder requirements that have worked so well to make Germany the world's most dynamic manufacturing exporter.

No Austerity! One of the follies that connected Bill Clinton to Barack Obama, via their heavily overlapping teams of advisers, was the use of budget austerity as a badge of virtue.

Franklin Roosevelt, after beginning with a pledge of budget balance, quickly learned better. Not so Clinton and Obama. Clinton began with a commitment to cut the deficit in half, and then by 1999 had pledged to end deficits entirely. By 2000, forecasters were predicting budget surpluses as far as the eye could see, to the point where serious economists were fretting about how the Federal Reserve would conduct monetary policy if there were no more Treasury debt to buy and sell. (George W. Bush made short work of Clinton's hard-won surplus with two gigantic tax cuts tilted to the rich.)

Obama also pursued budget balance. Long before the economy was on a path to sustainable growth, in late 2009 Obama's fiscally conservative advisers persuaded him to embrace deficit reduction rather than job creation as the paramount economic policy objective. This was bad economics as well as bad politics. At a time when progressive Democrats in the House were working hard to enact a second stimulus bill in December 2009 (which Obama opposed and let the Senate kill), Obama had already pivoted to budget austerity, creating the Bowles-Simpson Commission to come up with a fiscal straitjacket for the government. When the required supermajority of the commission could not agree on a formula, Obama worked with Republicans to devise a "sequester" that accomplished the same thing. Eventually, the economy did recover—on average—but much more slowly than it should have. Along the way, much damage was done, both to people's living standards and to Democrats' credibility as the party of the common American.

The next president, in the role of teacher, needs to offer a very different economics lesson. Borrowing money to serve long-deferred public needs is sensible policy. The government's capacity to borrow, of course, is not infinite. It needs to be complemented with tax reform to pay for increased public investment, so that large deficits created by tax giveaways to the right do not compound fiscal challenges and create excuses for cuts in needed and popular programs such as Social Security and Medicare. But the US public debt is nowhere near the point of causing increases in interest rates or inflation, or scaring off buyers of government securities, especially if used on productivity-enhancing projects such as rebuilding vital infrastructure.

Resisting the Undertow of Corporate Democrats

If a Rooseveltian president gets elected and takes this kind of agenda seriously, she will face fierce opposition not just from Republicans, but from corporate Democrats. The entire predatory business model of Wall Street will be at risk, and the financial industry will fight back. Many in the hedge fund and private-equity industry are Democrats. They have allies in Congress, though fewer than before the 2018 election. In August 2010, when the Obama administration raised the possibility of getting rid of the favorable tax treatment on hedge fund earnings, which are taxed at lower rates as capital gains, one prominent hedge fund executive, Steve Schwarzman of Blackstone, said, "It's like when Hitler invaded Poland in 1939." Schwarzman is a Republican and a friend of Donald Trump. But several billionaires in private equity and hedge funds are Democrats (and Democratic donors), including Bill Clinton's friend and longtime backer Ron Burkle, Quadrangle Group cofounder Steven Rattner, Carlyle Group cofounder David Rubenstein, and the several alums of the Obama administration mentioned earlier in this book, such as Tim Geithner. These and other corporate Democrats will resist financial reforms.

Silicon Valley was a huge supporter of both Obama and Hillary Clinton. With a few notable and heroic exceptions, tech billionaires tend to be liberal on social issues but fiercely resistant to the idea of government regulators constraining their business practices, however abusive. Democrats will need to break the Silicon Valley donor habit. One hopeful sign is that California, home of tech, has an effective state government led not only by Democrats but by progressive ones. And there are more voters than moguls. Khanna manages to get elected to Congress from Silicon Valley as an economic progressive.

Corporate Democrats in both Houses worked with Republicans to weaken the Dodd-Frank Act. It was a corporate Democrat, Joe Lieberman, who denied President Obama the needed sixtieth vote in the Senate for a more robust and politically defensible version of the Affordable Care Act, leading to protracted and enervating negotiations with Republicans and with health care industry special interests, and a much weaker and more convoluted law.

The good news is that the ranks of corporate Democrats are dwindling, and agendas are being set mainly by progressives. When Trump's tax bill, his one legislative success, was before Congress, not a single Democrat broke ranks to support it, despite the importuning of corporations that stood to gain handsomely. Under both Bush and Reagan, as many as a third of congressional Democrats voted for Republican tax cuts heavily tilted to the upper brackets.

In the December 2018 fight over the Speakership, corporate Democrats in the House associated with strategist and "triangulator" Mark Penn concocted one bogus alliance of convenience after another in the quest to replace the progressive Nancy Pelosi with a more centrist House Speaker. They were faced down. In March, it was reported that Penn had been to the White House to see Trump, gravitating to his natural home. The only way to defeat the financial influence of corporate Democrats is to take the case to the people, and to build overwhelming public support for a true reform agenda.

A Democracy Agenda

Along with substantive legislative goals, the next administration will need to pursue a democracy agenda. Much of this can be carried out at the state level, but there is a key federal role. Two prime candidates are efforts to limit the damaging impact of big money, especially (undisclosed) dark money, and to revive the Voting Rights Act. A measure to reverse the damage of the Supreme Court's *Shelby County v. Holder* decision—a voting-rights restoration act—has been introduced in every Congress since 2013.

Though the court struck down the preclearance provision of the Voting Rights Act in *Shelby*, Justice Roberts was careful to leave open the possibility of a revived Act. The court left intact Section 5, which allows preclearance. But it rendered the provision inoperative by holding that Section 4, specifying jurisdictions that require Justice Department approval of voting-system changes, had been overtaken by events. Roberts specifically left open the possibility of Congress devising a different system in response to new evidence—which the suppressors of the franchise have now provided in spades. Even Justice Roberts will have to recognize all of the creative forms of carefully targeted voter suppression that have proliferated since 2013. One variant of a new Voting Rights Act would apply preclearance across the board, so that the high court could not claim, as Roberts did, invidious regional discrimination.

In addition, the first bill that the Democrats introduced in the new Congress of 2019, designated "HR 1," is a measure, drafted by Representative John Sarbanes of Maryland and supported by the Democratic leadership, that links democracy reforms with anticorruption measures. The bill, called the For the People Act, reads like a compendium of all that ails American democracy, and how to begin remedying it. Among other measures, it provides for automatic voter registration— eligible citizens are considered registered unless they opt out; prohibits purges of voter rolls; strengthens voting-system security; ends partisan gerrymandering; provides 6-to-1 federal matching funds for small-donor campaign contributions; requires candidates for president and vice president to disclose ten years of tax returns; requires disclosure of the sources of dark money; and a good deal more. The bill passed the House, 234–193, in early March, on a party-line vote. Senator Mitch McConnell pronounced the measure dead on arrival in the Senate and called it the "Democratic Politician Protection Act"—a backhanded acknowledgment that in a normal democracy without voter repression, the Democrats would be the majority party.

Polling shows that majorities in excess of 80 percent support anti-corruption and pro-democracy reforms.

Beyond the Conservative Lock on the Courts

One of the factors that has depressed many progressives is the fact that conservative courts are likely to overturn many reforms, even if they pass Congress. The Roberts court has been inventive, in both senses of the word, in fashioning new doctrines and claiming that they reflect the original intent of the founders. One of the most egregious is what Justice Elena Kagan all too aptly termed "weaponizing the First Amendment"—the extreme solicitude for corporate free speech as a bulwark against certain kinds of regulation and the assertion that corporations are entitled to all the liberties of citizens. Many observers of the Supreme Court contend that the court is headed toward a pre-1937 view of the Constitution's commerce clause: that unless an activity is literally in interstate commerce, the federal government is barred from regulating it.

Even with this premise, however, there is a great deal of latitude for progressive legislation. There is much that Congress can do using its power to tax and spend, which most constitutional scholars view as bulletproof, even given the Roberts court. A fine case in point is the Affordable Care Act. Chief Justice Roberts was under pressure from conservatives on and off the high court to find the ACA unconstitutional. Instead, his ruling split the difference, holding that the Act's coercive formula, which was intended to require states to expand Medicaid with federal matching funds, violated the commerce clause, but that most of the Act was constitutional under Congress's power to tax and spend.

There are two tactical lessons here for Democrats. First, tax-and-spend does give Congress very broad latitude to create progressive programs, even with conservative courts. Nobody has ever challenged Medicare or Social Security as unconstitutional overreach. Second, simpler is better, not just as policy and as ideology, but as judicial bulletproofing. Had Congress simply expanded Medicare, rather than devising a convoluted mess of mandates and matching funds, using private insurers to carry out public goals, no constitutional challenge would have gotten to first base.

In addition, in several areas where conservative courts have inventively mucked up intended forms of regulation, Congress can restore good regulation simply by clarifying congressional intent. For example, in Chapter 5 I mentioned the abuses of the Federal Arbitration Act, where conservative courts have mangled the intent of the statute by allowing corporations to demand that employees and consumers sign away rights as a condition of employment. There is no constitutional issue here. Congress simply needs to clarify that the purpose of the statute is not to vitiate other legislatively specified rights.

Similarly, in the area of antitrust enforcement, conservative courts have contrived a doctrine holding that if abusive price increases cannot be demonstrated to be the result of mergers and other anti-competitive practices, then there is no antitrust violation. But, as a number of antitrust scholars have pointed out, Congress could easily make clear that the so-called price test is not the only test and that other anticompetitive practices are antitrust violations per se. The courts would have to go along.

And in the area of financial regulation, practices permitted and prohibited to financial corporations have long been the prerogative of Congress. If Congress wanted to pass legislation that discouraged banks from growing to larger than a certain size, it could do so by increasing reserve requirements for very large banks; there is no constitutional obstacle. Congress, as noted, could also close the loophole that permits hedge fund and private-equity abuses. Even in the period before 1937, when a very conservative court overturned several pieces of New Deal legislation, it did not interfere with Roosevelt's extensive schema for regulating banks and securities.

In addition, there are several measures that a new administration could take using executive powers to carry out existing laws that have long been deemed constitutional. For instance, under the Bayh-Dole Act of 1980, the federal government has the right to require that any drug developed with partial help of federal funding (virtually every major drug) be sold at reasonable retail cost or be licensed to generic producers. The government has used this power in only a handful of public health emergencies, but it could use the power more widely to stop price gouging.

I do not mean to minimize the damage that rightwing courts

can and will do. They are wedded to the idea that political donations equal free speech. They are moving to revive a pre-1937 version of the commerce clause. In its infamous *Janus* ruling of June 2018, the Supreme Court overturned settled law and held that freedom of association precluded public-sector unions from requiring nonmembers in bargaining units represented by unions to pay dues. Affirmative action as we know it could be struck down. Likewise the reproductive protections of *Roe v. Wade*.

Even so, my point is that there are plenty of areas for creative legislation that even this court is not likely to overturn. And with a Democratic administration serving two terms, the Roberts court and its hard-right majority would not last forever.

Hardball, Softball, or "Smartball"?

Some commentators, such as Harvard law professor Mark Tushnet, author of a seminal essay titled "Constitutional Hardball," argue that Republican abuses of the courts have now become so extreme that the time has come for the next administration to enlarge the Supreme Court, as Roosevelt attempted to do in 1937. Tushnet and others make the case on two grounds. First, many federal judges were appointed and confirmed using tactics that lack legitimacy—Republicans blocking Democratic judicial nominations, and railroading Republican ones. Second, extreme doctrines propounded by rightwing courts have been based on sheer partisan and ideological expediency. Justice Neil Gorsuch, in particular, has no business sitting on the high court; the seat properly belongs to Obama's nominee,

Merrick Garland, a moderate who was not even given the courtesy of a hearing.

Legal scholar Ian Millhiser, a reluctant and mainstream advocate of court packing, bases his case on the fact that the Roberts court has issued decision after decision upholding cynical measures intended to undermine the right to vote—and that the franchise is a more fundamental element of democracy than the size of the Supreme Court (which has been regularly altered by statute). As recently as 2013, Republicans tried and failed to reduce the size of the DC Circuit Court of Appeals, the most important federal appellate court after the Supreme Court, from eleven judges to eight, to prevent President Obama from filling three vacancies.

The history of Roosevelt's supposed defeat when he sought to enlarge the Supreme Court is more complex than the headline. In 1937, fresh from a landslide reelection and fed up with a conservative court overturning several key pieces of New Deal legislation, Roosevelt embarked on his ill-fated court-packing plan, which would have increased the size of the court to as many as fifteen judges. I say the plan was ill-fated because it offended even key Democratic legislators, and it was withdrawn before it was given a vote.

Yet, most scholars of the court have concluded that the scheme did its job. In March 1937, as the court-packing plan was being considered, a key member of the court's conservative bloc, Justice Owen Roberts, switched sides, voting to uphold the constitutionality of a Washington State minimum-wage law. That ruling marked the end of the so-called Lochner era, named after the case that had overturned a New York wage-and-hour law as a violation of the commerce clause. Roberts's prudent conversion, which deflated the pressure for enlarging the court, came to be known as "the switch in time that saved nine."

Could the same thing happen today? In some respects, the current court is even more ferociously ideological than the one that so aggrieved Roosevelt. Yet the current Justice Roberts has repeatedly signaled concern for the integrity of the court as an institution. Many Roberts watchers believe that he cast the decisive vote in the 5–4 decision to uphold the Affordable Care Act because he concluded that on an issue as politically fraught as Obamacare, the court must not kill the law if the Republicans could not kill it legislatively.

In a case on appeal from an appellate court in December 2018, Roberts offended three of the court's most hard-core conservatives by refusing to provide the fourth vote for Supreme Court review of cases in which states sought to bar Planned Parenthood from state Medicaid programs. His action let stand lower-court rulings protecting Planned Parenthood.

In another December 2018 case, Roberts voted with the court's liberals to let stand a lower-court ruling prohibiting Trump from carrying out an order to deport all asylum seekers who had crossed the border illegally. Roberts has a good political ear. He is already anticipating possible Democratic efforts to challenge the court's legitimacy and perhaps enlarge it. He is also plainly repulsed by Trump's overreach.

Long before either Justice Roberts, Finley Peter Dunne, in his incarnation as the fictional character "Mr. Dooley," spoke wisdom when he declared in 1901, after one unexpected court turnabout, that "no matter whether the Constitution follows the flag or not, the Supreme Court follows the election returns."

Assuming that a progressive administration governs, and governs effectively, beginning in 2021, one can well imagine the current Justice Roberts emulating his 1937 namesake and prudently limiting efforts of the other four conservative justices to wield novel doctrines in order to overturn legislation. If not, then constitutional hardball and even court packing could be on the table, and Roberts knows it.

As for other hardball tactics, the Democratic House beginning in 2019 modeled the right balance of a return to usual legislative courtesies, combined with strategic resolve. Democrats need to enact progressive legislation by having the votes, not by playing dirty. But they also need to resist the counsel to move to the center in the quest for an illusory common ground.

If Democrats can bring over some Republican votes to progressive legislation, so much the better. For instance, until Trump made the bill untouchable, several key Republicans were supportive of comprehensive immigration reform. Given the shellacking that Republicans took in the 2018 midterms and the presumed Democratic victory in 2020, as well as the support for immigration reform in the suburbs, several dozen House Republicans, as well as the Republican senators whose terms are up in 2022, may reconsider. It's reasonable to have bipartisan consultations on a potentially bridgeable issue like immigration. On the other hand, it makes no strategic sense to compromise with Republicans on an issue such as a national $15-an-hour minimum wage, or a public or buy-in option under Medicare. If some Republicans want to support the president's bill, that's great. If not, let them explain the negative vote to their constituents.

There are times when a conciliator or consolidator is what the republic needs. Examples are a president like Dwight Eisenhower, who accepted much of the New Deal; or Gerald Ford, who in his brief presidency sought to restore bipartisanship; or, in some respects, George H. W. Bush, who collaborated with Democrats on environmental and tax legislation. But this emphatically is not one of those times. Our democracy is in dire peril. The stakes for 2020 are rivaled only by those of 1860.

Binding Up the Nation's Wounds

The next president will need the integrity of Lincoln, the gifts of Franklin Roosevelt as a source of narrative leadership and philosophical clarity, combined with the legislative genius of Lyndon Johnson, and the capacity to inspire hope of Kennedy or Obama. Our president will need to be resolute in her own goals and values. She will need to navigate between the Scylla of hyperpartisanship and the Charybdis of naïve conciliation to define a new national interest and build majority support.

If the next president governs well, one salutary side effect could be the long-delayed fracturing of the current Republican Party—into one major party of normal conservatives of the sort who used to predominate, and one minor fringe party of the far right. Even progressive Democrats should recognize that the American Republic needs a two-party system that practices the usual give-and-take of debate and compromise. Our republic cannot function if one of its two major parties is an antisystem party bent on destroying democracy. Today's Republican legislators will endure everlasting shame for having protected a president they knew to be unfit for office. As much as we need a Democratic Party to restore economic hope to ordinary Americans, we need a Republican Party that is principled and sane.

Perhaps the most difficult and urgent challenge will be to damp down the hatreds so cynically stoked by Donald Trump. A new president can begin to accomplish this by showing that she is genuinely on the side of the common American, and by starting to deliver tangible help as well as respect. There will still be haters, but they will not loom quite so large or so fearsome.

We must believe that American democracy is not quite done for. America, in Lincoln's words, could enjoy a new birth of freedom in 2020. But that will not happen automatically or passively through the swing of some historical pendulum. It will take inspired radical leadership, mass organizing, and citizen mobilization of the kind that we see only in America's finest hours.

ACKNOWLEDGMENTS

I appreciate the fine work of the editorial team at Norton, especially Drake McFeely, copy editor Stephanie Hiebert, publicist Kyle Radler, and assistant editor Bee Holekamp. Thanks are also due once again to my friend and agent, Ike Williams.

My colleagues at the *American Prospect* served as sources of insight and sounding boards for many of the ideas and arguments in this book. The germ of the basic theme has appeared in several *Prospect* articles. This year I stepped down after thirty years of leading the *Prospect*. I will continue writing and editing. I've learned a great deal from my *Prospect* colleagues, especially Paul Starr, Harold Meyerson, David Dayen, Gabrielle Gurley, Mike Stern, and innumerable writers.

I appreciate the insights of students and colleagues at Brandeis University's Heller School, particularly Lisa Lynch, David Weil, Mike Doonan, Janet Boguslaw, and Bob Tannenwald.

Among friends, colleagues, sources, and mentors, thanks to Ian

Bassin, Jared Bernstein, Josh Bivens, Heather Booth, Paul Booth, Dan Cantor, Josh Chafetz, Frank Clemente, Chuck Collins, Bob Creamer, E. J. Dionne, Peter Dreier, Joseph Fishkin, Carolyn Fredrickson, Shanti Fry, Justin Gest, Martin Gilens, Todd Gitlin, Liza Goitein, Arthur Goldhammer, Anna Greenberg, Stanley Greenberg, Steve Greenhouse, Jacob Hacker, Stephen Heintz, Roger Hickey, Arlie Hochschild, Dan Hopkins, David Howell, Derrick Jackson, Deborah James, John Judis, Ira Katznelson, Dennis Kelleher, Randall Kennedy, Celinda Lake, Thea Lee, Denis MacShane, Michael McDonald, Tom McGarity, Heather McGhee, Ian Millhiser, Guy Molyneux, Yascha Mounk, Bill Moyers, David Orr, Ben Page, Richard Parker, Robin Parker, Frank Pasquale, Scott Paul, Tom Perriello, Paul Pierson, Robert Pollin, David Posen, Jed Purdy, John Shattuck, Anat Shenker-Osorio, Heidi Shierholz, John Sides, Damon Silvers, Ganesh Sitaraman, Bill Spriggs, Joseph Stiglitz, Katherine V. W. Stone, Zephyr Teachout, Ruy Teixeira, Richard Trumka, Richard Valelly, Wendy Weiser, Rob Weissman, Fred Wertheimer, Mike Wessel, and Sid Wolfe.

Thanks also for research help from Andy Tisdel and Emily Erdos.

Special thanks to Derrick Jackson, John Judis, Randall Kennedy, Heather McGhee, Harold Meyerson, Miles Rapoport, Ganesh Sitaraman, and my wife, Joan Fitzgerald, for reading portions of this book.

I am blessed with a family that is a source of emotional, intellectual, and political sustenance. My children, sons-in-law, and daughter-in-law relentlessly engage me in political discussion and are always teaching me something. Thanks to Gabriel, Jess, Shelly, Lori, Vince, and Jack. And to Gordon, Darlene, Ben, and John.

As always, thank you to Joan for so many more things than I can express here.

NOTES

≈

Introduction

xiii **"It starts with your sitting silent":** James Comey, "How Trump Co-opts Leaders Like Bill Barr," *New York Times*, May 1, 2019.

xv **"The accumulation of all powers":** Alexander Hamilton, John Jay, and James Madison, *The Federalist* (New York: Modern Library edition, 1961), 313.

Chapter I: Progressive Economics as Democratic Renewal

2 **"All economic indicators indicate":** Chris Cillizza, "It's NOT the Economy, Stupid!" CNN Politics, September 17, 2018, https://edition.cnn.com/2018/09/17/politics/trump-economy-poll/index.html.

2 **"The slower a county's economic growth":** Ben Casselman, "Stop Saying Trump's Election Had Nothing to Do with Economics," FiveThirtyEight, January 9, 2017, https://fivethirtyeight.com/features/stop-saying-trumps-win-had-nothing-to-do-with-economics.

3 **The Pew Research Center consistently finds:** Amina Dunn, "Partisans

Are Divided over the Fairness of the U.S. Economy—and Why People Are Rich or Poor," Pew Research Center, October 4, 2018, http://www. pewresearch.org/fact-tank/2018/10/04/partisans-are-divided-over-the -fairness-of-the-u-s-economy-and-why-people-are-rich-or-poor.

6 **Many commentators have thus insisted:** Mark Lilla, *The Once and Future Liberal: After Identity Politics* (New York: Harper Collins, 2017).

6 **Political scientist John Sides and colleagues:** John Sides, Michael Tesler, and Lynn Vavrick, *Identity Crisis: The 2016 Campaign and the Battle for the Meaning of America* (Princeton, NJ: Princeton University Press, 2018).

6 **Rather, what occurred in 2016:** Sides et al., *Identity Crisis*, 7.

11 **"This removed a crucial moderating element":** Bruce Ackerman, *The Decline and Fall of the American Republic* (Cambridge, MA: Harvard University Press, 2012), 17.

12 **"invisible primary":** Marty Cohen et al., *The Party Decides* (Chicago: University of Chicago Press, 2008).

13 **As several scholars have persuasively demonstrated:** The two classic works on asymmetrical extremism are Jacob Hacker and Paul Pearson, *Off-Center* (New Haven, CT: Yale University Press, 2005); and Thomas E. Mann and Norman J. Ornstein, *It's Even Worse Than It Looks* (New York: Basic Books, 2013).

14 **"Transformational leaders":** Doris Kearns Goodwin, *Leadership in Turbulent Times* (New York: Simon and Schuster, 2018), 235.

15 **Public opinion shifted in Roosevelt's direction:** Doris Kearns Goodwin, *The Bully Pulpit* (New York: Simon and Schuster, 2013).

15 **Political scientist Kay Scholzman:** Kay Schlozman, Henry E. Brady, and Sidney Verba, *Unequal and Unrepresented* (Princeton, NJ: Princeton University Press, 2018).

16 *Affluence and Influence:* Martin Gilens, *Affluence and Influence* (Princeton, NJ: Princeton University Press, 2012).

18 **"Progressives come to Congress":** David Dayen, "House Progressives Are Facing an Unexpected Problem in the Quest for Committee Power," Intercept, November 21, 2018, https://theintercept.com/2018/11/21/progressive -caucus-congressional-progressive-caucus.

21 **"The weakening of our democratic norms":** Steven Levitsky and Daniel Ziblatt, *How Democracies Die* (New York: Random House Penguin, 2017), 9.

21 **"In our view, the idea that Democrats":** Levitsky and Ziblatt, *How Democracies Die*, 215.

21 **"even if Democrats were to succeed":** Levitsky and Ziblatt, *How Democracies Die*, 217.

24 **"You define a new center by winning":** Jedediah Purdy, interview with the author, August 21, 2018.

Chapter 2: Democracy: A Damage Assessment

27 **The CIA supported the National Student Association:** Karen Paget, *Patriotic Betrayal* (New Haven, CT: Yale University Press, 2015).

28 **According to an exhaustive review:** Liza Goitein, "In a Crisis, the President Can Invoke Extraordinary Authority," *Atlantic*, January–February 2019.

29 **"To my Republican colleagues":** Adam B. Schiff, "An Open Letter to My Republican Colleagues," *Washington Post*, February 21, 2019, https://www .washingtonpost.com/opinions/adam-schiff-an-open-letter-to-my-republican -colleagues/2019/02/21/9d411414-3605-11e9-af5b-b51b7tt322e9_story .html?utm_term=.33251b8967ff.

30 **Later, as a Supreme Court justice:** Jay S. Bybee, "Printz, the Unitary Executive, and the Fire in the Trash Can: Has Justice Scalia Picked the Court's Pocket?" *Notre Dame Law Review* 77 (2001): 269–288, https://scholars.law .unlv.edu/facpub/348.

30 **Reagan issued 250 signing statements:** Bruce Ackerman, *The Decline and Fall of the American Republic* (Cambridge, MA: Harvard University Press, 2012), 90.

31 **Under Sunstein's direction, OIRA gutted:** Robert Kuttner, "Obama's Obama," *Harper's Magazine*, December 2014.

32 **Among Yoo's more outrageous inventions:** "Torture Memos," Wikipedia, accessed December 4, 2018, https://en.wikipedia.org/wiki/Torture_ Memos.

33 **"What has been the response of business":** Thwink.org, "The Powell Memo with Commentary," accessed December 4, 2018, http://www.thwink.org/sustain/articles/017_PowellMemo/index.htm.

35 **This string of rulings was intensified:** Citizens Take Action, "Supreme Court Decisions," accessed December 4, 2018, https://citizenstakeaction.org/supreme-court-decisions.

36 **As Theda Skocpol's research has shown:** Theda Skocpol, *Diminished Democracy* (Norman: University of Oklahoma Press, 2004).

36 **"long civic generation":** Robert Putnam, *Bowling Alone* (New York: Simon and Schuster, 2000).

38 **Jane Mayer detailed in an investigative piece:** Jane Mayer, "Trump TV," *The New Yorker*, March 11, 2019.

40 **45 percent of Americans get their news:** Elisa Shearer and Jeffrey Gottfried, "News Use across Social Media Platforms 2017," Pew Research Center, September 7, 2017, http://www.journalism.org/2017/09/07/news-use-across-social-media-platforms-2017.

40 **This weakening of the factual press:** Robert Kuttner and Hildy Zenger, "Saving the Free Press from Private Equity," *American Prospect*, December 27, 2017, https://prospect.org/article/saving-free-press-private-equity.

41 **"the right to be let alone":** Samuel D. Warren and Louis D. Brandeis, "The Right to Privacy," *Harvard Law Review* 4, no. 5 (December 15, 1890), http://faculty.uml.edu/sgallagher/Brandeisprivacy.htm.

41 **A career Sears salesman could retire:** Nelson D. Schwartz and Michael Corkery, "When Sears Flourished, So Did Workers. At Amazon, It's More Complicated," *New York Times*, October 23, 2018, https://www.nytimes.com/2018/10/23/business/economy/amazon-workers-sears-bankruptcy-filing.html.

43 **The rise of the market and the increase:** Statistics from Roberto Stefan Foa and Yascha Mounk, "The Signs of Deconsolidation," *Journal of Democracy*, January 2017.

43 **Half a century ago, the political sociologist:** Barrington Moore, *The Social Origins of Dictatorship and Democracy* (Boston: Beacon Press, 1966).

45 **The political scientist Richard Valelly:** Richard M. Valelly, *The Two Reconstructions: The Battle for Black Enfranchisement* (Chicago: University of Chicago Press, 2004).

47 **the Affordable Care Act consumed 25 days:** E. J. Dionne, Norman J. Ornstein, and Thomas E. Mann, *One Nation after Trump* (New York: St. Martin's Press, 2017), 80.

48 **"floor preemption":** Thomas O. McGarity, "Trumping State Regulators and Juries," *American Prospect*, Spring 2017.

51 **"Any guy that can do a body slam":** "Trump on Gianforte: 'Any Guy That Can Do a Body Slam . . . He's My Kind of Guy,'" MSN, October 19, 2018, https://www.msn.com/en-us/video/l/trump-on-gianforte-any-guy-that -can-do-a-body-slamhes-my-kind-of-guy/vp-BBOAdZQ.

51 **"We have to come together and send":** Sarah Westwood, "Trump on Suspicious Packages: 'Threats or Acts of Political Violence Have No Place' in US," CNN, October 24, 2018, https://www.cnn.com/2018/10/24/politics/ trump-suspicious-package-response/index.html.

51 **"false flags, carefully planned for the midterms":** Kevin Roose, "'False Flag' Theory on Pipe Bombs Zooms from Right-Wing Fringe to Mainstream," *New York Times*, October 25, 2018, https://www.nytimes .com/2018/10/25/business/false-flag-theory-bombs-conservative-media .html.

52 **"It's happening in October":** Rush Limbaugh, "A Day like This Sure Seems to Counter the Mob Narrative That's Been Sinking Democrats," *Rush Limbaugh Show*, October 24, 2018, https://www.rushlimbaugh.com/ daily/2018/10/24/a-day-like-this-sure-seems-to-counter-the-mob-narrative -thats-been-sinking-democrats.

52 **"Don't let Soros, Bloomberg and Steyer":** Devan Cole, "House Majority Leader Deletes Tweet Saying Soros, Bloomberg, Steyer Are Trying to 'Buy' Election," CNN, October 28, 2018, https://www.cnn.com/2018/10/28/ politics/tom-steyer-mccarthy-tweet/index.html.

54 **In her exhaustive study of the impact:** Kathleen Hall Jamieson, *Cyberwar* (Oxford: Oxford University Press, 2018).

55 **Indeed, as the political scientist Suzanne Mettler:** Suzanne Mettler, *The Submerged State* (Chicago: University of Chicago Press, 2011).

56 **The result was a stealth demolition of government:** For a hilarious and deeply disturbing account, see Michael Lewis, *The Fifth Risk* (New York: W. W. Norton, 2018).

57 **During his first two years, the tally:** Glenn Kessler, Salvador Rizzo, and Meg Kelly, "President Trump Made 8,158 False or Misleading Claims in His First Two Years," *Washington Post*, January 21, 2019, https://www .washingtonpost.com/politics/2019/01/21/president-trump-made-false-or -misleading-claims-his-first-two-years/?utm_term=.624a318acb61.

Chapter 3: Averting Tyranny

63 **Nixon tried to explicitly politicize the IRS:** Robert Kuttner, "The Taxing Trials of IRS," *New York Times*, January 6, 1974.

64 **"get her tit caught in a big fat wringer":** Katharine Graham, "The Water-gate Watershed: A Turning Point for a Nation and a Newspaper," *Washington Post*, January 28, 1997, https://www.washingtonpost.com/wp-srv/ national/longterm/watergate/stories/graham.htm.

66 **204 out of 665 major presidential appointments:** Michael Lewis, *The Fifth Risk* (New York: W. W. Norton, 2018).

67 **The 500-page report:** *A Review of Various Actions by the Federal Bureau of Investigation and Department of Justice in Advance of the 2016 Election*, Office of the Inspector General, US Department of Justice, June 2018, https://www.justice.gov/file/1071991/download.

67 **Other key agencies continued to be defended:** Robert Bazell, "Science under Siege," *American Prospect*, November 12, 2018, https://prospect.org/ article/science-under-siege.

68 **In late November 2018, thirteen major agencies:** "Fourth National Climate Assessment, Volume II: Impacts, Risks, and Adaptation in the United States," US Global Change Research Program, accessed January 25, 2019, https://nca2018.globalchange.gov.

75 **It could effectively repeal:** *New York Times v. Sullivan*: Oyez, "New York Times v. Sullivan," accessed December 19, 2018, https://www.oyez.org/cases/1963/39.

78 **He relented temporarily when McGahn warned:** Michael S. Schmidt and Maggie Haberman, "Trump Wanted to Order Justice Dept. to Prosecute Comey and Clinton," *New York Times*, November 20, 2018, https://www.nytimes.com/2018/11/20/us/politics/president-trump-justice-department.html?action=click&module=Top%20Stories&pgtype=Homepage.

79 **Trump: "If I win":** Debate between presidential candidates Donald Trump and Hillary Clinton, *NBC News*, October 9, 2016, https://www.nbcnews.com/video/trump-i-am-going-to-instruct-my-attorney-general-to-get-a-special-prosecutor-782417987718.

80 **An egregious case is Trump's effort:** Michael Wines, "Inside the Trump Administration's Fight to Add a Citizenship Question to the Census," *New York Times*, November 4, 2018, https://www.nytimes.com/2018/11/04/us/wilbur-ross-commerce-secretary.html.

82 **the Reagan administration drastically curtailed:** Robert Pear, "Conservatives Demand a 'Defunding' of the Left," *New York Times*, October 2, 1983, https://www.nytimes.com/1983/10/02/weekinreview/conservatives-demand-a-defunding-of-the-left.html.

84 **An internal investigation subsequently found no abuses:** "Lois Lerner," Wikipedia, accessed December 19, 2018, https://en.wikipedia.org/wiki/Lois_Lerner.

85 **There were calls in rightwing circles:** David Kaiser and Lee Wasserman, "The Rockefeller Family Fund Versus Exxon," *New York Review of Books*, December 8, 2016.

86 **"the potential manipulation of tax exempt 501 c 3 organizations":** The author has a copy of the letter.

86 **"The law is totally on my side":** "Donald Trump's New York Times Interview: Full Transcript," *New York Times*, November 23, 2016, https://www.nytimes.com/2016/11/23/us/politics/trump-new-york-times-interview-transcript.html?hp&action=click&pgtype=Homepage&clickSource=

story-heading&module=b-lede-package-region&region=top-news&WT
.nav=top-news&_r=0.

86 **the "President cannot obstruct justice":** Mike Allen, "Exclusive: Trump
Lawyer Claims the 'President Cannot Obstruct Justice,'" Axios, December 4, 2017, https://www.axios.com/exclusive-trump-lawyer-claims-the
-president-cannot-obstruct-justice-1513388369-032ba40d-55c3-42d6
-bdf9-d6399ed7a2ce.html.

86 **"When the President does it":** "Nixon Interviews," Wikipedia, accessed
January 31, 2019, https://en.wikipedia.org/wiki/Nixon_interviews.

86 **"so-called judge":** Amy B. Wang, "Trump Lashes Out at 'So-Called Judge'
Who Temporarily Blocked Travel Ban," *Washington Post*, February 4, 2017,
https://www.washingtonpost.com/news/the-fix/wp/2017/02/04/trump
-lashes-out-at-federal-judge-who-temporarily-blocked-travel-ban/?utm_
term=.5c3e1bcabab3.

86 **"There is no such thing as judicial supremacy":** "Full Miller Interview:
'There's No Such Thing as Judicial Supremacy,'" *NBC News*, February
12, 2017, https://www.nbcnews.com/meet-the-press/video/full-miller
-interview-there-s-no-such-thing-as-judicial-supremacy-875527747603.

88 **"The Trump White House fundamentally does not agree":** Dan Hinkel,
Annie Sweeney, and Bill Ruthhart, "The Difference with This Round of
Chicago Police Reform? A Federal Judge," *Chicago Tribune*, July 28, 2018,
https://www.chicagotribune.com/news/local/politics/ct-met-chicago
-police-reform-consent-decree-20180727-story.html.

88 **"We do not have Obama judges or Trump judges":** Robert Barnes, "Rebuking Trump's Criticism of 'Obama Judge,' Chief Justice Roberts Defends Judiciary as 'Independent,'" *Washington Post*, November 21, 2018, https://www
.washingtonpost.com/politics/rebuking-trumps-criticism-of-obama-judge
-chief-justice-roberts-defends-judiciary-as-independent/2018/11/21/6383
c7b2-edb7-11e8-96d4-0d23f2aaad09_story.html?utm_term=.2e863a3872ae.

88 **"Sorry Chief Justice John Roberts":** Barnes, "Rebuking Trump's
Criticism."

89 **In February 2019, a third such ruling:** Adam Liptak, "Supreme Court

Blocks Louisiana Abortion Law," *New York Times*, February 7, 2019, https://www.nytimes.com/2019/02/07/us/politics/louisiana-abortion-law-supreme-court.html.

90 **"almost ought to be illegal":** Jennie Neufeld, "Trump Says Flipping 'Almost' Should Be Illegal," Vox, August 23, 2018, https://www.vox.com/policy-and-politics/2018/8/23/17772540/trump-flipping-almost-illegal-manafort-cohen.

91 **"Under the fundamental rule":** Scott Bomboy, "Explaining the Presidential Self-Pardon Debate," National Constitution Center, *Constitution Daily* (blog), June 4, 2018, https://constitutioncenter.org/blog/explaining-the-presidential-self-pardon-debate.

91 **"Individual-1":** *United States of America v. Michael Cohen*, "The Government's Sentencing Memorandum," filed December 7, 2018, http://apps.washingtonpost.com/g/documents/world/read-prosecutors-sentencing-recommendation-for-michael-cohen/3340.

92 **"multiple acts of misconduct":** Fernanda Santos, "Contempt Ruling Rebukes Sheriff Joe Arpaio of Arizona, *New York Times*, May 13, 2016, https://www.nytimes.com/2016/05/14/us/arizona-sheriff-joe-arpaio-ruling.html.

92 **"Was Sheriff Joe convicted for doing his job?":** Dara Lind, "The Real Reason Trump Pardoned Joe Arpaio," Vox, August 25, 2017, https://www.vox.com/2017/8/25/16207446/trump-arpaio-pardon.

93 **The legal motion contended:** *United States of America v. Joseph M. Arpaio*, "The Protect Democracy Project, Inc.'s Motion for Leave to Participate as *Amicus Curiae*," filed September 11, 2017, https://3coziq40vafz1kqd5812oc8r-wpengine.netdna-ssl.com/wp-content/uploads/2017/09/Protect-Democracy-Project-Arpaio.pdf.

97 **Congress has the constitutional authority:** Jack Maskell, *Postponement and Rescheduling of Elections for Federal Office*, CRS Report for Congress, Congressional Research Service, October 4, 2004, https://fas.org/sgp/crs/RL32623.pdf.

97 **"I fear that if he loses the election in 2020":** Dylan Scott, "Michael Cohen's Parting Shot: I Fear What Happens if Trump Loses in 2020,"

Vox, February 27, 2019, https://www.vox.com/policy-and-politics/2019
/2/27/18243686/michael-cohen-testimony-closing-statement.

97 **The election of 2000 was effectively stolen:** Oyez, "Bush v. Gore," accessed
February 10, 2019, https://www.oyez.org/cases/2000/00-949.

98 **"lies about like a loaded weapon":** *Korematsu v. United States*, 323 U.S.
214 (1944), Justia, accessed January 31, 2019, https://supreme.justia.com/
cases/federal/us/323/214/#tab-opinion-1938225.

98 **If Trump's more outlandish claims:** Liza Goitein, "In a Crisis, the President
Can Invoke Extraordinary Authority," *Atlantic*, January–February 2019.

99 **"Whether the autocrat is deliberate":** Ian Bassin, interview with the
author, November 1, 2018.

Chapter 4: Suppression Meets Mobilization

102 **All told, the turnout rate:** United States Elections Project, "2018 November General Election Turnout Rates," accessed December 12, 2018, http://
www.electproject.org/2018g.

103 **The decline between the presidential year:** Andrew Hacker, "Hopeful Math," *New York Review of Books*, September 29, 2018, https://www
.nybooks.com/articles/2018/09/27/hopeful-math-democrats.

104 **Even so, turnout in 2018 was below:** United States Elections Project, "2018
November General Election Turnout Rates."

105 **Act Blue, the umbrella group:** Thomas B. Edsall, "The Lobbyists Blocking
Nancy Pelosi and Her New Majority," *New York Times*, January 10, 2019,
https://www.nytimes.com/2019/01/10/opinion/pelosi-trump-lobbying
-democrats.html?action=click&module=Opinion&pgtype=Homepage.

105 **Democratic House candidates raised $923 million:** OpenSecrets.org,
"Election Overview," Center for Responsive Politics, accessed December
12, 2018, https://www.opensecrets.org/overview.

106 **Much of the volunteer energy:** Lara Putnam and Theda Skocpol, "Middle America Reboots Democracy," *Democracy*, February 20, 2018, https://
democracyjournal.org/arguments/middle-america-reboots-democracy.

107   **In Kansas, where Democrat Laura Kelly:** Daniel Block, "Rural Voters Delivered Democrats Key Victories in 2018," *Washington Monthly*, November 9, 2018, https://washingtonmonthly.com/2018/11/09/rural-voters-delivered-democrats-key-victories-in-2018.

107   **In small rural counties, Tester received:** Block, "Rural Voters Delivered."

108   **In addition to the 40 Democrats who flipped:** "U.S. House Election Results 2018," *New York Times*, accessed December 12, 2018, https://www.nytimes.com/interactive/2018/11/06/us/elections/results-house-elections.html.

109   **In the 1880s and 1890s:** Carol Anderson, *One Person, No Vote* (New York: Bloomsbury, 2018), 4.

109   **That exclusion persisted until the 1960s:** Jack Maskell, *Postponement and Rescheduling of Elections for Federal Office*, CRS Report for Congress, Congressional Research Service, October 4, 2004, https://fas.org/sgp/crs/RL32623.pdf.

110   **With enactment of the Voting Rights Act:** Anderson, *One Person, No Vote*, 26.

111   *The Triumph of Voting Rights in the South:* Charles S. Bullock III and Ronald Keith Gaddie, *The Triumph of Voting Rights in the South* (Norman: University of Oklahoma Press, 2009).

112   **"trench warfare":** Randall Kennedy, interview with the author, January 10, 2019.

112   **"massive resistance":** James H. Hershman Jr., "Massive Resistance," Encyclopedia Viginia, accessed February 8, 2019, https://www.encyclopediavirginia.org/Massive_Resistance.

113   **In the early 1970s, the state of Mississippi:** Ari Berman, *Give Us the Ballot* (New York: Farrar, Straus and Giroux, 2015), 88–92.

113   **"I believe in states' rights":** "Transcript of Ronald Reagan's 1980 Neshoba County Fair Speech," *Neshoba Democrat*, November 15, 2007, http://neshobademocrat.com/Content/NEWS/News/Article/Transcript-of-Ronald-Reagan-s-1980-Neshoba-County-Fair-speech/2/297/15599.

114   **In 1978, the US Commission on Civil Rights:** Berman, *Give Us the Ballot*, 132.

114 **That predisposition changed with:** Oyez, "City of Mobile v. Bolden," accessed February 4, 2019, https://www.oyez.org/cases/1978/77-1844.

115 **"Racially discriminatory motivation":** Oyez, "City of Mobile v. Bolden."

115 **Nixon had named four new justices:** See discussion in Berman, *Give Us the Ballot*, 134.

115 **All were eventually acquitted:** Anderson, *One Person, No Vote*, 35.

116 **The dramatic reversal came:** Oyez, "Shelby County v. Holder," accessed February 4, 2019, https://www.oyez.org/cases/2012/12-96.

117 **"Any racial discrimination in voting":** Oyez, "Shelby County v. Holder."

117 **"Throwing out pre-clearance when it has worked":** Oyez, "Shelby County v. Holder."

118 **All told, according to a comprehensive study:** Brennan Center for Justice, "New Voting Restrictions in America," accessed December 12, 2018, http://www.brennancenter.org/new-voting-restrictions-america.

119 **According to voting scholar Carol Anderson:** Anderson, *One Person, No Vote*, 72.

119 **"exact match" legislation:** Sean Keenan, "There Are 53,000 Pending Voters in Georgia. They Can Still Vote. Here's What You Need to Know," *Atlanta*, October 16, 2018, https://www.atlantamagazine.com/news-culture-articles/53000-pending-voters-georgia-still-vote-what-to-know.

120 **Between 2012 and 2016, Georgia also:** Anderson, *One Person, No Vote*, 78–79.

120 **In the 2014 midterms, black turnout:** Ruy Teixeira and John Halpin, "Democrats Can and Should Expand the Map to Georgia and Arizona in 2020," *American Prospect*, March 1, 2019, https://prospect.org/article/democrats-can-and-should-expand-map-georgia-and-arizona-2020. See also Vann R. Newkirk II, "In the Georgia Governor's Race, the Game Is Black Votes," *Atlantic*, October 12, 2018, https://www.theatlantic.com/politics/archive/2018/10/georgia-race-mired-minority-vote-suppression-charges/572854.

120 **Several academic studies yielded similar results:** Brennan Center for Justice, "Debunking the Voter Fraud Myth," January 31, 2017, https://www.brennancenter.org/analysis/debunking-voter-fraud-myth.

121 **Ferocious prosecutors charged Mason:** Ed Pilkington, "US Voter Suppression: Why This Texas Woman Is Facing Five Years' Prison," *Guardian*, August 28, 2018, https://www.theguardian.com/us-news/2018/aug/27/crime-of-voting-texas-woman-crystal-mason-five-years-prison.

121 **One of them, Olivia Reynolds:** Matt Elofson, "Olivia Reynolds Gets Two Years in Prison for Election Fraud," Dothan Eagle, September 15, 2015, https://www.dothaneagle.com/news/crime_court/olivia-reynolds-gets-two-years-in-prison-for-election-fraud/article_984e9262-5bbe-11e5-ada3-fbed589e9505.html.

122 **Wilson was let off with a misdemeanor:** Ben Strauss, "'Kris Kobach Came After Me for an Honest Mistake,'" Politico, May 21, 2017, https://www.politico.com/magazine/story/2017/05/21/kris-kobach-voter-fraud-investigation-prosecution-215164.

122 **Crosscheck, administered by Kobach's office:** "Interstate Voter Registration Crosscheck Program," Wikipedia, accessed December 12, 2018, https://en.wikipedia.org/wiki/Interstate_Voter_Registration_Crosscheck_Program.

123 **The commission then produced an amateurish study:** Eli Rosenberg, "Kris Kobach Used Flawed Research to Defend Trump's Voter Fraud Panel, Experts Say," *Washington Post*, August 7, 2018, https://www.washingtonpost.com/news/politics/wp/2018/08/07/experts-say-kris-kobach-used-flawed-research-to-defend-trumps-voter-fraud-panel/?utm_term=.4ae2222cf1d8.

124 **Thanks to this strategy:** See the discussion in David Daley, *Rat F**ked: Why Your Vote Doesn't Count* (New York: Liveright, 2017), the authoritative investigative work on project REDMAP and its consequences.

126 **"with almost surgical precision":** "United States Court of Appeals for the Fourth Circuit," document no. 16-1529, p. 11, accessed February 4, 2019, http://www.ca4.uscourts.gov/Opinions/Published/161468.P.pdf.

127 **"You've got to get out":** Steve Benen, "Trump Explicitly Makes 2018 Midterms a Referendum on His Presidency," MSNBC, *MaddowBlog*, September 24, 2018, http://www.msnbc.com/rachel-maddow-show/trump-explicitly-makes-2018-midterms-referendum-his-presidency.

Chapter 5: The Two Faces of Corruption

129 **Trump overruled a long-standing plan:** *Review of GSA's Revised Plan for the Federal Bureau of Investigation Headquarters Consolidation Project*, Office of Inspector General, US General Services Administration, August 27, 2018, https://connolly.house.gov/uploadedfiles/gsa_ig_fbi_hq_report.pdf.

129 **Meanwhile, representatives of forty:** "Profiting from the Presidency," Citizens for Responsibility and Ethics in Washington, accessed November 24, 2018, https://www.citizensforethics.org/profitingfromthepresidency.

130 **"little more than a checkbook":** Shane Goldmacher, "Trump Foundation Will Dissolve, Accused of 'Shocking Pattern of Illegality,' " *New York Times*, December 18, 2018, https://www.nytimes.com/2018/12/18/nyregion/ny -ag-underwood-trump-foundation.html.

131 **Ross shorted the stock:** Dan Alexander, "Lies, China and Putin: Solving the Mystery of Wilbur Ross' Missing Fortune," *Forbes*, June 18, 2018, http:// www.forbes.com/sites/danalexander/2018/06/18/lies-china-and-putin -solving-the-mystery-of-wilbur-ross-missing-fortune-trump-commerce -secretary-cabinet-conflicts-of-interest/#6593033a7e87.

132 **"The system is rigged":** Garance Franke-Ruta, "Elizabeth Warren: 'The System Is Rigged,' " *Atlantic*, September 6, 2012, https://www.theatlantic .com/politics/archive/2012/09/elizabeth-warren-the-system-is-rigged/ 262030.

134 **So complicit were Democrats:** "CNBC's Rick Santelli's Chicago Tea Party," YouTube, published by the Heritage Foundation, February 19, 2009, https://www.youtube.com/watch?v=zp-Jw-5Kx8k.

137 **When Sears Roebuck went bankrupt in 2018:** Davide Scigliuzzo, Katherine Doherty, and Lauren Coleman-Lochner, "Lampert to Get Another Chance at Keeping Sears Afloat," Bloomberg, January 16, 2019, https:// www.bloomberg.com/news/articles/2019-01-16/eddie-lampert-s-esl-is -said-to-win-sears-bankruptcy-auction.

138 **The story of private-equity abuse ending:** Eileen Appelbaum and Rosemary Batt, *Private Equity at Work* (New York: Russell Sage Foundation, 2014).

139 **There is a huge literature in political science:** Gallup, "Confidence in Institutions," accessed November 24, 2018, https://news.gallup.com/poll/1597/confidence-institutions.aspx.

139 **That support peaked in 1962:** Pew Research Center, "Beyond Distrust: How Americans View Their Government," November 23, 2015, http://www.people-press.org/2015/11/23/1-trust-in-government-1958-2015.

140 **Corruption, they feared, could undermine:** Zephyr Teachout, *Corruption in America* (Cambridge, MA: Harvard University Press, 2014).

140 **leaders may "by corruption . . . betray":** *Federalist Papers*, no. 10 (James Madison), 59.

140 **"an avaricious man might be tempted":** *Federalist Papers*, no. 75 (Alexander Hamilton), 487.

141 **Alexander Hamilton was blackmailed:** Ron Chernow, *Alexander Hamilton* (New York: Penguin, 2004), 368–69.

143 **"There has got to be in every ward":** Justin Kaplan, *Lincoln Steffens: A Biography* (New York: Simon and Schuster, 1974), 65.

143 **"honest graft":** William L. Riordon, *Plunkitt of Tammany Hall* (New York: E. P. Dutton, 1963), 3.

144 **Jacob Hacker presciently wrote:** Jacob Hacker, *The Great Risk Shift* (Oxford: Oxford University Press, 2006).

147 **Despite the plain intent of Congress:** Katherine V. W. Stone, "Signing Away Our Rights," *American Prospect*, March 5, 2011, https://prospect.org/article/signing-away-our-rights-0.

149 **The debt burden resulted in a precipitous decline:** "College Debt Deters Young Home Buyers," *Wall Street Journal*, January 17, 2019.

150 **In Los Angeles, the median house:** Richard Florida, "Where the House-Price-to-Income Ratio Is Most Out of Whack," CityLab, May 29, 2018, https://www.citylab.com/equity/2018/05/where-the-house-price-to-income-ratio-is-most-out-of-whack/561404.

151 **Even in the second quintile:** Jenny Schuetz, "Is the Rent 'Too Damn High'? Or Are Incomes Too Low?" Brookings Institution, December 19, 2017, https://www.brookings.edu/blog/the-avenue/2017/12/19/is-the-rent-too-damn-high-or-are-incomes-too-low.

153 **A poll conducted by the Kaiser Foundation:** Margot Sanger-Katz, "Even Insured Can Face Crushing Medical Debt, Study Finds," *New York Times*, January 5, 2016, https://www.nytimes.com/2016/01/06/upshot/lost-jobs -houses-savings-even-insured-often-face-crushing-medical-debt.html.

153 **there are still 28 million uninsured Americans:** "Key Facts about the Uninsured Population," Henry J. Kaiser Family Foundation, December 7, 2018, https://www.kff.org/uninsured/fact-sheet/key-facts-about-the -uninsured-population.

Chapter 6: Overcoming the Racial Fault Line

158 **"The Democrats—the longer they talk":** Robert Kuttner, "Steve Bannon, Unrepentant," *American Prospect*, August 16, 2017, https://prospect.org/ article/steve-bannon-unrepentant.

159 **"revive the American dream by curbing big government":** Guy Molyneux, "A Tale of Two Populisms," *American Prospect*, June 1, 2017, http:// prospect.org/article/tale-two-populisms.

159 **In a spring 2018 survey of voters:** Stan Greenberg, Page Gardner, and Nancy Zdunkewicz, "Trump & GOP Strategy Make Blue Wave More Likely: The Evidence," Democracy Corps, July 13, 2018, http://www .democracycorps.com/attachments/article/1088/Dcorps_WVWVAF_ Memo_7.13.2018_FOR%20RELEASE.pdf.

160 **Republicans quietly shelved the tax cut:** Stanley Greenberg, "The Broad Support for Taxing the Wealthy," *American Prospect*, June 20, 2018, http:// prospect.org/article/broad-support-taxing-wealthy.

161 **"Conservatives villainize African Americans":** https://www.demos.org/ sites/default/files/publications/Race_Class_Narrative_Handout_C3_ June%206.pdf.

164 **"I believe Medicare and Social Security":** "Colin Allred," *Dallas Morning News*, accessed February 21, 2019, https://voterguide.dallasnews .com/2018-general/candidates/486.

165 **These voters are the historic constituency:** Gerald F. Seib, "Both Parties, Realigning, Face Identity Crises," *Wall Street Journal*, February 26, 2019.

166 **"mobilize and call forth a new American majority":** Steve Phillips, "Do the Math. Moderate Democrats Will Not Win in 2020," *New York Times*, November 12, 2018, https://www.nytimes.com/2018/11/12/opinion/democrats -midterms-progressives.html.

167 **Some 28 percent of the electorate:** William Darity Jr., "The Latino Flight to Whiteness," *American Prospect*, February 11, 2016, http://prospect.org/ article/latino-flight-whiteness.

167 **As the Pew Research Center has demonstrated:** Mark Hugo Lopez, Ana Gonzalez-Barrera, and Gustavo López, "Hispanic Identity Fades across Generations as Immigrant Connections Fall Away," Pew Research Center, December 20, 2017, http://www.pewhispanic.org/2017/12/20/hispanic -identity-fades-across-generations-as-immigrant-connections-fall-away.

167 **In earlier times, the category of whiteness expanded:** Noel Ignatieff, *How the Irish Became White* (New York: Routledge, 1995).

167 **"Ethnic identity is fluid":** Jamelle Bouie, "Democracy Is Not Destiny," *Democracy*, no. 31, Winter 2014, https://democracyjournal.org/magazine/31/ demography-is-not-destiny.

167 **In Ohio, Indiana, Iowa, Michigan, Missouri, and Wisconsin:** Ruy Teixeira, "The Math Is Clear: Democrats Need to Win More Working-Class White Votes," Vox, January 29, 2018, https://www.vox.com/the-big -idea/2018/1/29/16945106/democrats-white-working-class-demographics -alabama-clinton-obama-base.

169 **"Heading into the 2020 election":** Thomas B. Edsall, "The Deepening 'Racialization' of American Politics," *New York Times*, February 27, 2019, https://www.nytimes.com/2019/02/27/opinion/trump-obama-race.html.

169 **"I have a problem, guys":** David Siders, "Harris Blasts Critics of 'Identity Politics,'" Politico, August 3, 2018, https://www.politico.com/story/2018/08 /03/kamala-harris-netroots-identity-politics-762254.

170 **"Before Barack Obama, niggers could be manufactured":** Ta-Nehisi Coates, "The First White President," *Atlantic*, October 2017, https://www .theatlantic.com/magazine/archive/2017/10/the-first-white-president-ta -nehisi-coates/537909.

171 **In December 2018, a long-planned women's march:** Farah Stockman, "Women's March Roiled by Accusations of Anti-Semitism," *New York Times*, December 23, 2018, https://www.nytimes.com/2018/12/23/us/womens -march-anti-semitism.html.

172 **While white America surely owes the descendants:** Eugene Scott, "Democratic Candidates Are Backing Reparations for African Americans. That Could Be Politically Risky," *Washington Post*, February 26, 2019, https:// www.washingtonpost.com/politics/2019/02/26/democratic-candidates -are-backing-reparations-african-americans-that-could-be-politically -risky/?utm_term=.0504e588feca.

172 **"We must confront the dark history of slavery":** Astead W. Herndon, "2020 Democrats Embrace Race-Conscious Policies, including Repa-rations," *New York Times*, February 21, 2019, https://www.nytimes .com/2019/02/21/us/politics/2020-democrats-race-policy.html.

173 **Not to be outdone, the *Washington Post*:** James Hohmann, "The Daily 202: Will Supporting Reparations Become a New Litmus Test for Democrats in 2020?" *Washington Post*, February 22, 2019, https://www.washington post.com/news/powerpost/paloma/daily-202/2019/02/22/daily-202-will -supporting-reparations-become-a-new-litmus-test-for-democrats-in -2020/5c6edc261b326b71858c6c02/?utm_term=.185517c25253.

174 **"In Trump's story, the reason why":** "Senator Elizabeth Warren at Net-roots Nation 2018," YouTube, published by Thomas Brown, August 3, 2018, https://www.youtube.com/watch?v=Sgkk6ZE_kWw.

175 **"Finally, during the 1960s":** Elizabeth Warren (website), "Warren Deliv-ers Commencement Address at Morgan State University," December 14, 2018, https://www.warren.senate.gov/newsroom/press-releases/warren -delivers-commencement-address-at-morgan-state-university.

176 **"First of all, he's got neo-Nazis":** German Lopez, "'The Racists Believe He's a Racist': Andrew Gillum Calls Out His Opponent for Florida Governor," Vox, October 25, 2018, https://www.vox.com/policy-and-politics/2018/10/25/18022094/gillum-desantis-florida-governor-debate-racists.

177 **"In October 2018, US Senator Elizabeth Warren":** Nayantara Sheroan Appleton, "Do Not 'Decolonize' . . . If You Are Not Decolonizing: Progressive Language and Planning beyond a Hollow Academic Rebranding," *Critical Ethnic Studies* blog, February 4, 2019, http://www.criticalethnicstudies journal.org/blog.

178 **In late 2018, the Trump administration:** Laura Meckler, Samantha Schmidt, and Lena H. Sun, "Trump Administration Considering 'Different Concepts' regarding Transgender Rights with Some Pushing Back Internally," *Washington Post*, October 22, 2018, https://www.washingtonpost.com/national/trump-administration-considering-different-concepts-regarding-transgender-rights-with-some-pushing-back-internally/2018/10/22/0668f4da-d624-11e8-83a2-d1c3da28d6b6_story.html?utm_term-.38e22ba57eb4.

180 **In New York, a room cleaner in a hotel:** Robert Kuttner, "A More Perfect Union," *American Prospect*, November 28, 2011, https://prospect.org/article/more-perfect-union-1.

182 **Large majorities also support:** Yoni Blumberg, "70% of Americans Now Support Medicare-for-All—Here's How Single-Payer Could Affect You," CNBC, *Make It*, August 28, 2018, https://www.cnbc.com/2018/08/28/most-americans-now-support-medicare-for-all-and-free-college-tuition.html.

182 **Pew found that 58 percent of Americans:** Drew DeSilver, "The Real Value of $15 Minimum Wage Depends on Where You Live," Pew Research Center, October 10, 2018, http://www.pewresearch.org/fact-tank/2018/10/10/the-real-value-of-a-15-minimum-wage-depends-on-where-you-live.

182 **According to Gallup, 62 percent of Americans:** Lydia Saad, "Labor Union Approval Steady at 15-Year High," Gallup, August 30, 2018, https://news.gallup.com/poll/241679/labor-union-approval-steady-year-high.aspx.

182 **Gallup also found broad majority support:** R. J. Reinhart, "In the News: Public Backs More Infrastructure Spending," Gallup, February 12, 2018, https://news.gallup.com/poll/226961/news-public-backs-infrastructure-spending.aspx.

183 **"Guarantee a $15 an hour income to all?":** "Progressive Populism Will Save the Democratic Party," Intelligence Squared, accessed December 19, 2018, https://www.intelligencesquaredus.org/debates/progressive-populism-will-save-democratic-party.

184 **"'For example' is not an argument":** Daniel Bell, speaking to the author at least three decades ago. This is apparently a variation of a Yiddish folk saying: "For example is not proof." "Discover Ideas about Jewish Proverbs," Pinterest, accessed December 19, 2018, https://www.pinterest.com/pin/210613720045550852.

185 **In the December 2018 fight over the Speakership:** Ryan Grim, "Who's the Mystery Man behind the Latest Pelosi Putsch? It's Mark Penn," Intercept, November 26, 2018, https://theintercept.com/2018/11/26/nancy-pelosi-speaker-no-labels-mark-penn.

185 **"is based solely on economic resentment":** Mark Lilla, *The Once and Future Liberal: After Identity Politics* (New York: Harper Collins, 2017), 125.

186 **"After a 2018 midterm election":** Jonathan Martin, "Democrats Want to Run on Issues in 2020. But Does Beating Trump Matter Most?" *New York Times*, January 14, 2019, https://www.nytimes.com/2019/01/14/us/politics/democratic-candidates-issues-2020.html.

186 **In 2004, when Democratic presidential candidate:** Peter Dreier and Kelly Candaele, "A Moral Minimum Wage," *Nation*, December 20, 2004, https://www.thenation.com/article/moral-minimum-wage.

189 **"the larger the Trump electorate":** *Monkey Cage* (blog), "Is Trump Country Really Better Off under Trump? No. It's Falling Further Behind," *Washington Post*, November 18, 2018, https://www.washingtonpost.com/news/monkey-cage/wp/2018/11/18/are-trump-voters-better-off-than-they-were-two-years-ago-especially-compared-to-clinton-voters/?utm_term=.0c8572d7483a.

191 **In early 2019, polls were showing:** Tax Axelrod, "Poll: 33% of Kentucky Voters Approve of McConnell," *Hill*, February 21, 2019, https://thehill .com/homenews/campaign/431002-poll-33-of-kentucky-voters-approve-of -mcconnell.

Chapter 7: The View from 2021

203 **"Other liberal presidents," Gerstle writes:** Gary Gerstle, *American Crucible: Race and Nation in the Twentieth Century* (Princeton, NJ: Princeton University Press, 2001). The quote is on page 7.

203 **"Where the citizens of a state are also compatriots":** David Miller, *Strangers in Our Midst* (Cambridge, MA: Harvard University Press, 2016), 23.

204 **"Nationalist sentiments can be the basis":** John B. Judis, *The Nationalist Revival* (New York: Columbia Global Reports, 2018), 35.

205 **In the booming postwar era:** CCH, "2013 CCH Whole Ball of Tax," accessed December 19, 2018, https://www.cch.com/wbot2013/029Income TaxRates.asp.

210 **A 2018 Brookings Institution study found that:** Clara Hendrickson, Mark Muro, and William A. Galston, *Countering the Geography of Discontent* (Washington, DC: Brookings Institution, 2018).

211 **The city of Chattanooga, where the TVA:** Jonathan Talpin, "Chattanooga Has Its Own Broadband—Why Doesn't Every City?" Daily Beast, July 24, 2017, https://www.thedailybeast.com/chattanooga-has-its-own -broadbandwhy-doesnt-every-city.

212 **In the pilot program described by Hochschild:** Arlie Hochschild, "The Coders of Kentucky," *New York Times*, September 21, 2018, https://www .nytimes.com/2018/09/21/opinion/sunday/silicon-valley-tech.html.

214 **According to data from Catalist:** Harold Meyerson, "The Democratic Imperative," *American Prospect*, Winter 2019.

217 **According to a study by the Open Markets Institute:** David Leonhardt, "The Monopolization of America," *New York Times*, November 25, 2018, https://www.nytimes.com/2018/11/25/opinion/monopolies-in-the-us.html.

218 **Amazon, Apple, Google, Facebook, and Microsoft:** David Dayen, "The New Economic Concentration," *American Prospect*, Winter 2019.

220 **Lina Khan, a young scholar:** Lina M. Kahn, "Amazon's Antitrust Paradox," *Yale Law Journal* 126, no. 3 (January 2017).

223 **"It's like when Hitler invaded Poland in 1939":** Courtney Comstock, "Steve Schwarzman on Tax Increases: 'It's Like When Hitler Invaded Poland," Business Insider, August 16, 2010, https://www.businessinsider .com/steve-schwarzman-taxes-hitler-invaded-poland-2010-8.

224 **In March, it was reported that Penn:** Annie Karni, "Mark Penn, Ex-Clinton Loyalist, Visits Trump, and Democrats Are Not Pleased," *New York Times*, March 1, 2019, https://www.nytimes.com/2019/03/01/us/politics/ mark-penn-trump-clinton.html.

225 **The bill, called the For the People Act:** "H.R. 1," 116th Congress, 1st Session, January 3, 2019, https://www.brennancenter.org/sites/default/files/ legislation/HR%201_TheForthePeopleAct_0.PDF.

226 **"Democratic Politician Protection Act":** Mitch McConnell, "The Democratic Politician Protection Act," *Mitch McConnell: Senate Majority Leader*, January 29, 2019, https://www.republicanleader.senate.gov/newsroom/ remarks/the-democrat-politician-protection-act-.

226 **Polling shows that majorities in excess of 80 percent:** Ella Nilsen, "House Democrats Officially Unveil Their First Bill in the Majority: A Sweeping Anti-corruption Proposal," Vox, January 4, 2019, https://www.vox .com/policy-and-politics/2018/11/30/18118158/house-democrats-anti -corruption-bill-hr-1-pelosi.

226 **"weaponizing the First Amendment":** "Kagan, J., Dissenting, Mark Janus, Petitioner *v.* American Federation of State, Country, and Municipal Employees, Council 31, et al.," Supreme Court of the United States, June 27, 2018, https://www.supremecourt.gov/opinions/17pdf/16-1466_2b3j.pdf.

229 **"Constitutional Hardball":** Mark V. Tushnet, "Constitutional Hardball," Georgetown University Law Center, 2004, https://scholarship.law .georgetown.edu/cgi/viewcontent.cgi?article=1557&context=facpub. See also James Fishkin and David E. Pozen, "Asymmetric Constitutional Hardball,"

Columbia Law Review 118, no. 3 (2018), https://columbialawreview.org/content/asymmetric-constitutional-hardball.

230 **Yet, most scholars of the court:** Barry Friedman, *The Will of the People* (New York: Farrar, Straus and Giroux, 2009).

231 **"no matter whether the Constitution":** Howard Gillman, Mark A. Graber, and Keith E. Whittington, "The Republican Era—Foundations/Scope/Extra-territoriality," in *American Constitutionalism*, vol. 2: *Rights and Liberties*, chap. 7 suppl., http://global.oup.com/us/companion.websites/fdscontent/uscompanion/us/static/companion.websites/9780199751358/instructor/chapter_7/dunnesupreme.pdf.

INDEX

≈